LEX POPULI

THE CULTURAL LIVES OF LAW

Austin Sarat, Editor

The Cultural Lives of Law series brings insights and approaches from cultural studies to law and tries to secure for law a place in cultural analysis. Books in the series focus on the production, interpretation, consumption, and circulation of legal meanings. They take up the challenges posed as boundaries collapse between as well as within cultures, and as the circulation of legal meanings becomes more fluid. They also attend to the ways law's power in cultural production is renewed and resisted. Among the topics of books in *The Cultural Lives of Law* series are law and popular culture, legal consciousness, literary analysis of law, the self-understandings of legal actors, celebrated trials, the regulation of artistic and cultural life, and historical and ethnographic treatments of law and national identity.

WILLIAM P. MACNEIL

Lex Populi

The Jurisprudence of Popular Culture

STANFORD UNIVERSITY PRESS

Stanford, California, 2007

Stanford University Press
Stanford, California

Printed in the United States of America on acid-free,
archival-quality paper

Library of Congress Cataloging-in-Publication Data

MacNeil, William P.
   Lex populi : the jurisprudence of popular culture / William P.
MacNeil.
      p. cm.—(The cultural lives of law)
   Includes bibliographical references and index.
   ISBN-13: 978-0-8047-5367-8 (cloth : alk. paper)
   ISBN-10: 0-8047-5367-9 (cloth : alk. paper)
   1. Culture and law.   2. Sociological jurisprudence.   3. Popular
culture.   4. Law—Psychological aspects.   I. Title.
K487.C8M33 2007
340′.115—dc22   2006036365

Typeset by Newgen in 10/14.5 Minion Roman

To my parents,
John Angus and Viberta Marie MacNeil

Contents

Acknowledgments

Lex Populi has been long in the making and would never have made it into print but for the support, encouragement, and enthusiasm of any number of people. First and foremost, I owe to Austin Sarat an enormous debt of gratitude for his scholarly advice and assistance. I would like to thank Amanda Moran, Jared Smith, and Mariana Raykov of Stanford University Press for their efforts on my behalf, and the press's anonymous reviewers for their helpful comments. I would also like to thank Rosemary Hunter and Justin Malbon, successive deans of the Griffith Law School in Brisbane, Australia, and especially Richard Johnstone, director of the Socio-Legal Research Centre, for all their aid, financial and otherwise. Several members of the Griffith faculty provided much of the initial inspiration of this book, and I would like to thank them in turn: for introducing me to the Harry Potter series, Shaunnagh Dorsett (now of the Faculty of Law, Victoria University of Wellington, New Zealand); for screening *The Castle* for me at her home in Brisbane, Bridget Cullen-Mandikos; for innumerable conversations about law and the image, Merran Lawler, Shaun McVeigh, and Christine Morris. Students, as well, played a significant role in the development and completion of this text, and thanks go to my Legal Fictions classes, both at Griffith and Hong Kong Universities. Stephen Burton is singled out especially for his Lacanian loucheness and devil-may-care *jouissance*. But I could not have seen this project through without the invaluable technical, research, and critical assistance of Chantelle Williams, Karen Beattie, and particularly, Tim Peters, student stalwart of the Griffith Law School, conference confrère, and fellow Tolkienista! To Tim—and Chantelle and Karen—I am truly grateful for all your help.

Several of this book's chapters have appeared in earlier versions. Chapter One, "Kidlit as Law 'n Lit: Harry Potter and the Scales of Justice," was first published in 2002 in *Law and Literature*. A version of Chapter Two, "You Slay Me! Buffy as Jurisprude of Desire," came out in a special 2003 issue of *Cardozo Law Review*. Chapter Five, "One *Recht* to Rule Them All! Law's Empire in the Age of *Empire*," originally appeared in 2004 in a chapter in *Studies in Law, Politics, and Society*. Chapter Six, "Precrime Never Pays! Law and Economics in *Minority Report*," made its digital debut in 2005 in the e-journal *Continuum*. A version of Chapter Seven, "It's the Vibe! The Common Law Imaginary Down Under," appeared in 2004 as a chapter in *Law's Moving Image*. I would like to thank, in turn, the editors of the above publications: Peter Goodrich, Penny Pether, and Richard Weisberg; Jeanne Schroeder and Renata Salecl; Andrew Kenyon and Peter Rush; Christy Collis and Jason Bainbridge; and finally, Leslie Moran, Elena Loizidou, Emma Sandon, and Ian Christie. Thanks, additionally, to the various anonymous reviewers involved with those journals.

Versions of the chapters mentioned above, as well as some hitherto unpublished ones, were delivered orally at a variety of conferences, lectures, and seminars sponsored by the following institutions: American University, Amherst College, Australian National University, Birkbeck College London, Cardozo Law School, Griffith University, Institute of Postcolonial Studies–Melbourne, LaTrobe University, McGill University, Queensland College of Art, Smith College, Tate Gallery London, University of Connecticut, University of Kent, University of Melbourne, University of Pennsylvania, University of Queensland, University of Sydney, and University of Texas-Austin. I would like to thank the audiences of each, and all organizers: Pamela Adams, Anita Allen-Castellito, Scott Beattie, Paul Berman, Robert Burrell, Andrew Byrnes, David Carlson, April Chrzanowski, Michael Coper, Lynda Davies, Maria Drakopoulou, Ian Duncanson, Kirsty Duncanson, Mary Farquhar, Vicki Farrington, Miranda Feldman, Susan Sage Heinzelman, Rosemary Hunter, Richard Johnstone, Gloria Lappin, Max Lieskewicz, Cressida Limon, Desmond Manderson, Jan McDonald, Shaun McVeigh, Naomi Mezey, Les Moran, Brendan O'Conner, Ann Orford, Penny Pether, Alain Pottage, Jennifer Rutherford, Renata Salecl, Austin Sarat, Jeanne Schroeder, and James Boyd White.

Friends and friendly communities have given me intellectual support and emotional succor during the writing of this book. Much was written while I enjoyed the scholarly hospitality of the departments of Political Science and Jurisprudence at Amherst College in Amherst, Massachusetts, as the Loewenstein Visiting Fellow in

Jurisprudence. To the members of those two departments and to the Loewenstein fellowship program, I am profoundly grateful. The Department of Law at Birkbeck College London, and on the other side of the Atlantic, Cardozo Law School in New York City, have been welcoming of both myself and my work, and I would like to thank them collectively. McGill University in Montreal, Quebec, as well, opened its doors to me, and I extend my warmest thanks to Desmond Manderson for making that possible. Other colleagues and friends who have given me advice, encouragement, and support include: Orit Kamir (Israel); Isobel Findlay, Rebecca Johnson, and Anne McGillvray (Canada); Anne Barron, Alison Diduck, Tatiana Flessas, and David Seymour (England); and Michele Goodwin (USA). In Australia, I would like to thank the following people: in Melbourne, particularly, my fellow Slayerettes, Peter Rush and Alison Young, as well as Derek Dalton, Judy Grbich, and Juliet Rogers; in Sydney, Peter Hutchings; in Brisbane, Paul Barclay, Bede Roshan de Silva-Wijeyeratne, Janine Brown, Fiona Kumar Campbell, John Dewar, Heather Douglas, Mary Keyes, and especially the Keyes-Liley clan (Clare, Josh, Caitie, Jordi—and now, Elise), Marett Leiboff, Jeffrey Minson, Aileen Moreton-Robinson, Brad Sherman, Bronwyn Statham, Mark Thomas, Kieran Tranter, Graeme Turner, and Rozzie Williams.

Two other intellectual debts, long outstanding, must be acknowledged: to Jane Millgate (Department of English, Victoria College, University of Toronto) and to William Twining (Faculty of Laws, University College London)—many thanks for teaching me how to "read" the respective texts of literature and law and for modeling so well the combined roles of scholar and teacher. Special thanks, as well, to more junior colleagues (meaning, all under age thirteen), especially Livingstone "Lili" McVeigh-Go, Zach and Felix Barclay, and last but certainly not least, my American nieces and goddaughters, Catherine Elizabeth and Carolyn Patricia Harding for their patience throughout and, indeed, enthusiasm for repeated viewings of the Harry Potter movies. Other family members deserve thanks: to my brother John MacNeil for introducing me to the work of Posner. To my brother Peter MacNeil and my sister, Mary Patricia Harding (née MacNeil), for accompanying me to innumerable screenings of, inter alia, the Tolkien trilogy—even when they thought I was just a step away from a dungeons 'n dragons cult. To my aunt and uncle, Charles Bernard and Jean MacLean, for sponsoring the mini–film festivals I organized while a law student at Dalhousie, at their home in Inverness, Nova Scotia. To my partner, Pam Adams, who not only organized, in her capacity as administrative officer of the Socio-Legal Research Centre at Griffith Law School, many of the talks on which this book's chapters are based, but patiently listened to them from embryonic form through to completion, all the while posing questions and offering suggestions with as much good humor as critical insight. But the debt of greatest and indeed longest standing is to the two people who introduced me to popular culture in the first place: in an outing to the University Cinema on Bloor Street in Toronto, Ontario, in 1963 to see Disney's *The Sword in the Stone*, my first and one of my favorite films. Interestingly, and quite fittingly, they are the very same people who accompanied me, in March of 2005 in Ann Arbor, Michigan, to the screening of the film that constitutes the final chapter of this book, *Million Dollar Baby*. They are, of course, my parents, John Angus and Viberta Marie MacNeil. To them, I dedicate this book with much love and affection.

List of Abbreviations

BtVS	*Buffy the Vampire Slayer* (TV series)
FC	*Fight Club* (DVD)
C	*The Castle* (DVD)
CILP	*A Clinical Introduction to Lacanian Psychoanalysis* (book)
CL	*The Concept of Law* (book)
HP&CS	*Harry Potter and the Chamber of Secrets* (book)
HP&GF	*Harry Potter and the Goblet of Fire* (book)
HP&PA	*Harry Potter and the Prisoner of Azkaban* (book)
LB	*Legally Blonde* (DVD)
LD	*Life's Dominion* (book)
LR	*The Lord of the Rings* (book)
LR-FR	*The Lord of the Rings: The Fellowship of the Rings* (DVD)
LR-RK	*The Lord of the Rings: The Return of the King* (DVD)
LR-TT	*The Lord of the Rings: The Two Towers* (DVD)
MDB	*Million Dollar Baby* (DVD)
MR	*Minority Report* (DVD)
PC	*The Paper Chase* (DVD)
SI	*The Sea Inside* (DVD)

LEX POPULI

Introduction

Toward an Intertextual Jurisprudence

This is a book about jurisprudence. Yet the jurisprudential texts under consideration are—to say the least—unorthodox. Tolkien, *Buffy the Vampire Slayer*, Harry Potter, and *The Castle* (Melbourne comic Rob Sitch's, not Franz Kafka's), to name just a few, are all referenced as exemplary instances of what I call *lex populi*—literally, "people's law" or, more loosely, "pop law." I turn to these literary, televisual, and cinematic texts of *lex populi* instead of more traditional academic sources such as journal articles or scholarly monographs, because I feel that contemporary pop culture has something important to say to and about jurisprudence, above and beyond what the mainstream legal academy has to offer. Indeed, current academic jurisprudence and its two reigning contemporary paradigms—"sociolegal studies" and "law and economics"—have to a large degree sidelined the discipline's canonical (and contemporary) issues, pursuing instead their own policy goals or efficiency analysis. Sidelined (if not silenced) by the jurisprudential mainstream are questions that ask, for example: What is the nature of postmodern justice? Can rights be revivified in the wake of critique? Should the law's moral foundations be rethought in terms of ethics? Of course, these concerns continue to be central to the "critical" margins of the legal academy—feminists, race theorists, queer theorists, postmodernists—but with respect to the official discourse of jurisprudence (and law), they remain just that: marginal. *Lex Populi* holds out the prospect for a much broader, more public debate around these issues. The various media highlighted in this book not only reach a much larger audience than standard legal texts, but potentially, and even more democratically, they also help restore topics of jurisprudential import—justice, rights, ethics—to where they belong: not with the economists, not with the sociologists, not even with the philosophers, but rather with the community at large.

It is precisely this recontextualization of jurisprudence from the specialist to the generalist interpretive community that this book attempts. And that recontextualization—the popularization of jurisprudence and the jurisprudence of popular culture—entails and is predicated on the production of a new *intertext*, one that enables a rethinking of the culture of law and the law of culture. Producing that intertext is, I will argue, a unique mode of analysis, of interpretation, and of *reading*, and what this book in part proposes is nothing less than a practical demonstration of how to read *jurisprudentially*. In so doing, I hope to repay some of the theoretical debt that jurisprudence (and law-and-literature) so clearly owes to literary criticism, cultural studies, and Continental philosophy. For far too long, jurisprudence has been content to absorb the lessons of these disciplines' versions of textual theory—of the play of the sign, the dissemination of meaning, the deconstruction of the logos—without propounding its own *topoi*, let alone interpretive paradigms. Such *topoi*, of course, jurisprudence has in abundance: in such highly contested notions as form versus substance, law's normativity, rights and responsibilities, judicial discretion, property as theft, the politics of law, and the "reasonable (wo)man." This book will explore some of these *topoi* in a series of close readings largely organized around the principal schools of jurisprudence.

Thus liberal legalism and its issues of the Rule of Law, rights, and justice are addressed in Chapter One, "Kidlit as Law 'n Lit: Harry Potter and the Scales of Justice," based on *Harry Potter and the Goblet of Fire*,[1] the fourth in J. K. Rowling's remarkable series of teenage witchcraft and wizardry. There, Hogwarts is revealed as a site of substantive injustice, not only for its unequal treatment of the house elves but also for the procedural irregularities compromising its trials of the Death-Eaters. This woeful state of affairs raises the question: Is the magic kingdom—that is, liberal legality for which the kingdom is so clearly a metaphor—worth fighting for? That question continues to bedevil all reformist projects, not only Hermione's fight for elf rights but also any liberal agenda that seeks to work within the law, utilizing it as a (dubious) mechanism for change. By way of contrast, the changeless patterns of natural law—"higher law" characterized as either divine, philosophical, or psychoanalytical—are engaged in Chapter Two, "You Slay Me! Buffy as Jurisprude of Desire," based on the cult TV series, *Buffy the Vampire Slayer*.[2] Here, Buffy is variously analogized to Antigone, Aquinas, and Kant, figures of the natural law tradition that the Slayer "stakes" symbolically, all the while instantiating an alternative: that is, the Law of Desire as "extimate," both within and outside of us, and imaged in the trope of the demon (inner demons and demon lovers, for example).

Natural law, and its semio-psychoanalytic transmogrification by Buffy, is succeeded by an analysis of positivism-as-*psychomachia* in Chapter Three, "The First Rule of Fight Club Is—You Do Not Talk About Fight Club!: The Perverse Core of Legal Positivism." This chapter unpacks, in some detail, the rule fetishism of H.L.A. Hart in terms of David Fincher's film, *Fight Club*,[3] which, in its story of a split subject fighting itself, gestures toward the "perverse core" of positivism and its endless, internal battle between the law and morality. This Lacanian/Žižekian-inspired reading of positivism gives way to a more political—at times Schmittian—analysis in Chapter Four, "One *Recht* to Rule Them All! Law's Empire in the Age of *Empire*." Here, Tolkien's *Lord of the Rings*—both the Jackson films[4] as much as the original text[5]—are read, respectively and collectively, as allegories of the Kelsenian *grundnorm* as revived and retheorized by Michael Hardt and Antonio Negri's *Empire*.[6] That *grundnorm*, or basic norm, is conjured up, oddly enough, by the destruction of the Ring, a casting away of the posited law, itself analogous to *Empire*'s recuperation of a new, dematerialized law: rights discourse. Read from this vantage, the real empire that emerges at the end of Tolkien's text is not so much Sauron's as Aragorn's, with Gondor standing in as a fantasy, fancy-dress version of the American imperium: consensual yet oppressive, peaceful but always at war: that is, a friend *and* an enemy, at one and the same time.

Empire accedes to law and economics in Chapter Five's "Precrime Never Pays! Law and Economics in *Minority Report*." In this chapter, Law and Economics' claims to act *ante facto* are exposed as equally obscurantist as the PreCogs' claims in *Minority Report*[7] to predict precrime. Thus an irrationality, according to this chapter, is driving this most putatively "rational" of jurisprudential movements, a chiasmus that takes its most extreme (il)logical form in Law and Economics' attempts to construct a "jurisprudence of antijurisprudence." Such antijurisprudence would reduce law to nothing more than a set of disincentives to "inefficiency," a cluster of behavior-modifying sticks with which to beat *homo economicus*' "free choices." Law and Economics' paradox of "forcing one to be free" finds its filmic corollary, so this chapter will argue, in the stun guns of the PreCrime police squads, and indeed, the authoritarianism—the unregulated "nightwatchman state" having produced the overprescribed "nightmare state"—for which they are so clearly symbols (as much as agents).

From this "far right" of the juridico-political spectrum, Chapters Six and Seven take a sharp left, turning to critical legal studies (CLS) and the "politics of the

law," particularly as exposed by the gender and race critiques of its epigones: critical legal feminism and critical race theory. The former—critical legal feminism's
gender critique—informs Chapter Six's "Critically Blonde: Law School as Training for *Her*steria," which examines *Legally Blonde*[8] as a response to and critique
of both formalist (rule-bound, hierarchical) and CLS-style (rule-skeptical, antihi-
erarchical) legal education, offering, impliedly, a feminist alternative to the hitherto phallic arena of the law school. The latter—the race critique of critical race
theory—underpins Chapter Seven's "It's the Vibe! The Common Law Imaginary
Down Under," which takes the reader away from the Anglo-American pop littoral
to the distant antipodes. Aussie cult comedy, *The Castle*,[9] is the focus here, and this
chapter will examine how this film satirizes issues of property, ownership, and race
in contemporary Australia. These topics remain paramount for the "lucky country," especially in the wake of the 1992 landmark *Mabo* decision,[10] recognizing the
native title of Indigenous Australians. In its story of the Kerrigans, a working-class
Melbourne family fighting for possession of its soon-to-be expropriated home,
The Castle reflects (in its citation of *Mabo*) but also refracts (given the Kerrigans'
undeniable whiteness, despite their insisted affinity for Indigeneity) these issues,
posing and reposing the question: Who owns Australia?

Chapter Eight, the last substantive chapter, ends fittingly enough on the theme
of endings and the notion of the right to die as dramatized in two films: American
Oscar winner *Million Dollar Baby*,[11] and the Spanish film *The Sea Inside*.[12] Both
were released in the United States during the legal trials of Terri Schiavo, the life-in-
death case that gives this chapter its title, "Million Dollar Terri: The Culture of Life
and the Right to Die." Each of these films airs, in unusual and thought-provoking
ways, the pros and cons of termination as played out in the ethical, political, and
legal debates over Terri Schiavo's court-ordered termination, and might suggest
an alternative to the stark divide in that case between the sacred and the secular,
between faith and freedom. From here, the conclusion, "Whither Lex Populi?" will
review the preceding chapters' close readings and will speculate on the theoretical
and practical consequences of the intertextual jurisprudence of *lex populi*.

That intertextual jurisprudence is itself a product of context, of institutional,
interdisciplinary, and discursive networks of scholarship spanning (at least) three
continents: Australia, Europe (particularly the United Kingdom), and North
America (particularly the United States). These networks are as much a product of
biography (I have lived, studied, and worked in all three jurisdictions) as they are
of two forms of globalization, one historical, the other current. Historical global-

ization, of course, finds its force in the very real legal and linguistic influences of the now (formally) defunct British Empire: namely, common law and the English language, both of which continue, at least in symbolic terms, to color much of the world's map as pink. Add modern globalization to this, the more contemporary version of imperialism promoted by the *Pax Americana* and the most benign form of which is ideological: its pop culture (especially *legal* pop culture) and its *lex populi*–dominating texts, images, and screens around the globe. These two tremendously colonizing juggernauts (for what is globalization if not a new form of colonization?) collide, like tectonic plates, in the pop culture imaginary of my adoptive country, Australia.

That nation, poised as it is on the fault lines of Anglo-American *lex populi*, has become a trailblazer in the academic analysis of this cultural legal phenomenon, producing cutting-edge scholarship that crosses the boundaries between, for example, law and art (Alison Young[13]), law and music (Desmond Manderson[14]), law and film (Judith Grbich,[15] Mary Farquhar[16]), and law and television (Suzanne Christie,[17] Jenni Milbanke,[18] Isabel Karpin[19]). Of late, an excellent anthology has appeared—Margaret Thornton's *Romancing the Tomes: Popular Culture, Law, and Feminism*[20]—collecting and collating many of these perspectives. This exciting research, and the lively debate that it generates, finds a welcome and welcoming home in the annual Conference of the Law and Literature Association of Australia (LLAA). This moveable feast, currently under the aegis of Association president Peter Rush (of Melbourne), was the initiative of what might be called a "first wave" group of law-and-literature scholars such as Terry Threadgold[21] (now of Wales), Penny Pether[22] (now of Villanova, Pennsylvania), Larissa Behrendt[23] (of Sydney), and Peter Hutchings[24] (previously of Hong Kong; now of Sydney). Now in its second decade—and into its second and even third wave of scholars (Derek Dalton,[25] Kirsty Duncanson,[26] Merran Lawler,[27] Mark Rosenthal,[28] and Kieran Tranter,[29] for example), this conference is one of the principal venues of what might be called global "cultural legal studies," attracting speakers and attendees from countries like Great Britain and the United States—in short, countries toward which Australia has a long history of "cultural cringe," a tradition that is now (pleasantly) reversed.

Not that Britain is without its equivalent movement (think of the work of Steve Redman,[30] or law-and-film duo, Guy Osborn and Steve Greenfield[31]), venues (such as the annual Critical Legal Conference, or 2003's Law and Popular Culture Symposium at University College London), and organs of publication (such as

Law & Critique). Indeed, that nation's cultural legal scene has proved to be one of the most intellectually open, innovative, and nonhierarchical in the common law world, a reality very much at odds with a popular (mis)representation—David Lodge?—of the British academy as static, stale, and Oxbridge dominated. Perhaps one of the saving graces of British cultural legal studies has been the (deafening?) *silence* of Oxbridge, a default enabling the different voices of London, of Lancaster, and of Kent to be heard. And heard they most definitely have been, like "the mouse that roared," punching well above their weight in true Dunkirk style. Nowhere is that voice of cultural legal difference more strongly and keenly expressed than in the work of a group of three wise men, whom I call, with all due deference, the "magi of Bloomsbury": semiotician Peter Goodrich[32]; philosophe Costas Douzinas,[33] and the late, great "crit," Ronnie Warrington.[34] Among them—and with able and admirable assistance from Kent's Peter Fitzpatrick—they have established what, in a sobriquet with no overstatement, might be hailed the "Birkbeck School." Based at London University's avant-garde law school, Birkbeck College, this school or movement has broadened its initial cultural base from law-and-literature (still well and worthily represented by Maria Aristodemou[35] and Wales-based, Birkbeck-trained Melanie Williams[36]) to include law and film (Les Moran[37]), law and architecture (Piyel Halder[38]), and law and aesthetics (Adam Gearey[39]). Other affiliated members of this school, although not directly associated with Birkbeck, would include "Northern" scholars such as Sue Chaplin[40] (law and literature), David Seymour[41] (law and film), and Angus McDonald[42] (law and aesthetics), as well as a sprinkling of diasporics, such as Los Angeles–based Irishman, Bill Grantham[43] (law and film).

As energetic and go-ahead as the British scene is—including its European fellow travelers: think of Finland's Ari Hirvonen[44] and Panu Minkinnen[45]—it pales, in terms of sheer volume, when one crosses the Atlantic to that society of (juristic) spectacle, that land of (law's) moving image, the United States. There, cultural legal studies builds upon and takes off from a well-established and even entrenched law-and-literature movement, elegantly represented by such distinguished luminaries as James Boyd White[46] (Michigan), Robert Ferguson[47] (Columbia), Robin West[48] (Georgetown), Peter Brooks[49] (Yale), and Wai Chee Dimock[50] (Yale). What characterizes the current American scene, however, is the free-for-all that cultural legal studies has inaugurated in its hitherto decorous law-and-lit debates (about the Constitution as text, the legal judgment as polyphonic, and Melville as jurisprude, for example), whereas now all manner of media are up for grabs. This has led to an explosion of inquiry, debate, and commentary on not just literary but also filmic, televisual, artistic, musical, and digital texts. Leading the charge here are the movie-and-TV brigade, spearheaded by scholars like Anthony Chase,[51] Carol Clover,[52] Paul Bergman,[53] David Black,[54] and of course, Richard Sherwin[55]—to name but a few. But the directorial honors, orchestrating and organizing cultural legal studies, must go to that contemporary Cecil B. DeMille of academe, that auteur of Amherst College, Austin Sarat.[56] A sociolegal scholar of capacious interests—as comfortable with anti–death penalty activism as he is with interpreting *Unforgiven*[57] or *The Sweet Hereafter*[58]—Sarat, more than anyone else, has put cultural legal studies on the American (and global?) map.

Joining Sarat in this enterprise are a host of interesting and innovative American and Canadian scholars: Texas literary critic Susan Sage Heinzelman,[59] Berkeley rhetorician Marianne Constable,[60] and Victorianist Hilary Schor[61] (USC); legal historian Martha Umphrey[62] (Amherst); Russian literature specialist Harriet Murav[63] (Illinois); postcolonialist Nasser Hussain[64] (Amherst); political theorist Tom Dumm[65] (Amherst); race theorists Kendall Thomas[66] (Columbia), Stephen Best[67] (Berkeley), and Michele Goodwin[68] (DePaul); Holocaust scholar Lawrence Douglas[69] (Amherst); criminologist Marianna Valverde (Toronto)[70]; legal philosophers Nomi Stolzenberg[71] (USC) and Roger Berkowitz[72] (Cardozo); and critical-cultural legal feminists Rebecca Johnson[73] (Victoria), Marie-Claire Belleau[74] (Laval), Orit Kamir[75] (Michigan/Hebrew University), and Naomi Mezey[76] (Georgetown). With this sort of backing, Sarat and company have managed to corral one of the most impressive and increasingly international groups of scholars investigating the "cultures of law" in an annual jamboree, the Conference of the Association for the Study of Law, Culture, and the Humanities. That conference has in turn produced a journal, the London-published and American- and Australian-funded *Law, Culture, and the Humanities: An Interdisciplinary Journal*, a new organ for this sort of cultural legal scholarship and a worthy competitor to Britain's *Law & Critique* (edited by Costas Douzinas and the rest of the Birkbeck School) and Australia's *Law, Text, Culture* (edited by Rick Mohr of the University of Wollongong).[77]

Noteworthy in this, my "Cook's tour" of contemporary interdisciplinary scholarship in progressive law, is a similar and shared phenomenon, observable in all three jurisdictions: that is, "culture" has replaced "critique" as not only le mot juste but also the fulcrum of millennial legal studies. The reasons for this change are complex, but some of the etiology of this shift can surely be traced to the critical project's crisis of leadership, its "Young Turks" (especially in America), now aging, sidelined, and ironically open to precisely the same sort of critique that they launched against the previous generation of formalist legal professoriate for being ideological prisoners of their whiteness, their maleness, and their privilege. Another possible reason might be found in the (inevitable?) splintering of critique's identity politics into ever smaller, even more cellular units of "intersectionality." But whatever the specific cause, there is no denying the exhaustion of critique nor the end of its jurisprudential sway. Indeed, that end might be just a small ripple in a much broader current: that is, the "end of theory"—or at least the high theory of the postmodernist moment and its concerns with language's indeterminacy, history's power struggles, or ethics' regard for the Other.[78] For the era of post-theory has largely turned its back on Levinasian pieties, Foucauldian capillaries, and Derridean *différance*, opting instead for a distinctive mode and a new mise-en-scène of interpretation. Not for the posttheoretical are those "scenes of reading" so precious to high theory and revolving around the canon of Heidegger and Rousseau, Bentham and Descartes, Buber and Maimonides. Instead, its privileged site is one that leaves the socio-Symbolic of the philosophy seminar, substituting in its stead the Imaginary of global popular culture.

After all, the "theoretical" success story (succès de scandale?) of this, our post-theoretical, even antitheoretical, age is none other than Slavoj Žižek[79] and his Slovenian cohorts (Mladen Dolar,[80] Alenka Zupančič,[81] and last but certainly not least, Renata Salecl[82]) who look to, say, the films of Hitchcock for a staging of Lacanian psychoanalysis: the "impossible embodiment" of *Psycho*,[83] the gaze of *Rear Window*,[84] and the *objet petit a* in *Notorious*,[85] for example. Of course, reading Hitchcock psychoanalytically is a familiar, even overfamiliar, interpretive move of the likes of cinema studies and cultural studies. And that would seem to portend not theory's end, but its spectral, indeed uncanny return (the return of the repressed?). Žižek and company are all too aware of, even archly self-conscious about, this kind of "eternal recurrence" of theory. But the real point being made by the "Slovenian School"—if it can be called that—is that such a return is anything but the effect of such a predictable hermeneutical maneuver as "psychoanalytic reading" (let alone deconstruction, the archaeology of knowledge, or discourse analysis). That sort of analysis is, for them, absolutely otiose and totally beside the point, because Hitchcock is not only enacting the psychoanalytic in his films (for example, the high-camp, Dal*iesque* dream sequence of *Spellbound*[86]), he is also putting it on the couch, palpating its symptoms, and exploring its unconscious traumas. In short, Hitchcock's films are *reading* psychoanalytic theory, turning the interpretive tables so that the popular culture object explicates the theoretical subject.

A similar such volte-face is precisely the second part of this book's project. That is, I propose not only to read popular culture jurisprudentially, but also to fully examine the extent to which jurisprudence is read "otherwise" by popular culture. Thus I hope to do for jurisprudence what Žižek, Salecl, and others have done for Lacanian psychoanalysis: to see it anew and thereby lay the groundwork for a renewal. Such a renewal will begin not in the standard sources of jurisprudence—the law library stacks with their law reviews and monographs, textbooks and crammers' aids, all rehearsing well-worn debates (Hart-Fuller,[87] Fish-Dworkin,[88] and the rest)—but rather in popular culture's mediation of law's Imaginary, in its science fiction and fantasy literature, in its teen films and "indie" (independent) comedies, in its cult TV and mass-appeal Oscar winners. In so doing, I recognize that I cross not only disciplinary boundaries (jurisprudence-cultural studies), but generic ones.

Moving just as recklessly as I did across jurisdictions—from Oz to Blighty to the Land of E Pluribus Unum—this text shifts and swerves, back and forth, from the page to the screen; or in Lacanese, from the Symbolic (of words, of texts) to the Imaginary (of reflections, of mirror images). This kind of reckless abandon, however, is defensible because it is precisely the sort of peripatetic movement *lex populi* not only solicits but enacts, its principal effect being the very erasure of the distance between the word and the image. Think of the Harry Potter series, which, for all its much-touted "literariness" (puns, anagrams, and other forms of wordplay), has all too easily, even effortlessly, made the transition to cinema (and the wonderfully remunerative digital world of video games!). Or consider Buffy, the vampire slayer, who has been given a new lease on life (returning from the grave?) by the "novelization" of her post-TV escapades,[89] long after the end of her series. The same can be said of *The Lord of the Rings* (do we mean Tolkien's or Jackson's?) or *Fight Club* (Palahniuk's or Fincher's?) and others. So in a sense, *lex populi* has eroded and even brought down the "Berlin Walls" that cultural studies, literary criticism, and legal theory have erected between genres (as well as between jurisdictions, be they spatial or discursive), producing instead a heady mix—an intertext—of textual, imagistic, *and* jurisprudential enjoyment.

That very freighted term *enjoyment*[90]—or more technically, *jouissance*,[91] a term that in French connotes the erotic, even obscene, in contradistinction to the more prim *plaisir*[92]—brings me full circle, back to my principal objective as well as argument, announced at the opening of this Introduction. To reiterate: it is my contention here that popular legal culture, what I call *lex populi*, carries with it an enjoyable supplement or excess—what might be called, by Žižek, via Miller via Lacan, a "remainder of the Real."[93] Though often equated with a brute, Thing-like materiality, the "Real" here turns out to be nothing less than the emptiest of empty ciphers, that most symbolic of symbolic fictions: namely, jurisprudence. This is a startling, indeed astonishing reversal not only of standard (vulgarized?) Lacanian theory but also of the usual demystifying *doxa* of "critique," which hitherto (especially in the 1980s) contented itself with the (now routine) exposure, à la cod-Lacan, of the Real's "Thing": that is, *das Ding* of politics lurking behind the Symbolic Law's letter, constraining and controlling it, and ultimately even cannibalizing it.

Here, I want to not only reverse critique's causal relationship—recasting the letter as supporting, even symptomatizing the image or the object/Thing—but also alter its effect. Instead of merely exposing (and thereby presumably wishing it away?) the "symptom" of jurisprudence, I want to encourage and indeed model for readers how to "enjoy" it, be they Hogwarts wannabes or die-hard Slayerettes, Tolkienistas or Fincher fans, Spielberg devotees or Elle Woods' fashion victims, Aussie "ocker" or American "bubba" working-class heroes. That enjoyment is as necessary as it is desirable because it points a way forward, beyond the stale palliatives of either the economy or sociology of the law, toward a reimagined legality, one informed by and turning on a juris-*jouissance* as much as a juris-*prudentia*. And nowhere is that promise of juristic enjoyment more tantalizing than the one held out by global popular culture. For it is in the realm of *lex populi*, with all of its imaginative possibilities, all its limitless fantasies, that, as Dr. Strangelove might put it, one can stop worrying and learn to love legal theory. It is to this recuperation, this recovery of love—a love of juridical knowledge, of the *philosophia* of *nomos*—that my text, *Lex Populi*, dedicates itself in the hopes that all of us—scholar, student, spectator—can finally, ultimately, and at long last *jouis* jurisprudence!

CHAPTER ONE

Kidlit as Law 'n Lit

Harry Potter and the Scales of Justice

Harry Potter's Legal Legerdemain: The Jurisprudence of Magic and the Magic of Jurisprudence

As many of his young fans would put it, "Harry Potter is magic!" That fashionable youth culture expression is for once entirely warranted because it captures our hero's extratextual (oc)cult following as a worldwide publishing phenomenon, as much as it does his intratextual practices as a wizard-in-training. For Harry Potter is, literally, enchanting. From his first appearance in the kickoff volume of J. K. Rowling's remarkable series, *Harry Potter and the Philosopher's Stone*,[1] Harry and his teenybopper cohort of sorcerer's apprentices—Hermione, Ron, Neville, Seamus, and the rest—have cast a spell over legions of supposedly print-allergic, digitally dependant children, bewitching them on behalf of the "pleasure of the text" instead of the spiel of the video. In the second and third follow-ups—*Harry Potter and the Chamber of Secrets*[2] and *Harry Potter and the Prisoner of Azkaban*[3]—they have continued to charm that original readership as well as new, largely adult audiences. Principally, those Tolkien-, Lewis-, and Blyton-reared baby boomers, long alienated by the exile of "the fantastic" not only from the best-seller lists but from children's literature as a whole. With the publication of the fourth installment, *Harry Potter and the Goblet of the Fire*,[4] this broadening of readership, adult or otherwise, continued apace; though it complicated and even contested some of the unflattering and patronizing media images of Rowling's series as escapist whimsy, nostalgic for the conservatism of the Shire, Narnia, or Mallory Towers.[5]

For here, in her fourth offering, Rowling first addresses—so I contend—one of the least whimsical of readerships in terms that are anything but backward looking or conformist: namely, *lawyers*[6]—especially those of a critical persuasion.

Not that the legal profession directly figures in the text's characterological system in the way, say, journalism is satirized in Rita Skeeter, the odious queen of tabloid tittle-tattle. Or for that matter, the way bureaucracy is lampooned in the unfortunately monikered Cornelius Fudge, the muddlingly mediocre Minister of Magic. But despite their absence as characters from the dramatis personae, lawyers nonetheless may be the novel's privileged implied readers because of their pervasive presence in the text's setting, language, and theme: what James Boyd White would call its "legal imagination"[7] and what in this text I call its *lex populi*. This imaginative vision is realized in the novel's representation of the law's principal forensic process, the trial and its Rule of Law imperatives as dramatized in the tribunals of the Death-Eaters and detailed in the next section of this chapter. It is developed in the text's repeated referencing of that now-dominant juridical idiom, *rights*, especially in the running gag about Hermione's efforts to emancipate the house elves, and again in its implicit evocation of jurisprudence's controlling value, *justice*—the very norm that I contend Hogwarts supposedly stands for, but so desperately lacks. Justice, rights, and the Rule of Law: that is the juridical triune, the nomological three-in-one of legal theory generally, and liberal legalism in particular, that this seemingly simple "kidlit" text takes up and narrativizes. It does so, moreover, with Rowling's characteristic mixture of the serious and the satirical, the critical and the celebratory, to the extent that *Harry Potter and the Goblet of Fire* is propelled out of the "genre ghetto" altogether (by a Nimbus 2000?) and into the stratosphere of *lex populi*'s emerging canon of "law-and-lit."

Hogwarts as Nuremberg: The Pensieve's Vision of Judgment

A law-and-lit reading of this kidlit text would begin however, at the story's end. A back-to-front interpretive strategy is justified because in Chapter 30—near the concluding Chapter 37, ironically titled "The Beginning"—the reader is immersed, vicariously, in the novel's legal imagination. There Harry plunges, like an inadvert diver "thrown forward and pitched headfirst" (HP&GF, p. 508), into the undecidably aqueous or gaseous "bright, whitish silver" (HP&GF, p. 507) swirl of Albus Dumbledore's "pensieve." This object is a magical, rune-decorated "shallow, stone basin" (HP&GF, p. 506), secreted away in the headmaster's study, upon which our hero stumbles after a debriefing session following his disturbing encounter with the now clearly deranged ministerial official, Bartemius Crouch, Sr. The pensieve is one of those portmanteau puns, typical of Rowling's humor (like Diagon Alley), that works both as a referent, descriptive of its object, and as a sign, phonically autoreferencing itself. Quite literally, the pensieve, as the orthography of the second syllable indicates, is a *sieve*, screening out "excess thoughts" and "memories" (HP&GF, p. 519). But as the first syllable's *pen* indicates, the pensieve is holder, as Dumbledore explains, containing these thoughts for later reflection. Then, their "patterns and links" will be processed, mulled over mentally (HP&GF, p. 519); hence, the *pensiveness* of the pensieve. But the pensieve affords more than just an opportunity to reexamine past memories and thoughts; it enables one to actually reexperience them, restaging these moments of *temps perdu*, like some returned, hitherto repressed trauma, suggesting that the pensieve is not unlike, in its structure and function, the Freudian unconscious.

This similitude, of course, is not the text's first gesture in the direction of psychoanalysis. After all, throughout the novel, Harry has been plagued by a series of psychic events that Freud called "the royal road to the unconscious": namely, dreams—or more precisely here, nightmares. The first of these occurred at Privet Drive, home of the dreaded Dursleys (HP&GF, ch. 2); the second, at Hogwarts in the unlikely confines of Prof. Trelawney's bogus Divination class (HP&GF, ch. 29). Both nightmares herald the return of Voldemort, the Dark Lord, whose growing power is somatized in the symptomatic throbbing of Harry's fabled forehead scar. But Harry's nightmares, on both occasions, differ markedly in content, as well as in their source and effect, from the memories vouchsafed him by Dumbledore's pensieve. While the nightmares are criminally violent in the extreme, replete with near-Tarantino*esque* scenes of murder (that of Riddle House's hapless muggle caretaker, Frank Bryce; HP&GF, p. 19) and torture (in the Cruciatus curse performed on Voldemort's shape-shifting factotum, Wormtail; HP&GF, pp. 500–501), the pensieve's memories are models of order—specifically, *law* and order. For they consist of three long-past trials at law of putative Death-Eaters, the Dark Lord's erstwhile minions. First, that of Igor Karkaroff, the Blofeldian headmaster of Durmstrang, Hogwarts' ruthless *Mitteleuropa* rival in athletics and scholastics. Second, that of the aptly named Ludo Bagman, former Quidditch star now turned sports impresario for the Ministry of Magic, compering any and all events of a gaming (read, gambling) nature, such as the World Quidditch Cup and the Triwizard Tournament. Finally, there is the trial of a kind of Death-Eating "Gang of

Four," the most recalcitrant of Voldemort's followers, of whom one prominent member is Crouch's renegade son, Barty Jr.

None of these trials, however, tells either Harry or the reader anything new in terms of plot development. They merely confirm what the text has strongly hinted at, if not disclosed outright. For example: that Karkaroff was a Death-Eater, imprisoned for it, and released only when he grassed on his former associates in crime by turning state's evidence (all of which we know, courtesy of the fugitive Sirius Black, who early on warned Harry off Karkaroff and the entire Durmstrang mob; HP&GF, p. 291). That Ludo Bagman is a compulsive punter who plays fast and loose with any and all rules when money is involved (think how all too eager he is to "help" Harry by passing on insider information, prior to each event of the tournament so that his odds-on favorite will win the Triwizard and his punt with the goblins; HP&GF, pp. 307, 389). That the Crouch family was destroyed by Barty Jr.'s treachery: his father's career compromised, his mother dead of grief, and himself dying in prison (again, a cautionary tale told by Sirius in one of his clandestine visits to Hogwarts in his role as Harry's godfather and guardian; HP&GF, pp. 456–59). Nothing startling here, at least in causal terms of who, what, or why. All of which points to a thematic rather than structural function for the pensieve's trial scenes in the narrative as a whole.

What these trial scenes thematize is the kind of world that Hogwarts—and magic—represent. Namely, one that is subject to the Diceyan-like "Rule of Law,"[8] that lynchpin of liberal legalism where no one is above the law, even if they are Barty Crouch, Jr., and where everyone is entitled to the same procedures—in this case, trial by jury (twelve wizards strong and true?). The presence of the jury at these trials heightens this thematic of legalism and provides a sharp contrast to the insidious trials by ordeal meted out by that demonic parody of the "Rule of Man," Lord Voldemort. He is the would-be sovereign that kills through command and whose sanctions work almost as brutally against those who obey him (think of Wormtail's sacrificed hand during the resurrection ceremony; HP&GF, pp. 556–57) as those who oppose him (like Neville's parents, the Longbottoms, whom he has driven insane; HP&GF, pp. 523–24). Here, I argue, is the raison d'être for the pensieve's curial representations; they drive home an important jurisprudential point about Hogwarts and indeed the magic kingdom as a whole. That, despite the unsettling carceral presence of Azkaban in its midst—now, more than ever, under the rule of the Dementors, a spiritual gulag—the realm of witches and wizards remains committed, as the trials demonstrate, to resolution rather than revenge, adjudication rather than attack—or, as the late Jacques Derrida might put it, the "force of law"[9] rather than the law of force.

Or is it so committed? After all, force is present in spades in the brusque court-room strong-arming of Barty Crouch, Jr. His pathetic, repeated cries of "Mother, I didn't do it" (HP&GF, p. 517) evoke among the jury neither "the quality of mercy" nor a call for clemency, but rather a vengeful, almost sadistic "savage triumph" (HP&GF, p. 516). Admittedly, you couldn't find an accused more deserving of this kind of treatment than Barty. Think of his litany of criminal escapades, recited during his "veritaserum"-induced confession (HP&GF, p. 593): the covert break from Azkaban (HP&GF, p. 594); the abduction and impersonation of Mad-Eye Moody (HP&GF, pp. 591–92); the attempt on Harry's life (HP&GF, p. 589). All carried out by Barty in the aid of and fanatical devotion to Voldemort: "It was my dream, my greatest ambition, to serve him, to prove myself to him" (HP&GF, p. 597). Thus Barty's cries of innocence here ring far from true, calling to mind the disturbed psychopathology of that other mother-fixated killer of popular culture, Norman Bates, and warranting, even justifying the use of the most extreme force. Still there is something deeply unsettling about a life sentence callously meted out to a teenager in the most ham-fisted way imaginable, "being dragged away" by the Dementors, whose "cold, draining power was starting to affect him" (HP&GF, p. 517). But the real sticking point is that Barty is not only denounced, but de-nounced by his own father, an intrafamilial betrayal recalling those treacheries rife under Hitler and Stalin in which party loyalty trumped blood ties. This betrayal raises a strong suspicion that what Harry witnesses here in the pensieve is not a bona fide judicial proceeding but rather one of those curial performances beloved of totalitarian regimes: namely, the show trial, where legality is staged as a show of governmental force. Precisely, in fact, what the Ministry of Magic under witch-finder-general Bartemius Crouch, Sr., seems to have done here.

For all that is bad in Barty Jr.'s trial, however, things are worse with the pro-ceedings against Karkaroff and Bagman, thoroughly undermining the dignity of the court and its processes. The trial of Karkaroff, for instance, is more a police in-terrogation than a judicial proceeding, with an unctuous, favor-currying accused plea-bargaining his way out of Azkaban: "'Crouch is going to let him out,' Moody breathed quietly to Dumbledore. 'He's done a deal with him'" (HP&GF, p. 511). The deal consists of an exchange for information, Karkaroff naming the names of his erstwhile Death-Eating comrades: Dolohov, Rosier, Travers, and even, in one last desperate effort, Severus Snape, Hogwarts' obstreperous Potions master and the bane of Harry's and indeed Gryffindor's existence (HP&GF, pp. 511–13)! An even more unedifying juridical spectacle is the "indulgence" with which Ludo Bagman is treated at his trial (HP&GF, p. 514). He is all too easily exculpated as the "innocent dupe" of the Philby-like ministerial mole, Augustus Rockwood. "Not one person raised their hand" for a vote for guilty, and he is even congratulated by one of the jury for his "splendid performance" in the last Quidditch match (HP&GF, p. 515). So much for the equality of treatment under the law, which here seems shot through with judicial bias, operating far too leniently for some (for sporting stars like Bagman), but all too severely for others (like Barty Jr.). And which, in its utter indifference to the principle of "like cases being decided alike"—the fulcrum of the Rule of Law, stare decisis—is suggestive of the worst features of the Rule of Man and its capricious, arbitrary, and erratic "palm tree justice."

So the vision of judgment that emerges from the pensieve's rebus is a grimly forbidding one: of a society judged and found wanting. Wanting in the very legality it purports to stage; because here, in the trial tactics of forced confessions (Barty Jr. under the veritaserum) and grudge informers (Karkaroff), this society resembles nothing less than a police state. Now, one could argue, as indeed Sirius Black does, that this a-legality, even antilegality, is an extreme but necessary response to an emergency situation, a "policing of crisis," as Stuart Hall[10] would put it. For these trials occur in the aftermath of Voldemort's first appearance, his rise to power having bred "terror everywhere . . . panic [and] confusion." Against this dire backdrop, the magic kingdom's chances for survival would have been remarkably slight, or so Sirius seems to imply, if it did not fight "violence with violence." But the danger, Black continues, is that these temporary "harsh measures"—turning the Aurors, for example, into a kind of crack SAS squad with "powers to kill rather than capture"—may have become permanent (HP&GF, p. 457).

This situation threatens to transform, if not the whole society, then at least the hitherto rule-bound, but ultimately benign, Ministry of Magic into something "as ruthless and cruel as many on the Dark Side" (HP&GF, p. 457). Already, Cornelius Fudge travels in state, with the Dementors acting as a kind of praetorian guard (whose loyalty is highly uncertain, given that Voldemort himself considers them his "natural allies"; HP&GF, p. 564). Fudge even goes so far, in the wake of the debacle of the Triwizard Tournament, to bring them into Hogwarts itself, where they dispense their "rough (in)justice" to the likes of Barty Crouch, Jr.: "It had administered its fatal kiss to Barty Crouch. It had sucked his soul out through his mouth. He was worse than dead" (HP&GF, p. 610). Naturally, Dumbledore stands firm against the Dementors and the kind of "discipline and punish" they represent; he says to Barty Crouch, Sr.: "The first and most essential step is to remove Azkaban from the control of the Dementors" (HP&GF, p. 614). So his attitude is consistent with and remains unchanged from *Harry Potter and the Prisoner of Azkaban*, where even on their security patrols he forbade the Dementors' presence on Hogwarts' school grounds. "Dumbledore won't let them into the school," says Lupin (HP&PA, p. 140), a bar that functions as a kind of quarantine, immunizing the student body against the Dementors' malign influence, even spiritual pollution.

Training for Hierarchy? Hogwarts and the Alchemy of Rights and House-Elfery

What complicates this Dumbledorean strategy of inoculation is that, in *Harry Potter and the Goblet of Fire*, Hogwarts itself is exposed as always/already infected by injustice. It might not be as rank as that of the Dementors; but it is severe enough to call into question Dumbledore's (and Hogwarts') claims of occupying the high moral ground. For if the Dementors abuse the prisoners in their charge, literally feeding off their life force (chi?), then Hogwarts, too, is implicated in an exploitative arrangement. But here they feed off their charges *figuratively* in that they are fed *literally* by "them." I refer, of course, to the house elves. No Tolkien*esque* sprites of high estate here; instead, as implied by their name—*house* elf—these are the lowest of domestic help. Previously, house elves have intruded in the series in the curious shape of Harry's little friend, Dobby, distinguished by his "enormous, green, tennis-ball-shaped eyes . . . pencil-shaped nose . . . bat-like ears [and] long fingers and feet" (HP&GF, p. 327). The friendship is surprising, given that Dobby is the house elf of the haughty, high-born Malfoys, those gentry recusants of the Dark Arts, and the family of Harry's nemesis, Draco. As fans of the series will remember, however, Dobby, with the assistance of Harry, "tricked" his way into freedom in *Harry Potter and the Chamber of Secrets* (p. 328). That trickery, and Dobby's release from servitude was represented as an inevitable and even natural progression. For in that volume, house elves were depicted as historical anachronisms, throwbacks to another time. Like the nurses of Shakespearean drama, or the old retainers and mammies of romance novels—with whom they share the structural function of supplying rather broad comic relief—house elves were feudal superfluities of the "old wizarding famil[ies]," otiose fixtures of, as Ron points out, "big old manors and castles and places like that," with little or no relevance to the modern world of witchcraft and wizardry (though Mrs. Weasley wishes she had one "to do the ironing"; HP&CS, pp. 27–28). So the suggestion in *Harry Potter and the Chamber of Secrets* is that the house elves, like the Giants, are a dying breed, the few remaining ones—like Dobby—soon to secure their manumission.

Nothing, of course, could be further from the truth, as *Harry Potter and the Goblet of Fire* all too clearly demonstrates. For there, house-elfery is exposed as alive and well, indeed flourishing, and at no less a place than Hogwarts itself, which runs as smoothly as it does because of the seemingly invisible, but tireless efforts of the elves: "You do realize," orates an outraged Hermione, "that your sheets are changed, your fires lit, your classrooms cleaned, and your food cooked by a group of magical creatures who are unpaid and enslaved" (HP&GF, p. 210). Hogwarts thus mimics the worst aspects of the ancien régime of the Malfoys, and their "Upstairs, Downstairs" ethic. For Hogwarts house elves are outfitted in livery (in tea towels emblazoned with the "Hogwarts' crest"; HP&GF, p. 328); consigned to, and "rarely leaving the kitchen by day"; and generally being neither seen nor heard, "the mark of a good house elf." Indeed, Hogwarts goes one better than the Malfoys (the Ste. Evremondes of the magic kingdom?) by indenturing more house elves than anyone else: "the largest number in any dwelling in Britain," observes the Gryffindor ghost, Nearly Headless Nick. "Over a hundred" (HP&GF, p. 161). Compounding this "oppression of a hundred slaves" is the deep denial, as the language of pop psychology would have it, with which Hogwarts seems to regard its complicity. Evidencing this denial is the omission, in "one thousand pages" of its official *Hogwarts: A History*, of any reference to the elves, a silence that Hermione condemns as the worst sort of revisionism: "biased" and "selective" (HP&GF, p. 209).

So something is most definitely rotten in the state of Hogwarts, complicating and even contesting its meritocratic claims. For as Napoleon said of the First Empire, so too Hogwarts says of itself: that it is a realm in which *la carrière ouverte aux talents* (the career is open to talent) whether one is from a background that is pureblood (like Ron), mixed (like Harry), or muggle (like Hermione). But far from being a school of wizarding that is beyond reproach, Hogwarts reproduces all the status inequities of the wider society within which it is situated. Its "slave labour" (HP&GF, p. 162)—as Hermione, calling a spade a spade, characterizes house-elfery—resonates with overtones of racial discrimination (signaled in "slave") as much as with class oppression (conveyed in "labor"). For this is a world in which race as much as class is determinative, thereby contextualizing Rowling's fiction as very much a work of postimperial, multiracial, fin-de-siècle Britain, and why it has so much resonance in a world of globalized multiculturalism that is anxious to rewrite its history of racist segregation, stereotyping, and ghettoization. Hence, the presence in the text—unthinkable in earlier children's fiction of, for example, the eminently Waspy "Secret Seven" or "Famous Five"—of characters of color, such as the British-born Chinese (BBC) Cho Chang, or the Afro-Caribbean Angelina Johnson.[11] But this Hobsbawmian "(re)invention of tradition"[12] that Rowling engages in here—depicting Hogwarts as a very grand public school, but with the distinction of black and Asian students—more *displaces* than replaces racism, projecting its worst caricatures of racial "Otherness" onto the house elves. Described as "beaming, bowing, and curtseying" (HP&GF, p. 329)—terms reminiscent of either wide-eyed Uncle Toms or giggling Oriental houseboys—the house elves parallel in their subservient status ("House elves does what they is told"; HP&GF, p. 90) the treatment meted out to and behavior expected of all subaltern subjects—be they black, yellow, or brown—by white mythology's race power.

The allegory of race does not stop with the house elves. Consider, for instance, the case of Hagrid, Hogwarts' larger-than-life gamekeeper and instructor in the Care of Magical Creatures, who feels obliged to offer Dumbledore his resignation when Rita Skeeter "unearths evidence" (HP&GF, p. 381), published in the *Daily Prophet*, exposing him as a "half giant" (HP&GF, p. 373) "*passing*" as a wizard, an epithet that evokes memories of the Empire and its half-castes. For the world of witches and wizards has its own version of the old colonial color bar, tabooing relationships like that of Hagrid's parents—a wizard father and a Giantess mother, the Wagnerian "Fridwulfa" (HP&GF, p. 381)—as a "miscegenation" that even Ron euphemizes as "not very nice" (HP&GF, p. 374). Now Harry, having grown up in the muggle Dursley world of 4 Privet Drive may be oblivious to the niceties of birth adverted to here: "Who cares? . . . There's nothing wrong with Hagrid" is his reaction. But Ron, as the progeny of a pureblood wizarding family—however down at the heels—is certainly not oblivious to the implied hierarchies and understands immediately why Hagrid has kept his less than "respectable" parentage so quiet. This is because the Giants, like the werewolves and vampires, have been hounded from Hogwarts' midst, hunted down as putative Voldemort supporters by the Aurors, and considered so "vicious" as to be irredeemable. Indeed, so ingrained is this prejudice that even someone as secure in their social position as the magnificent Mme. Maxime, the towering headmistress of the Francophone and -phile Beauxbatons, denies her origins as a half-giantess, as other large persons might justify their weight: as nothing more than "big bones" (HP&GF, pp. 373–35).

One person who makes no pretense about how she feels about Hogwarts' finely calibrated race and class hierarchy is Hermione Granger. A subject that she knows from firsthand experience, having endured the schoolyard taunts of "mudblood"—a racist put-down for the muggleborn—from Draco Malfoy's high-caste clique of Slytherin snobs (think of the repellently hooray Henrietta-ish Pansy Parkinson) and slobs (the prehensile duo of Goyle and Crabbe). In fact, much of the latter half of the narrative is concerned with Hermione's retaliation against the Slytherin mob's malicious mouthpiece, poison-pen *journo* Rita Skeeter, for disseminating these kinds of racist slurs against her and especially Hagrid. But Hermione's antiracism is about more than just personal reprisal; for her, to misquote Sheila Rowbotham, "the personal" is the occasion for "the political."[13] And the political that Hermione introduces into the hitherto apolitical world of Hogwarts is nothing less than the "politics of the law"[14]: that is, the quintessentially legalist agenda of what Mr. Weasley calls "elf rights" (HP&GF, p. 125), in this instance pursued through her activist pressure group, the "Society for the Promotion of Elfish Welfare," acronymized as S.P.E.W. (HP&GF, p. 198).

It is here in the narrative that Rowling indulges her own not-inconsiderable flair for political satire, having as much fun at the expense of the agitprop of the 1960s and 1970s New Left, with their "manifesto[s]" and "badges" (HP&GF, p. 198)—though now in the service of the Goon-ish "House Elf Liberation Front" (HP&GF, ch. 29)—as with the politically correct campus politicians of the 1980s and 1990s and their obsessions over quotas (for example, one of S.P.E.W.'s longterm goals is "trying to get an elf into the Department for the Regulation and Control of Magical Creatures because they're shockingly underrepresented") and concern with speech codes (think of Hermione's arched eyebrow over Ron's phrase "working like a house elf") (HP&GF, p. 198). But this kind of humor begins to wear a bit thin, especially when it starts to take on a distinctly Skeeter*esque* tone of vitriol, describing Hermione, in the least flattering of terms, as "vociferous," "badgering," and "glowering," and her campaign as one for which even her closest confreres—Harry and Ron—exhibit a distinct "lack of enthusiasm" (HP&GF, p. 210). What remains unclear, however, is *why* Harry and Ron are unenthusiastic about Hermione's efforts to combat racism through a revivified rights discourse. Does that imply, a fortiori,[15] that Harry and Ron are content with and even supportive of the prevailing status quo, however racist, because it redounds to their advantage as white male wizards? Rowling's text suggests not, because it goes out of its way to parody the kind of right-wing rationalizations of racial inequity often proffered by the privileged in defense of their privileges: namely, that the subaltern actually enjoy their symptom of servitude, subordination, and second-rate citizenship. "We've met them [the elves], and they're *happy*. They think they've got the best job in the world" (HP&GF, p. 211). So claim the Weasley twins, George and Fred, hitherto concerned solely with sport, pranks, and money: in short, Jack-the-lad spoofs of the bloke-y, Richard Branson–like public schoolboy, and as such, hardly the best judge of elf welfare.

The problem, though, is that the behavior of the house elves confirms rather than contests the twins' argument. For example, consider how "delighted" the house elves are when Ron, then on a foray into the Hogwarts kitchen, comments "Good service" after being presented with a tea tray groaning with elf-prepared goodies (HP&GF, p. 329). "False consciousness" is Hermione's rather predictable retort: the house elves only think they are content because they are "uneducated" and "brainwashed" (HP&GF, p. 211). They will soon be put to "rights"—that is, rights to "wages," "holidays," and "proper clothes" (HP&GF, p. 161)—with the shining example of Dobby before them, now working on contract at Hogwarts: "I think this is the best thing that could have happened to those elves," opines Hermione in top "head girl" form. "Dobby coming to work here . . . The other elves will see how happy he is being free, and slowly it'll dawn on them that they want that too" (HP&GF, p. 334). But the difficulty with Hermione's model worker—a kind of elvish Lei Feng—is that Dobby himself feels that, as far as freedom goes, there can be too much of a good thing. For instance, when Dumbledore offered to pay him ten Galleons a week—a standard wizarding wage, but for an elf an *embarras de richesses*—Dobby "beat . . . him down" (HP&GF, p. 331) to one Galleon, thereby exchanging the slavery of unpaid domestic service for what Marxists would call "wage slavery." This is hardly the movement from the realm of necessity to that of freedom.

In light of this, where then lie the text's—and by extension Rowling's—sympathies, be they social, political, and last but certainly not least, legal? Do they lie with the Weasley twins and the organic conservatism of the wizarding caste they represent? Namely, that the traditional bonds of master and slave, of wizard lord and house-elf serf are best left alone, untouched, and intact because reforms, like emancipation, bring with them the greater threat of what Habermas might call "juridification"—in the form of rights discourse—which, more often than not, creates more problems than it solves. This very Burkean view of "law and society" seems borne out by the doleful plight of Winky, Hogwarts' other free elf. She is at loose ends because of her dismissal from the Crouch family's service, having contravened the "Code of Wand Use" by being in possession of Harry's wand (HP&GF, p. 119). The fact that she was unconscious and that the wand was planted on her by Barty in the confusion precipitated by Voldemort's conjured "Dark Mark" at the close of the World Quidditch Cup is no mitigation, occasioning her inadvertent and unlooked-for freedom (HP&GF, p. 116). "Freedom" in this context means for Winky "disgrace" and a source of "shame" (HP&GF, p. 331), hysterically "acted out" by "screaming" and "beating her tiny fists" (HP&GF, p. 330). "Pining" for the only "home" (HP&GF, p. 446) she has known—that of her hereditary masters, the Crouches—Winky anesthetizes herself against self-recrimination (after all, her secret charge, Barty Jr., did escape from her at the match) with a six-bottle-a-day Butterbeer habit, ending up a disheveled, teary, and sodden pariah among the Hogwarts' house elves. "We are sorry you had to see that," chime the house elves when Winky, now a weepy drunk, passes out; "we is hoping you will not judge us all by Winky" (HP&GF, p. 467).

So much for liberalism's equal rights, Rowling seems to say here. For the freedom they bring is double edged, enabling at one and the same time the flourishing self-improvement of Dobby and the sinking stupor of Winky, in much the same fashion as Anatole France once said of the "majestic egalitarianism" of the Rule of Law, which forbids the rich and the poor alike to sleep under the bridges of Paris.[16] This suggests that Rowling's jurisprudential position is more complex than either the *arrière-garde* benevolence of the Weasleys or the militant activism of Hermione, and constitutes something of a "third way" in its politics. A clue to its path may be found in the very identity of Winky herself, who is referred to repeatedly as "her," though initially there is some ambiguity about her sex: "Its voice was higher even than Dobby's had been, a teeny, equivalent squeak of a voice, and Harry suspected—though it was very hard to tell with a house elf—that this one might be female" (HP&GF, p. 89). Thus, Winky is first and foremost a gendered subject, the daughter of a long matrilineal line ("I is looking after the Crouches all my life, and my mother is doing it before me, and my grandmother is doing it before her"; HP&GF, p. 332), who speaks, as the text insists, in a "different voice" from her male partner Dobby. This difference is more than just literally vocal; it extends figuratively to outlook, attitude, and even ways of knowing in the broad sense of Carol Gilligan's celebrated metaphor of a "different voice."[17] For Winky and Dobby seem to differ on every issue: For him, wages are a point of pride ("Dobby wants paying now!"; HP&GF, p. 329), while for her, they are "unbecoming . . . a house elf" (HP&GF, p. 90). For him, disclosures about ex-masters are exercises in blunt honesty (the Malfoys, admits Dobby, are "bad Dark wizards"), while for her, they smack of the rankest betrayal ("You ought to be ashamed of yourself, Dobby, talking that way about your masters"; HP&GF, p. 332).

Male house elves are from Mars, female house elves are from Venus? The text seems to cock a satirical snook at the current battle of the sexes in exchanges like these; but they might also point to a more serious proposition, long maintained by critical legal feminists.[18] That what may work for men—contract, autonomy, rights—may not even speak to, let alone address women's concerns of connection, community, and context and will often result in a juridico-political "silencing" even more final and forceful than the one Winky keeps as a "good house elf" over her "master's secrets" (HP&GF, p. 467). So here the narrative airs a wider hermeneutics of suspicion, rife in and bedeviling critical legal circles, that rights discourse, and indeed the law itself, might be highly problematic strategies for change, something that you can't live with, and can't live without. For how do you change a system's status inequities—its gender, race, and class "intersections"[19] overdetermined in the figure of Winky—through the very instrument of those inequities, namely the law? Or to reformulate the question in terms of agency rather than structure: How do you name someone as a legal subject—that is, the bearer of rights—without negating her through the lack that the law installs in its severance of feudalism's ties?[20] In short: Is the law a symptom or a solution? a hindrance or a help? a friend or a foe? That seems to be the philosophical anxiety driving the novel's very ambiguous representation of rights and, perforce, the law.

Avant la loi: Judging J. K. Rowling

The text's anxieties about the law may in fact be rooted as much in practice as in philosophy, hinting at J. K. Rowling's own legal woes. Of course, the usual intellectual property problems of pirated copies persist in copyright-averse Asian jurisdictions, for example.[21] Not that the West is any better, although the legal issue there concerns the series' "magical" properties—specifically, whether Harry Potter is an advert for the occult, luring preteens away from what *The Simpsons'* Ned Flanders would call the "Good Book" and the numbing fundamentalism that in this instance forms its interpretive community.[22] Calls for banning the series from schools and public libraries have been heard in—where else?—a number of states in the American "Bible Belt"[23] by decidedly (un-)Christian Coalitions (and condemned, quite rightly, by mainstream church leaders, be they Roman

Catholic, Anglican, or mainline Protestant). But the real source of Rowling's troubles, until 2002, was a federal lawsuit launched in the U.S. District Court by Rowling and Scholastic, Inc., the American publisher of the Harry Potter series (along with Time-Warner, Hasbro, and Mattel). The suit was in response to intellectual property rights asserted against Rowling—first by letter, then by counterclaim—by a Pennsylvania-based children's fantasy writer, Nancy Stouffer.[24] Stouffer's counsel argued, inter alia, trademark and copyright violation of the word "muggle," which she claimed to have coined first in her 1984 book, *The Legend of Rah and the Muggles*.[25] Although "muggle" has a very different meaning in Stouffer's text (where it signifies tiny, hairless mutants in a postnuclear holocaust future) than in Rowling's (where it signifies nonwizarding humanity), this etymological similitude was deemed sufficient by Stouffer and her counsel to initiate litigation. But the similarities, they contend, did not stop there. According to the lawsuit, both texts had characters named Potter (though in Stouffer's *The Legend of Rah and the Muggles*, the first names are Larry and Lilly rather than Harry and Lily).[26] Finally, the names Nevil and Nimbus were also claimed to have first occurred in her work, presumably providing the models for characters (Neville Longbottom, the Billy Bunter-ish class klutz of Gryffindor) and/or contraptions (Nimbus 2000, the state-of-the-art Quidditch broomstick) in the Harry Potter series.[27]

Theft? Certainly that was the crass criminal accusation that lay behind all the motions, suits, claims, and counterclaims about infringement, dilution, unfair competition, and the rest. Simply, that Rowling had *stolen* Stouffer's ideas. "Coincidence!" was the comeback of Rowling's publishers, quick off the mark to dismiss Stouffer's claims as "completely meritless."[28] "Fraud" was the court's final decision, lambasting Stouffer for her evidence tampering, convenient vagueness, and ungrounded allegations.[29] Not only did the court find in favor of Rowling and Scholastic; it awarded, as a punitive sanction, a monetary amount of US$50,000 and "costs" against Stouffer on the grounds that she had "engaged in a pattern of intentional bad faith."[30] Indeed, what I find interesting about the case is the way in which it sidesteps another, allied issue, one that turns not so much on the stark contrast of property's theft-ownership nexus but rather on what might be called *lex populi*'s problematic of "appropriation." That is, can there ever be a wholly original act of literary invention? Contemporary literary theory would argue negatively, holding that all writing, especially good writing, is a form of appropriative plagiarism.[31] A point with which, most certainly, Rowling would concur; she has made no secret of her sources,[32] principally, the work of the Oxford "Inklings"

(Lewis, Tolkien, and that ilk)[33] and the school sagas of Enid Blyton.[34] This was the extremely distingué company that transatlantic arriviste and adventuress, Stouffer, attempted to join—and in which, I feel, she may yet have a place. But to be absolutely clear, I am *not* arguing that Rowling infringed Nancy Stouffer's (bogus) intellectual property rights. I *am* pointing out that "muggle" appeared first in Stouffer's oeuvre, and only secondarily in Rowling's. Plagiarism? Certainly not is my retort; because appropriation, however plagiaristic it may seem, always works a transformation. Nowhere more so than in Rowling's putative appropriations of the great tradition of children's literature—and possibly its not-so-great tradition, in the form of Stouffer. Not for nothing is the controlling leitmotiv of the Harry Potter series one of "transfiguration," because these spells (*"Riddikulus,"* for one) bring about a metamorphosis (at one point changing the shape-shifting creature, the boggart into an image of a cross-dressed Snape, to the delight of Neville Longbottom in *Harry Potter and the Prisoner of Azkaban*, pp. 103–4). This transformative process functions as a metaphor for Rowling's literary method, one that weaves canonical echoes and resonances, literary allusions and attributions into a wholly new intertextual fabric.

Justice for All? Transfiguring the Magic Kingdom

If that is the case here, then the real issue becomes whether courts, indeed the law itself, can distinguish between plagiarism and appropriation, derivation and innovation, as much as guilt and innocence. This uncertainty as to the law's judgment shifts the jurisprudential concerns that I have explored so far in this chapter away from critique and its overarching question of whether to mobilize the blunt instrument of the law for social change, to the essentially postmodern question of whether the law as a forensic device is capable of rendering any kind of determination. Uncannily enough—and this may be the truly astounding coincidence of the series—*Harry Potter and the Goblet of Fire* anticipates and even preempts proleptically this jurisprudential shift in its representation of a legal system that cannot tell, with any conviction, who is a Death-Eater and who a White Wizard: in short, it cannot tell who is good and who is evil. This is not to suggest, as some vulgar relativist might, that the world the narrative depicts is beyond good and evil because, without any doubt whatsoever, there is radical Evil here (distilled in its purest form in Lord Voldemort), as much as there is Good (figured in the Gandalf*esque* Dumbledore).

But the point *Harry Potter and the Goblet of Fire* seems to make is that it is no longer possible to tell authoritatively—legally or otherwise—who is good and who is evil, because evil in this world is a corollary, even a result of, the good: Voldemort himself was a product of the Hogwarts system as the poor scholarship boy, Tom Riddle—the uncanny double, interestingly enough, of Harry Potter.[35] All of which raises a greater uncertainty here: not whether Voldemort should be resisted—clearly he must be—but whether that world, with its admixture of good and evil, is one worth fighting for. Class distinctions, racial discrimination, gender bias: all the social evils depicted at Hogwarts and throughout the magic kingdom suggest *not*. If, however, the evil of Voldemort outweighs the social evils represented at Hogwarts, rendering this a cause worth the fight, then changes *must* come, as Dumbledore suggests at the close of the narrative in his Churchillian plan for a "popular front" against the Dark Lord, involving not just his continental, European Union wizarding allies—the Beauxbatons and Durmstrang contingents (HP&GF, p. 627)—but also the Giants (HP&GF, p. 614), possibly the vampires, and even the elves (!).

But the situation could just as easily go the other way. Now that he has risen from his strange, twilight state of life-in-death and reassumed human form (HP&GF, p. 558), Voldemort might appear at any moment, like Lenin at the Finland Station in Petrograd, declaring "All power to the Giant and Vampire Soviets," urging elvish workers of the world to throw off their chains, and marshalling broad Death-Eater support for the construction of the Dark Arts order. If our embattled band of wizards and witches—Harry, Dumbledore, Sirius, Ron, Hermione, even Snape!—is to combat this threatened coup d'état and its looming civil war, then Rowling's "imagined community"[36] of Hogwarts' world must be *reimagined*. It must go beyond the bumbling "governmentality" of the Ministry of Magic (which keeps fudging the issue under Cornelius Fudge), beyond the forbidding carcerality of Azkaban (and its demented and dementing wardens, the Dementors), and even beyond the law, be it the old order's ethic of duty (with everyone—wizards, house elves, Giants—in their proper stations) or the critical language of rights (and its attendant problems of "misrecognizing" some, such as Dobby, at the expense of others, such as Winky).

Yet where is this community to go in search of a *lex populi* vision of a more equal society, a fairer world? Surely it must turn to the imaginary of Justice itself, with Iustitia at its center, her blindfold loosened so that she might balance not just one against one, but the one against the many, form against substance. What might this sighted Iustitia's magic kingdom look like? I would hazard a guess that it would be a place in which slurs like "mudblood" are unutterable and house-elf indenture unthinkable, in which a Giant heritage (or half-heritage) would be a point of pride, and unearned privilege, like that of the Malfoys, a disgrace. It would be a place in which inclusiveness prevails and in which difference is not only tolerated but encouraged. Of course the law, in the form of rights—enforceable through the Rule of Law—would have to be involved to some extent in these sweeping changes. But the point *Harry Potter and the Goblet of Fire* seems to be making is that the law is not enough—at least in its classical liberal legal formulation. Indeed, if change should and must come to Hogwarts, then that community must broach and tap into the transformative potential of substantive justice with its capacity to look beyond formal equality and to trade off entitlement against right, need against desire. Such justice remains, as Jacques Derrida might say, *à venir*—to come—even in the subsequent texts of *Harry Potter and the Order of the Phoenix*[37] and *Harry Potter and the Half-Blood Prince*.[38] I hope, therefore, that the controlling trope of the last of the books—hitherto, "the Philosopher's Stone," "the Chamber of Secrets," "the Prisoner of Azkaban," "the Goblet of Fire," "the Order of the Phoenix," and "the Half-Blood Prince"—is Harry Potter and "the Scales of Justice."

CHAPTER TWO

You Slay Me!

Buffy *as Jurisprude of Desire*

Network Necromancy and the Discreet
Charm of *Buffy the Vampire Slayer*

Why is a TV show like *Buffy the Vampire Slayer*[1] so bloody brilliant, when others in the same time slot, age demographic, and generic vein, like *Charmed*,[2] are so utterly charmless? This contrast is as odd as it is striking: odd, because *Charmed* and *Buffy* exhibit many of the same dramatic features in terms of characters, setting, and most to the point, narrative content. Both programs, for example, showcase ensemble casts of high-profile teen or twenty-something actors.[3] Each series makes the most of its California location, staging a kind of *echt* "West Coastness."[4] And most significantly, both TV shows take the occult as their principal motif and overarching thematic, while exploring that magical brief with varying degrees of specificity or generality.[5] Despite this quantitatively measurable similitude, however, *Buffy* so decidedly rocks, while *Charmed* bites, for at least one reason that goes above and beyond more obvious ones of better scripting, tighter story lines, flashier special effects, abler acting, and more likeable characters. What is this reason?

I would like to suggest in this chapter that the main reason why *Buffy* is so much "buffer" than *Charmed* lies in the former's intellectual appeal over the latter. Intellectual appeal? Of something as farcical sounding as *Buffy the Vampire Slayer*? But before the reader consigns the series—and this chapter's claim—to the same televisual dustbin as such witless prime-time efforts at adolescent Grand Guignol as *Sabrina the Teen-Age Witch*,[6] consider for a moment the website titled

"All Things Philosophical on *Buffy the Vampire Slayer*."[7] There, any cyber-fan of the Slayer can jack onto, for example, the series' "moral ambiguities" and "ethical quandaries"—two of the website's categories—all the while cross-referencing each episode's metaphysical intertexts. So it would seem, if the Internet is anything to go by, that *philosophy* (!) is one of the mainsprings driving the critical as well as popular success of *Buffy*. One significant philosophical subdiscipline, however, is curiously and conspicuously absent from the digital and print commentary concerning the series. What the show's website and literary criticism fail to mention—an omission that this chapter seeks to rectify—is none other than the philosophy of law.

This claim for a legality of *Buffy*—let alone a legal philosophy—may strike even the most theory-friendly Slayerette as misdirected, if not out-and-out wrong. After all, no one goes to court in *Buffy*; no lawyers make any sort of appearance, even when charges are laid; and none of the characters (including Brainiac Willow) evince any sort of desire as undergraduates—let alone high school students—to apply to law school. So why read *Buffy* juridically at all? Especially when such a legal analysis is solicited so clearly, even commanded, by its spin-off, *Angel*?[8] There, strong representations of the law abound: detection (centered around Angel's agency of private investigators of the occult: Wesley, Cordelia, and friends), policing (in the figure of love interest and L.A.P.D. officer, Kate), and lawyering (with those satanic solicitors, Wolfram and Hart). None of *Angel*'s images of crime and punishment recur to the same curially dramatized extent in *Buffy*. This is not to say, just because *Buffy* lacks a *Law and Order* S.V.U. (Special Vampires Unit) overlay, that the series is a-legal or even antilegal. That highly dubious claim is precisely what some of the show's most vociferous critics on the cultural and religious right would argue, claiming it celebrates crime and incites transgressions of the law through teen violence, vandalism, and even vampirism.

This chapter will argue, to the contrary, that *Buffy* is intensely legalist in its issues; indeed, it is a paradigmatic instance of *lex populi*. But the law that *Buffy* engages takes a very different form from that of the conservative caricature of televisual trans(ag)gressivity (Beavis and Butthead with fangs?), or for that matter the street legal aspect of *Angel* (Bobbie Donnell in a cape?). The law as it appears in *Buffy* is more abstracted, even theoretical: in short, an interest that in the parlance of *lex populi* might be called jurisprudential. This more speculative characterization would explain the preoccupations in *Buffy* not only with such metajuridical conundrums as a "higher law"—its sources (in physical nature? in human nature?)

and its content (what is "good"? what, "evil"?)—but also with the question of the legal subject itself. That is, who is the *One* (the Chosen, the Slayer), and who, the Other (the vampires, the demons, the forces of darkness)? Or in legalese, who is intra vires [9] and who is ultra vires [10] the Law? Simply put, who is to live, and who is to die? All of which may suggest that in this bold staging of the Law's, and indeed life's, "tragic choices"—of lives sacrificed (of Buffy for her putative sister Dawn, the Key; and before that, of Kendra, Jenny Calendar, and even Angel himself), but also of love foresworn (which Buffy and Angel repeat in series 1, 2, 3, and so on)—*Buffy's* real concerns are ethical.

But an ethics of what? For as Alain Badiou [11] has shown, there is never an ethics unmodified. An ethics is always/already "for" and "of" something, like the famous (or, depending on your clinical persuasion, infamous) "ethics of psychoanalysis" of Jacques Lacan, with its prime directive, *Ne pas céder sur son desir* (Do not give up on your desire).[12] Here, the ethics that *Buffy* enacts is an ethics of jurisprudence, itself properly Lacanian to this *lex populi* extent. That is: the Law that Buffy qua Slayer desires is a Law of Desire that desires *differently*, a desire that traverses (slays?) the jurisprudential fantasies of either an external (natural) or internal (Kantian) law. Buffy as jurisprude-of-desire acts in order to *hail*, in the Althusserian sense of interpellation,[13] a new legal subject. That subject is neither the *lex natura's* theologue (Antigone, Aquinas) of this chapter's next section, nor liberal legalism's philosophical rights-bearer (the Kant-Mill autonomous self). Rather it is what I call, following the *école freudienne*, the subject of *extimité* (extimacy).[14] That extimate subject is both and neither inside and/or outside the law, because it is saturated by a gap, a lack—a hole. And the staking of this hole, literalized in Buffy's vampire slaying, may point (pun intended) *lex populi* in the direction of a new juristic identity, undergirded by a jurisprudence of desire for *difference* and a different *desire*.

Death and the Maiden: Buffy as Postmodern Antigone?

If any device announces *the* jurisprudential subtext of *Buffy*—and specifically the jurisprudence of natural law—then it is the series' self-conscious Gothicism: graveyards, haunted houses, crypts, and such. This explicit referencing of genre situates the show's diegetic reality squarely within a natural law world of gods and monsters, of divinities and devils in which our heroine is the sole (Christological?) redemptive force. "In every generation there is a Chosen One. She, and she alone will fight the demons, the vampires, and the forces of darkness. She is the Slayer."[15] So goes the opening voice-over introducing the first episode of the series. And what this epigraphic dialogue drives home is not only the point of the Slayer's singularity ("Chosen One"; "She, and she alone"), but also her perpetual presence ("In every generation . . . "). This double coding of the Slayer—as unique as well as recurrent—renders Buffy a contempo-casual version of what German Idealism might call the "eternal feminine."[16] Thus "the gothic" is most definitely gendered here. Indeed, Buffy's slaying has a long gynocentric lineage, stretching back through time immemorial. From a 1970s Pam Grier look-alike, fighting Spike in one episode,[17] to a 1930s "Korean chick" mentioned by Sid the demon-hunting dummy[18]; from a 1920s Chicago gal to a Civil War widow, both featured in the opening voice-over of the first episode[19]: all the Slayers have been women. And each of these figures is anticipated by and issues from that *She*-style ur-Slayer, the Aboriginal-like Primitive, whom Buffy meets up with in her dreams in the episode "Restless."[20]

All these avatars of the Slayer—including, of course, Buffy herself—carry out that diktat from above, "Slay all vampires"—a ukase if not in clear contravention, then at least operating outside of state sanction and its monopolization of legitimate violence. This linking of a "higher law" ("Slay all vampires" as an imperative that takes priority over, even trumps posited law) with femininity (Buffy, and all those lineal femmes fatales before her) should suggest, to all jurisprudes worth their "philosophy of right," a strong analogue if not identity. Antigone the Vampire Slayer, or Buffy the postmodern Antigone? In either case, the series seems to go out of its Hegelian way to place Buffy within a natural law context and its founding theological mythos of "Death and the Maiden." For, of course, this school of jurisprudence, like that of *Buffy*, finds its originary moment, its writing *degré zéro* in the Sophoclean[21] story of a young woman who defies the *law* (that of man) in favor of the *Law* (that of God—or nature, or humanity): namely, in Princess Antigone's service to the will of Greek gods and their "higher law" mandating a proper burial of the dead, otherwise dooming the unburied to wander the earth as spirits, without admittance to the Isles of the Blessed. In giving her dead brother Polynices a proper burial—like the one accorded his sibling and killer, Eteocles—Antigone saves his soul from this fate of endless afterlife peripateia, thereby satisfying the dictates of divine justice. But in so doing, she violates Thebes' "command of the sovereign" forbidding such funerary rites for Polynices, a punishment imposed here owing to his treachery in taking arms against his native polis. Now, as much an outlaw as Polynices was, at least in the eyes of the state,

Antigone finds herself—like Buffy does in the first episode of Season 6 [22]—sentenced to living entombment by that embodiment of the "rule of man," her uncle, King Creon. Unlike Antigone, however, Buffy survives this and other near-death close calls; she "dies" at the end of Season 1 (drowning by the Master [23]) as well as Season 5 (the life force drained from her in her final showdown with Glory [24]) and yet lives to fight another day. Nonetheless, loose corollaries can be drawn here, analogizing slaying to the higher law of the gods (in defiance of the posited law of the state, or the Mayor), or analogizing Principal Snyder to King Creon, and the Slayer herself to the Princess.

What seals Buffy's identification with the natural law, however, lies in the medieval more than classical, jurisprudential parallels, which "Aquinianize" the series, so to speak, by situating its *lex natura* [25] of slaying ("Slay all vampires!") within a specifically theocratic institutional frame. Here, this Caesaro-papalist context is announced by the figure of Watcher, Rupert Giles, whose library of demonological and vampire folklore functions as a kind of occult equivalent of the scriptural *lex divina*. [26] And just as holy writ was safeguarded and made secure by *Ecclesia*, the Church, so too Giles's Foucauldian archive of magical power and knowledge is policed and patrolled by an ecclesial body: the Curia-like, nay, "Sacred Congregation for the Doctrine of the Faith"–style interpretive community, the synodical Council of Watchers. Such a sectarian characterization of the Council might seem at loggerheads with the Anglophile, even Anglican accent, attitude, and provenance of the individual Watchers. Giles, Quentin Travers, and of course, the ludicrous Wesley Wyndham-Pryce suggest more the See of Canterbury than that of Rome. But note the way in which the Council behaves: far from miring itself in any Church of England "via media" muddle, the Council acts with an "infallibility" worthy of Tridentine conciliarism; vetting, reprimanding, even recusing not just the Slayer but her Watcher (going so far as to relieve Giles of his duties in the fourth season) for any infraction of their highly persnickety notion of theological correctness.

But the problem with the Council and, indeed, the series' "theological correctness," is that it is so politically incorrect and in deep denial, if not actively engaged in repressing the law's ideological implications. Of course, this repression is precisely why *Buffy* is so much the master narrative of our postideological, "third way" times. [27] Times that, now more than ever in light of September 11, are intent on depoliticizing the etiology of world events, as much as the "politics of the law," by projecting a theological *weltanschauung* of the "ethics of the Good" [28] (read, Western values) against "radical evil" [29] (read, Islamic fundamentalism). This repression of legal ideology in favor of Manichean theology, however, is not entirely successful. Closure is never fully realized: another space, an alternative—potentially disruptive—scene intervenes. The nature of this space or scene, of course, is suggested in the many dream visions the series vouchsafes, dreams being the "royal road to the unconscious," as Freud teaches us.[30] But the unconscious that *Buffy*'s *Traumdeutung* points to is of a special type. Its dreamwork here is neither a portent of things to come (like Drusilla's vision of Ms. Calendar's computing counterspell for Angel in "Passion"[31]), nor a remembrance of things past (like that of James's 1950s *liebestod* with Miss Newman, replayed over and over again in "I Only Have Eyes for You"[32]). Rather it is a *wunsch* of alternate worlds and parallel universes, with radically different, even dystopian modes of legal sovereignty. Think of that worst-case scenario: Bizarro-Sunnydale ruled by vampires—The Master, Vamp Xander, and in a "star turn," Vamp Willow as polymorphous perverse dominatrix for bondage slave, "puppy" Angel—in that most chilling of the series' episodes, "The Wish."[33] Which suggests that what is being enacted here is a juridical version of what Fredric Jameson would call the "political unconscious"[34]: the very realm of repressed legal ideology hived off from—but never entirely hunkered down under—the conscious world of theological forgetting.

Yet the dream is not the only symptom in *Buffy* that marks the law's ideological "return of the repressed," crossing over and traversing that split between the political unconscious and apolitical legal consciousness. In fact, that very split is projected upon and literalized in the ideological fissures that become more and more apparent throughout the series in the theological edifice of the *Buffy* house of higher law, the Council. Far from presenting a united front of regular juridical routines and rationale—"like cases being decided alike," for example, as consistent with the Rule of Law—its magisterium is compromised, even riven. On one hand, it betrays a negligence (allowing a rogue Watcher like Gwendolyn Post to remain at large in "Revelations"[35]) that shades into complete ineptitude (dispatching an incompetent like Wesley to replace Giles in "Bad Girls"[36]). On the other hand, it displays a peremptoriness (relieving Giles of his Watcher's duties for taking too "fatherly" an interest in his charge, Buffy, in "Helpless"[37]) capable of astonishingly ruthlessness (utilizing SAS-style commando tactics to kidnap Faith and spirit her back to England for a pseudo-Slayer court-martial[38]). So wide is this rift that the Council (and its "higher law") begins to look less and less like the Roman Catholic Church (and its canon law) and much more like the cosa nostra (with its code of *omertà*). Or even more fantastical, like one of those underworld organizations beloved of action-adventure films and TV series—the Bond movies,[39] *The Man from U.N.C.L.E.*,[40] and *Get Smart*,[41] for example—that are everywhere and nowhere, mimicking in their cloak-and-dagger methods (agents licensed to kill) and evil genius "Mr. Bigs" (Ernst Stavros Blofeld as demonic parody of "Mother"), the "secret state" of the MI5 or the CIA, right down to their acronymic "S.M.E.R.S.H.," "T.H.R.U.S.H.," and "K.A.O.S."

However one may choose to characterize the Council—as Mother Church, Mafia, or Murder Inc.—one thing remains clear: in its factionalism and fanaticism, in its power struggles and wars of position, the Council is above all a site of political jockeying and source of ideological conflict. Nowhere more so than in defining the ambit of its central tenet: the "higher law" of slaying. Indeed, complicating the Council's already precarious juristic position, if not driving an even deeper wedge into its ever-widening politico-legal fault lines, is the figure of the Slayer herself. This is a somewhat surprising about-face because, as *the One*, she would appear to be the agent of suture nonpareil. Of course, Buffy is anything but the one and only Slayer, a function that keeps on dividing, as if by meiosis, first into two (the West Indian, Kendra, introduced in "What's My Line?, Part 1"[42]) and then into three (that outrageously improper Bostonian, Faith, who first appears in "Faith, Hope, and Trick"[43]) Slayers. Moreover, these improbable multiples of One not only double and triple Buffy, but they also proffer very different, even incompatible if not contestatory jurisprudential models of slaying. Kendra's rule-bound formalism provides a vivid contrast to Faith's ruleless nihilism. And both function as the opposite extremes to the median of Buffy's much more relaxed (realist?) style, neither all by the book (Kendra-as-positivist) nor entirely improvised (Faith-as-Crit), but more on the Llewellyn*esque* order of getting the "law job"[44] done.

All of which is to say, *how* you slay in the Buffyverse is contingent upon *who* is slaying. Further, *who* is slaying determines *what* is being slain, because much to Kendra's straitlaced shock (as a flagrant breach of her commitment to the letter of the law) and Faith's lascivious approval (as totally in keeping with her eroticization of violence), Buffy exceptionalizes one vampire. He is, naturally, Angel, that most seraphically named and partially redeemed of vampires, "cursed" by Romany hex with a soul. Indeed, Buffy not only refrains from slaying Angel, she also does everything in her power to save him, even breaking with the Council when it refuses him an antidote after his poisoned spearing in "Graduation Day, Part 1."[45] What's more, Buffy defies the Slayerettes themselves, and their not-unjustifiable concerns about her judgment in taking Angel in, when, soul restored, he returns in "Faith, Hope, and Trick,"[46] feral-like, from a harrowing in hell with the worst case of Catholic guilt on prime time. Thus slaying's target (all vamps, but one?) and tactics (formalist? nihilist? ad hoc?), as well as the Slayer's identity (Buffy? Kendra? Faith?) and the Council's nature (consensual or conflicted? good or evil?), chop and change so much, trim and turn so often that the "politics of the law"[47] begins to move to center-stage once more, legal ideology not just displacing but rendering unstable and ultimately undoing theology's "higher law."

Liberal Legalism's Specular Twins: Kant avec Sade; Buffy avec Spike?

But the series' ideological moment—and its disruptive radical indeterminacy, reminiscent of 1980s' Critical Legal Studies—is not merely destructive but properly deconstructive, in that it not only combusts but also constructs programmatic, jurisprudential alternatives to theology and its Law of Nature. Buffy's postconciliar career amply attests to this not-so-hidden juristic agenda, because no sooner does she take up slaying under her own aegis, then she begins enacting a particular, even peculiar kind of politics of the law, one with its own unique legal philosophical lineage. By way of contrast, the nature of law's politics here is underscored by Faith, the other "rogue slayer," whose raison d'être, as well as *raison d'état*, is summarized in Season 3's "Consequences"[48] by her neatly anaphoric, "I see. I want. I take." With this triumph of the will over reason, Faith effectively forecloses the Law, a *verferwung* (repudiation) guaranteeing her descent into madness, to the point where she ends up the psychotic minion of that figure of *hors-loi*, the Mayor. Unlike Faith, however, Buffy does not foreclose the Law as much as internalize it. In so doing, she realizes an *auto-nomos*, a self-government that looks something like an autonomic variation on the theme of liberal legalism and its organizing meta-law.[49] What is this meta-law? It turns out to be none other than a conflation of the jurisprudential formulae of those two great liberal (and legal) philosophes, John Stuart Mill and Immanuel Kant. Here, the former's "harm principle" ("The only purpose for which power can be rightfully exercised over any member of a civilised community, against his will, is to prevent harm to others"[50]) combines with the latter's "categorical imperative" ("Act as if the maxim of your action were to become through your will a universal law of nature"[51]). Together they produce a new "rule of recognition"[52] or *grundnorm*[53] of slaying, one that would run along the lines of: "Slay! But slay only those who intentionally vamp others!"

This injunction is thus classically liberal legal. It is at once *particular*—in that it is self-legislating, thereby releasing the individual's right to slay from the strictures of established structures (be they sacred or secular)—and *universal*, providing a

principled yardstick by which to measure all cases of vamping while simultane-
ously sanctioning slaying. It is from this convocation of opposites—of specific
right and general principle, of *gesetz* and *recht*—that liberal legality's Rule of Law
thematic obtains. Nowhere is this thematic of particularized universalism or uni-
versalized particularity—what Ronald Dworkin's Hercules might call "law as integrity"[54]—better put to the test then in "Bad Girls."[55] There, Faith accidentally
stakes the all-too-human Deputy Mayor Allan Finch, himself on the verge of de-
fecting to the Scooby Gang from the Mayor's inner circle of "sword and sorcery."
Faith's stunned reaction, and specious self-justification—of ends over means, of
utility over rights: that individual sacrifices must be made for and on behalf of the
"greatest good for the greatest number"[56]—boldly differs from that of her sister
Slayer. For Buffy endorses, absolutely and unequivocally, the value of the particular—the sanctity of human life, the centrality of the individual, the paramount
need to "take rights seriously"[57]—as the only means by which to realize the universal and any sort of higher purpose, particularly "Law's Empire"[58] of integrity
and its prevailing value of liberal autonomy.

At this juncture, the question arises as to why this jurisprudential "inward turn"
in *Buffy*, thereby detaching the Slayer from the theology of natural law's "great
chain of being" and resituating her squarely within the ideology of liberal legalism's self-government? Why a kind of slaying equivalent of the Kantian "Coper-
nican Revolution," exchanging the Council's autocracy for the Slayer's autonomy?
In short, why the change from outer command to an inner voice? This startling
juridical shift makes sense only when seen holistically in its overall popular as well
as youth cultural context, and within the law stories that circulate within each.
For what—or rather, *who*—is the legal underdog, the antiheroic jurisprude of
our postmodern times? One who turns out to be none other than that desiccated
descendant of nineteenth-century legal liberalism's autonomous individual. That
is, the figure of the "marginal man,"[59] the "outsider," or—with all due respects
to Oz—the "lone wolf," existing apart from and, on occasion, in conflict with
the social herd. A figure, who, nonetheless, is "Lacanianized" to the extent that
he proclaims, contra deconstruction's "bad infinity" of différance: "The Truth is
out there." Of course, true believer, Fox Mulder, and his less and less skeptical
scientific sidekick, Dana Scully, represent the televisual apogee of this typology of
"faith and good works." Both are forever searching for that sublime object of ideology—the alien body—that will seal the rupture in the Other, itself barred, sealed,
crossed out by the "X" of the series' eponymous FBI files.[60]

Buffy replicates, even clones, this science fiction-cum-supernatural scenario, starting in the fourth season's premiere, "The Freshman." [61] There, the scene and story line shift to campus life, with the Scooby Gang's admission and move to UC-Sunnydale. It is against this collegiate-Gothic backdrop that *The Parallax View*—[62] or *Three Days of the Condor*–style [63] narrative of "the Initiative" is played out. Like the apocryphal X-files of the FBI, the Initiative is a state-sponsored, highly covert operation under the direction of its own "smoking man": "psycho" psychology professor, Dr. Maggie Walsh. Walsh, like all mad scientists, is engaged in the typically overreaching and unquestionably doomed-from-the-start project of "alien resurrection," monstrously embodied and brought to life in that most "Other" of others, Adam—truly Frankenstein-like in his creation, but one that only the twentieth century could have produced. This is because, in his admixture of terror and technology, Adam betrays more the influence of Martin Heidegger as mediated by James Whale than that of Mary Shelley. Moreover, the traumatic "truth event" of Adam's animation, as Deleuze [64] and Badiou [65] might put it—and subsequent killing rampage: first, "Mummy," a.k.a. Dr. Walsh in "The I Team" [66]; then the small child he comes across in "Goodbye, Iowa" [67]—effectively reanimates Buffy's flagging career of slaying. Specifically, Adam provides Buffy with a Mulder-like focus (if not obsession), hitherto absent in a season that had gone—but for the truly terrifying "Hush" [68]—somewhat stale in its focus on dorm conundrums (obnoxious roomies like "Believe"-lovin' Kathy Newman in "Living Conditions," [69] for example, and one-night stands like "Stinky Parker Man" Abrams in "The Harsh Light of Day" [70]). With Adam's appearance, however, the differences between *Buffy* and *The X-Files* become as apparent as their similarities, nowhere more so than in how these programs' main characters position themselves with respect to the Other. Mulder and Scully, for example, want to annul themselves in the Other (either becoming or bearing aliens); while the Slayer must destroy this Other (Adam finally and climactically disposed of in "Primeval" [71] with the help of the Slayerettes) because it threatens to destroy the very notion of otherness itself.

The notion of otherness is precisely what is at stake in the autonomization of Buffy. This is so because the categorical imperative of slaying hails not only the choosing self ("Slay!") but also the chosen other ("but slay only those who intentionally vamp others"). And with the installation of this self-other dyad, the series exposes—and thereby undoes—liberal legalism's trumpeting of the primacy of the individual. For autonomy is revealed here as contingent, even dependent upon the moment of an(O)ther's recognition. That is, the "me" of liberalism (the One) is predicated upon and a result of the "not-me": namely, a double, or specular twin, reflected in an identic hall of mirrors. No wonder, then, that increasingly throughout *Buffy*, the vampires *reflect* (even though they have no reflection) the issues and interests of the characters: for example, Vamp Willow's lesbian chic as a prefiguration of Willow's own same-sex preferences, "outed" in Season 4. And this mirroring extends to the broader topics and trends of youth culture writ large: Drusilla as Euro-Goth, for example, or Harmony as a "blonde joke." But more than just reflect, the vampires *refract* the world of *Buffy*, giving back in reverse form its demands and desires. Crucial here is the figure of that mockney New Lad, the Billy Idol / Sid Vicious–like Spike, a.k.a. "William the Bloody." Initially introduced as a saturnine counterpoint to the sensitive Angel (and later, briefly, as a disabled foil to Angelus redivivus), Spike grows in stature throughout the series, becoming the Slayer's most persistent nemesis and outlasting even the Mayor. Indeed, one could go so far as to say that Spike becomes Buffy's Other, providing a kind of Sadean inversion of her Kantianism.[72] He mirrors—that is, reproduces but reverses—the Slayer's injunction, so that the prohibitive, "Slay! But only slay those who intentionally vamp another!" becomes the perverse, "Vamp, vamp, and vamp again because it feels so good." So Spike specularizes slaying back to front, transposing *jouissance* for *coupure*, enjoyment for the Law. In so doing, Spike-as-Other paradoxically performs a valuable moral function: more than any other character, he seems to secure the stability of the series' Imaginary, fixing its "quilting points" of good and evil, of friend and foe.

Or does he? After all, one of the series' most outrageous turnabouts is the transmogrification of Spike from archfiend and foe into something resembling an ally, if not an on-again, off-again amour. Of course, the mechanism by which this volte-face is effected is just that, *mechanical*: a device implanted by the Initiative that "defangs" Spike after his capture in "The Harsh Light of Day."[73] This device renders him, so to speak, neuter. Incapable of vamping, even when he escapes the Initiative's clutches (in "The Initiative"[74]), Spike takes shelter with the Scooby Gang (in "Pangs"[75]) and discovers, to his delight, that he can still take pleasure in inflicting pain because his cortical override is inoperative when it comes to demons. From there on, the former "Hostile 17" becomes a slaying ally—albeit a highly unreliable one—in the struggle against the Initiative. Though in covert contact and cahoots with Adam for much of Season 4, Spike rallies for the climactic showdown in "Primeval," throwing his lot in with the Scooby Gang at the last minute. In Season 5, Spike becomes an integral part of the Slayerettes. He exposes

Riley's kinky vamp addiction (in "Into the Woods"[76]), intercedes on Dawn's behalf (in "Crush"[77] and "The Gift"[78]), and even falls in love with Buffy herself (starting in "Out of My Mind"[79] and then developing in "Fool for Love"[80] and "Crush"[81]). Although initially unrequited and mediated—with a fitting Spike-like perversity, through the fetish of the Buffybot (see "Interventions"[82])—Spike's love (or at least, lust) is reciprocated in Season 6. Buffy and he not only snog at the end of "Buffy: The Musical"[83] but also have Slayer-sex in "Smashed."[84]

Now, if this sort of metamorphosis can happen to the "Big Bad" himself, then all bets are off as to anyone's identic determinacy in the series. All of which suggests that the series' Imaginary is not as secure as previously indicated. Rather than an Althusserian *salon des glaces* of clear-cut "hailing," the Imaginary here turns out to be more properly Lacanian, grounded in all the ambiguities of *méconnaissance*—or "misrecognition,"[85] in which a foe can become a friend and an enemy, a lover. This interdeterminacy of the Imaginary has repercussions not only for the series' intersubjective relations (who is the hero? Who, the villain?) but for the status in the show of *intra*subjectivity per se. That Spike can swap roles and change emotional registers with such seemingly mutable ease suggests that vampiric subjectivity is just as unsettled, just as uncertain, just as *conflicted* between unconscious *wunsch* and superegoic control as the divided self of human psychology. No wonder, then, that as the series progresses from its fourth, to its fifth, then sixth and final seventh seasons, Buffy stops slaying vampires because they turn out to be just like us—human. Even more human than human, because in Season 4 the vampires are the victims of an inhuman science, the eugenics experiments of the Mengele-like Walsh and her fascistic "initiative" to create an *uebermensch*, the superhuman Adam. That program, and the very inhumane humanity behind it, become the Scooby Gang's focus, a reorientation away from vampire slaying that continues apace in Season 5 with the introduction of a new, extrahuman nemesis, the god Glory.

But these in-, super-, or extrahuman threats do more than provide an alternative to slaying; they work together to reconfigure the Scooby Gang's group dynamics. No longer a praetorian guard with Buffy as primus inter pares, the Slayerettes emerge, by the end of Season 4 and throughout Seasons 5 and 6, as a genuine community, the intersubjectivity of which is marked by a dialectic of desire. That desire turns out to be, of course, the desire for another: a partner, a companion, a mate. Not surprisingly, the series' later seasons witness a flurry of couplings: Buffy with Riley (and Spike!?), Xander with Anya (with nuptials pending, then backfiring spectacularly), and the succès de scandale of the series, Willow with Tara (a sort of teen *Queer as Folk*[86]). But the real difference that desire makes here is in the desire for difference—*the* psychoanalytic problematic, if there ever was one—that shifts *Buffy* issues away from philosophy and the "Kant avec Sade" impasse it had landed itself in. What it turns toward is none other than *ethics*—which the psychoanalysis of Lacan, even more than the thought of Levinas, has defined as an *ethics of the Other*. The "Other" here, however, is not confined to the "significant others" pursued by the Scooby Gang. Those lowercase "others" are outside of the self; and are sought to complete it. While the uppercase "Other" sought here is both external and internal to subjectivity, and indeed is constitutive of it. This constitutive doubleness—both within and without the self—is captured in Jacques Lacan's term, *extimité*.[87]

Confronting Your Inner Demons: My Vampire, Myself!

Extimité is a Lacanian neologism (a compound of *intimité* and, variously, *externale, exterieur*), mentioned en passant in *The Ethics of Psychoanalysis*[88] and developed more fully in an essay of that name by Lacan's son-in-law and disciple, Jacques-Alain Miller.[89] For him, *extimité* is largely a clinical concept, enabling a more precise—that is, "logically consistent"[90]—understanding of the status of the *objet petit a* in analysis (principally, as the unconscious, the key meditating link in the relationship between analyst and analysand[91]). But what engages the attention of this chapter is the path *not* taken by Miller. Namely, the "ontic"[92] potential of *extimité* in redefining the subject in terms of the Other in anything but Levinasian terms, so that the "exterior is present in the interior . . . like a foreign body or parasite."[93] With this metaphor of the "alien within," Miller gives *extimité* a science fiction / horror definition, as if directly lifted out of a Sigourney Weaver film, taken up and gentrified by *Buffy the Vampire Slayer*. For by recasting it, *Buffy* renders benign the malignancy with which Ripley struggles (seemingly ad infinitum). Instead of creating a monstrosity that gestates in its host then bursts out of the body, destroying subjectivity in the process (whether on the starship, space station, or planet[94]), *extimité* remains both without and within the self, shaping, altering, and transforming the body politic as much as the body personal. Embodying *extimité*—as the Other-in-the-self and the self-in-the-Other—is the *objet petit a*[95] of the demonic itself, realized graphically and with high humor in the logo of the series' production house, Mutant Enemy. That is: a cartoon demonic homunculus, a small, human-shaped demon, the lurching "grrr, grrr" of which comically follows the credits of each episode.

Certainly, every character in *Buffy* displays, eventually, the impress of this demonic *extimité*. Indeed, the series reveals practically all the principal characters to be, literally, demons—or, at least, half-demons—a disclosure usually made as a consequence of, if not in the very act of, desiring (in flagrante delicto) their "demon lovers." This is the case for not only Angel (who loses his soul when he experiences what is euphemized as "true happiness": that is, slayer-sex with Buffy), but also Tara and Willow (who "out" themselves as witches, as much as lesbians, with their affair), Anya (formerly the 2,000-year-old Vengeance Demon, Anyanka, whose on-again, off-again engagement to "Zeppo" Xander Harris is the tragicomedy of Season 6), Oz (a werewolf whose lupine condition is aggravated, if not provoked, by desire), Cordelia (a seer, gifted to her by love interest, the now dead Doyle in *Angel*[96]), and even Buffy herself (who begins to mimic her inamorato Angel, acting as a kind of faux vampire by rising from her crypt in the opening episode of Season 6[97] when she returns—yet again—from the dead). So in desiring another's difference, each of the Slayerettes comes to know their difference within, their "inner demon." And even though they are demons at heart, the demonic turns out to be a difference to celebrate rather than slay, because it is *shared* and thus grounds for an identity that is social as much as psychic. If there is a demon *within* all the Slayerettes, then it is precisely this Other-in-the-self that undergirds and indeed drives the Slayerettes' desire for the demon *without*, linking opposite to opposite (of Slayer Buffy with vampire Angel, of witch Willow with werewolf Oz, and so on), and establishing them as a *socius* of *extimité*.

The paradox of this *extimité*—at once individual and social, different and identical, inner and outer—is that it is an *effect* of, not a bar to slaying. How is this so? How can a process like slaying, which, after all, combusts demons, vampires and more, also construct them? The answer lies in the figurative significance of slaying, a significance that is suggested, ironically, by its very literality, its very physicality. For the act of slaying—sighting, staking, and transmogrifying the undead into digitally generated ash—is on one hand the most corporeally material of sequences in *Buffy*, and the source of the series' tremendous grrrlpower appeal. But Buffy's slaying is so thoroughly stylized, so exaggeratedly "camp" with all of its contrived "chop suey" cinema choreography of back flips, sharp blows, and midair freeze-frames, à la John Woo, that it suggests, on the other hand, a meaning that is more if not wholly metaphorical rather than material. Take the most prominent example of slaying's metaphoricity: the way in which *staking*, as a cut puncturing the undead body, allegorizes but also instantiates signification's Law, which itself turns out to be none other than the law of *coupure*[98]—the "cut" of Law's letter, of language. In linking language to lancing, Law's letter to staking, *Buffy* breathes new life into the phrase and raises from the dead that old Hegelian-Kojevian *momento mori*—"the word is the murder of the thing" (*le mot est le meurtre de la chose*).[99] No wonder then that the staking of each vampire always elicits from Buffy a quip, a comeback, a mot juste—like "I'm Buffy and you're history."[100] Because, in her slaying, Buffy *is* the very embodiment of the murderous mot, dispatching in her executory cut the Thing of the vampire, and figuring the Law of the signifier itself.[101]

The problem, however, with this executory cut—and complicating its allegorization of the Law of the signifier—is that it results in *more* not fewer "things." Buffy's slaying increases, rather than decreases, the number of vampires. Another one pops up as soon as one is staked, much as one sign follows another in semiosis, generating a Symbolic organized around a fundamental antagonism. All of which means, of course, that in *Buffy*, the vampire turns out to be on the side of the signifier rather than the signified. This is because, in staking *das Ding*, the Thing of the vampire, Buffy reveals the phantasmatic thing within, the *objet petit a* of the "inner vampire," predicated on a lack in all of us—including the Slayerettes—and subject to the Law of Desire. For, indeed, it is desire's Law that activates Buffy's slaying, despite a compulsively repetitive quality, more suggestive of id's drive or, better yet, superego's *jouissance*[102] and its injunction, "Enjoy!"[103] Which is why, when it comes to the "culture wars," the religious and cultural right, parodied in Season 7 in the demonic figure of The Preacher,[104] always get the wrong end of the stick—or rather stake—in discussions of *Buffy*. Because the series is about anything and everything—the postnuclear family, the "indie" music scene, high school hierarchies, teen fashion, identity politics—except "enjoyment," and the realities of id-like violence (like Columbine), which its fantasies of the "theft of enjoyment"[105] sustain (all of which take the form that someone is enjoying more than me, *plus-de-jouir*). If it seems otherwise, then it is because the series *stages* "enjoyment"—in its vicious vampire attacks, its Sadean scenes of torture, its mounting body count—so that Buffy and her slaying can enact what the Lacanians might call la *traversée du fantasme*,[106] "traversing the fantasy" of blood, pain, and death occasioned by *jouissance*, and thereby end it. But the key point to keep in mind is that this end comes only *through* the Law and its active force of desire; because desire, by reason of the Law's cutting edge (*coupure*) of language and lack, excises enjoyment from the Symbolic through a rupture so deep it can never be wholly sutured.

This rend—in short, the appearance of the Real[107]—is ultimately fortuitous because, as every (at least, Lacanian) schoolchild knows, full Symbolic closure would foreclose identic reinvention under the Law, stabilizing subjectivity into a mortified fixity. Such stasis would bring the Law grinding to a halt, proscribing any extension of its ambit, shutting down its interpellation of new subjects of desire. Instead, it would "hail" static binaries like the immanent and the transcendent, the Kantian and the natural law subjects. Buffy shatters this nomological stasis. Through her staking and its perforation of the vampiric body—a stand-in for the body politic—she literally clears, through *coupure*, a Real space for the installation of lack.[108] A *hole* is drilled to make a *whole*, as it were. And through that w/hole, she ensures the perpetual reimagining of Law's subjects of desire. This is why Buffy is so very much a juridical figure, a *lex populi* icon for our postmodern times, because as murderer *and* mate of the vampiric Thing, she guarantees the persistence of Law—and indeed desire—in her very transgression of it. In fact, it is only through her (and others') desiring of that which is proscribed, interdicted, impossible—like Buffy's tabooed love for Angel—that the Law of Desire continues to operate at all, supplying other obscure objects of desire in the wake of its nonsatisfaction (Riley and Spike, for example), and in so doing sustaining the *extimité* of difference, both within (our "inner demons") and outside of us all (in our "demon lovers"). Which is why I conclude this chapter in the hope that Buffy, as *the* jurisprude of desire, keeps on slaying and, indeed, slays *me*: that is, enables my *extimité*—and the identic reinvention of juristic difference that it begets—by staking me to my phantasmatic core with a *coupure* that will expose the alien within, my "inner vampire" as it were, so much so that, echoing Nina Auerbach,[109] I can say "My vampire, myself!"

CHAPTER THREE

"The First Rule of Fight Club Is—You Do Not Talk About Fight Club!"

The Perverse Core of Legal Positivism

Lex Populi's Heavyweight Contender: *Fight Club* and the Pugilism of Legal Positivism

Fight Club[1] packs quite a punch, both literal and figurative. Literal, in that David Fincher's cinematic adaptation of Chuck Palahniuk's cult novel[2] is one of the most graphic depictions of fisticuffs on film; for sheer violence, it exceeds any of those ringside boxing films, from *Gentleman Jim*[3] to *Raging Bull*,[4] from the *Rocky*[5] series to the subject of the last chapter of this book, *Million Dollar Baby*.[6] Figurative, in that *Fight Club* is shadowboxing *with* and *as* none other than the concept of law itself. That concept, as I argue in the next section, turns out to be the jurisprudence of the rule as defined by Oxford legal philosopher Herbert Hart, in his midcentury bid for the championship of English legal theory. For if *Fight Club* is, as I believe it to be, *lex populi*'s heavyweight contender, it is because the film dramatizes and provides the central metaphor for the pugilistic slugfest that *is* legal positivism: with Hart and his rule system in one corner, and John Austin[7] and his command theory in another. The outcome of this juridical boxing match, however, remains highly contested to this day, with neither side taking the championship title. This draw arises because Hart never really solved what might be called the "scandal of legal positivism"—namely, the violence latent in its "command theory." Instead of replacing this violence with rules, he *displaces* it to the rule system itself, especially to the rule of recognition, rendering it riven by an ongoing brawl between law and morals. This displacement is allegorized in *Fight Club*'s tale of two fighters—who turn out to be the same pathologically perverse person. But oddly enough, as I conclude in the chapter's last section, this very disclosure of pathology is what delivers *Fight Club* from its sadomasochistic spiral, enabling it to separate itself, unlike Hart, from what I call, with a nod to Slavoj Žižek,[8] the "perverse core" of legal positivism. Thus the stakes are high in *lex populi*'s ringside rounds, because *Fight Club* may provide a solution to the impasse that afflicts an Anglo-American jurisprudence still fighting its way out from under the shadow of Herbert Hart: a cultural legal solution that, ironically, returns legal positivism to its violent origins.

The "H(e)art" of *Fight Club*:
The Law of Perversion and the Perversion of the Law

Where is the law in *Fight Club*? "Beaten to a pulp!" might be the wry retort of some critical legal wag. For Fincher's film goes out of its way to stress its *lawlessness*. Certainly the film compiles quite a rap sheet of summary and indictable offenses worthy of any convicted felon: from jaywalking to grand larceny, from breaking and entering to wanton vandalism, not to mention any and all manner of assault and battery (resulting in blackened eyes, broken teeth, bloodied mouths, and assorted gouges). However, these criminal transgressions occur within, and issue from a context that is recognizable as law*ful(l)*, meaning law saturated. That context is established in what I take to be the film's paradigmatic scene: the one set in the basement of Lou's Tavern, when Tyler Durden—the deranged narrator Jack's ego-ideal—proclaims for the first time to the punch-hungry men assembled there, "The first rule of fight club is—you do not talk about fight club!" (FC, ch. 15). What follows is a kind of Mosaic code of the fight club with eight additional "commandments," the second being a repetition of the first, "The second rule of fight club is—you do not talk about fight club!" This sort of iterative speech act is picked up and parroted, over and over again, particularly when the filmic center of attention shifts to Project Mayhem, a politicization of the fight club as an anarchist cell (though more rightist, paramilitary *Freikorps* than Spartacist Rosa Luxemburg) and committed to an agenda of sabotage, be it industrial, aesthetic, or absurdist. There, the Demolition Committee repeats, mindlessly and mantralike, "The first rule about Project Mayhem is that you do not ask questions!" (FC, ch. 27). The cumulative effect of these exclamatory expressions is to produce a precise jurisprudential definition of law: as proscription, prohibition, taboo.

Thus the law of *Fight Club* amounts to a kind of ban, its much-repeated bar—"no talking," "no questions," "no . . . "—recalling the Ten Commandments ("Thou shalt not . . . "), but also that of the ur-analyst, Freud and his "No! in thunder" to incest and parricide. *Fight Club* returns to Freud—and Moses—however, in order to transform them, articulating an alternative kind of jurisprudence, very different from that of the Freudo-Mosaic negative bar. Instead, *Fight Club* substitutes a definition of law that turns on positive precept. For the legal lynchpin of Tyler's "declaration of fights," his core nomological element is none other than the sine qua non of positivism: namely, *the rule*. Now, the rule and all it conveys (good sportsmanship, fair play, and the rest), would seem to be light-years away, at least jurisprudentially, from the violence of *Fight Club*. After all, rules import a measure of order, routine, and reason at sharp variance with *Fight Club*'s pugilistic free-for-alls. But despite the "mischief," "mayhem," and "disinformation" that the fight clubs (and Project Mayhem) wreak, they continue to abide by their own rules. In fact, the last thing to be broken in *Fight Club*, more than arms, jaws, or noses, are the rules as laid down by Tyler. For they enable the game to be played and thereby sustain Jack's hallucination. So there is most definitely a juristic method to Jack's madness, a legal logic to his lunacy. Which raises the question: What kind of madness is so methodical? What sort of lunacy is so logical?

Psychoanalysis, at least in its Lacanian register,[9] provides a useful heuristic here. This is because Lacanian psychoanalysis, as detailed in *A Clinical Introduction to Lacanian Psychoanalysis*, defines the pathological psyche in terms of a misfiring *nomos*: that is, the Law of the Father's Name, and its socio-Symbolic failure (CILP, p. 170). Precisely how that Law fails determines, in turn, the aberrant condition of the psyche, as mapped out by Lacan: repression leads to neurosis (CILP, pp. 112–14); disavowal, to perversion (CILP, pp. 167–69); foreclosure, to psychosis (CILP, pp. 78–81). This failure of the Law is offset in each case by some form of its spectral "return": as a symptom (CILP, pp. 114–15) (neurosis), as pere-version (CILP, pp. 181) (perversion), as "the Real" (CILP, pp. 84–85) (psychosis). *Fight Club* traces all three forms of Law's uncanny recurrence, ranging from the symptomatic (Jack's insomnia) to "the Real" of his delusion (Tyler, but also Marla? Bob?). But only one of these reappearances is distinguished by intensification, indeed an amplification, of the law: namely, perversion. The suggestion is startling, if not in and of itself perverse. For isn't perversion marked by a vicious disregard for the Law, in its "no-holds-barred, *jouissance*-seeking activity," as Bruce Fink succinctly puts it (CILP, p. 180)? After all, isn't the pervert par excellence the Marquis de Sade, who fantasized a ferociously cruel *jouissance*, endlessly transgressing the Law? But according to Lacan, the irony of perversion—Sade's no less than anyone else's—is that this perpetual transgression doesn't so much end the Law as call it into being by constantly appealing to it to *legislate:* that is, to establish legal limits on the pervert's own brutal *jouissance*. Thus the end-game of perversion is not so much violence—be it sadism, masochism, or other permutations—as the *structural constraints* on violence in the form of law. In short, perversion fetishizes the law.

In so doing, perversion promulgates its own law, a yoking together of psyche and *nomos* that *Fight Club* vividly dramatizes in its rule-bound scenes of sadomasochism. That point has been made elsewhere and at some length by others, principally Žižek.[10] My point here, and contribution to this debate, however, is this: if there is a "law of perversion" in *Fight Club*, then the film equally suggests by way of implication that there is a "perversion of the law": that is, a perversity inherent in, even innate to its key jurisprudential formulation, the posited rule. That is why *Fight Club* is such a powerful example of *lex populi*, because it drives home the point that there is a "perverse core" at the "H(e)art" of legal positivism itself. I set off "heart" as shown because the word phonically duplicates and invokes its homophone: namely, Herbert Hart, the great twentieth-century exponent of legal positivism and, by my lights, the real jurisprude underwriting and informing *Fight Club*'s legal subtext. So much so that I make the provocative claim here that Herbert Hart and Tyler Durden are two sides of the same coin, whose union,[11] like those of the primary and secondary rules in Hart's *The Concept of Law* (CL, p. 91), constitutes one of the great legal fictions of *lex populi*.

How, though, are these two exceedingly different figures—and the antithetical theories of law they embody—related? The equation seems and *is* ludicrous. On the one hand, there is all-time bad boy, Tyler Durden, promoter and impresario of visceral affect, of physical blow, played to lounge lizard perfection, all Sunset Boulevard "street cred" and drug dealer chic, by Hollywood "himbo" Brad Pitt (in a performance that forever lays to rest any dismissals about Pitt being just another pretty face). On the other hand, there is the wry and dry denizen of the Oxford high table, Herbert Hart—Wittgensteinian, ordinary-language advocate, and latter-day disciple of cognitive *begriffsjurisprudenz*.[12] The former is all action; the latter is all thought. Thus to reformulate the opposition of my opening question in a slightly more philosophical key: How is the instantiation of law's body (Tyler) related to that of law's mind (Hart)? The connection, I hazard, lies in their shared notion of the rule. Like Tyler, Hart propounds a concept of law that places rules—indeed, posits them, jurisprudentially, front row and center: "(without) the idea of a rule . . . we cannot hope to elucidate even the most elementary forms of law" (CL, p. 78). Thus both Tyler and Hart, if I may be permitted a pseudo-Dworkinism, "take rules seriously."

An outraged positivist, *à la Hartienne*, might very well object, arguing with no uncertain justification that Hart's idea of the rule of law is designed to have precisely the opposite effect of Tyler's. Instead of facilitating the fight club's perverse form of aggression, Hart's rules are intended to mitigate their coerciveness, muting their threats, physical or verbal. "Rules," he wrote in *The Concept of Law*, "must contain in some form restrictions on the free use of violence, theft, and deception" (CL, p. 89). Which is, of course, precisely the position of the pervert, for whom the law is just such a restriction "on the free use of violence" and also necessary to one's ongoing enjoyment of that violence. But to give the angry positivist his due, Hart goes further than this, propounding a notion of rule that seemingly outlaws the perverse violence—indeed, the sovereign sadism—at legal positivism's core. Rules can do so because they operate, according to a different juridical logic, an "internal point of view" (CL, p. 87), which is inimical, purportedly, to the not-so-latent violence in the posited law. Ironically, this position pits Hart as a contender within his own cerebral fight club—that of jurisprudence—duking it out, at least metaphorically, for the legal positivist championship with that nineteenth-century heavyweight, John Austin, and his "command theory of the law." That theory, according to Hart, launched English jurisprudence on its "record of failure" (CL, p. 78) by reducing the law to little more than a particularly vicious armed assailant—no better than, say, Tyler Durden when he holds the hapless Raymond Hessel at gunpoint, taunting and teasing him with imminent death and extracting from him, in his halting English, a terrified confession (FC, ch. 24).

This primal scene of gangsterism is evoked several times in *The Concept of Law* (pp. 19, 20, 21, 22, 80–81), becoming its master trope and functioning as a metaphor writ large for the command theory. For behind all of Austin's rhetorical persiflage about "imperation," "signification," and "address"—let alone his additional Benthamite blather about "utility"—stands, according to Hart, a mortifying imago of the law: "a gunman who says to the bank clerk, 'Hand over the money or I will shoot'" (CL, p. 19). The effect of this deadly utterance, issuing from such a malign prosopopoeia, is to demystify the command theory, turning its political nexus of sovereign and subject into the criminological one of perpetrator and prey. For the sovereign's command now looks like a criminal's *threat* (Tyler), while the subject's habitual obedience resembles nothing so much as a frightened victim's *compliance* (Raymond). But what troubles about this scenario of violence is that Hart seems to have little or no trouble with it; certainly no objections along the lines of *lex iniusta non est lex*. Indeed, if anything, Hart seems attracted by the violence of this traumatic scene, compulsively, repetitively returning to it. Why? Because, I would argue, this scene stages not only a crime—but also a crime of passion, one that solicits an erotic investment. That *crime passionnel* is the classically "perverse" one of sadomasochism, with the sovereign cast as sadist, and the subject cast as masochist. Seen from this nosological point of view, the sovereign's commands are revealed as nothing more than perversion's "invocatory drive"[13] at its most overbearing, barking out orders through that "part-object," the voice of the bondage Master. The subject's obedience turns out to be the masochist's submission to the bondage Master's domination, his disciplinary "whips and chains" coded here as a gun.

Given this (ob)scenario's phantasmatic pull, no wonder Hart has no problems with violence here. Or for that matter, in that of another, more fiendish S&M scene, Nazi law (CL, 204–5), the violence of which Hart seems remarkably detached from (and perhaps secretly cathected to?) in his ongoing debate with Lon Fuller. Surprisingly (or not), Tyler Durden turns out to be much more a moralist of the law-as-violence, holding a gun to Raymond's head in order to make him a *better* person by forcing him, by means of the toughest of "tough love," to face up to and realize his heart's desire: to become a veterinarian (FC, ch. 24). All of which proves the truth of the adage that you have to be cruel to be kind: folk wisdom that is verified by Lacan's characterization of the sadist as one, like Tyler, who (cruelly) searches for but (kindly) releases the *objet petit a*—the obscure object of desire—in the Other. Hart, however, is neither cruel nor kind enough to do this to or for the Other, remaining entirely indifferent as to whether humanity is better or worse: "angels" or "devils" (CL, p. 191), as he puts it. For the sadist's active attachment, anything but indifferent, is not the role in which Hart is cast here; rather his position is one of masochistic passivity, an inert "sub" who nonetheless longs for a "dom"—a Master—to materialize the Law and thereby indefinitely sustain the scene of suffering. A masochist is nothing if not persistent in his passivity, clamoring for the continuity of submission. As such, it comes as no shock that, along with its "inaccuracy," Hart's principal objection to the command theory seems to be its failure to account for law's "persistence" (CL, p. 50) and authority's "continuity" (CL, p. 50) (embodied, for example, in the problematic succession of King Rex and his successors; CL, pp. 51–54, 67–68).

This may be why, as the basis for his concept of law, Hart turns to a jurisprudential foundation that envisages the reason for rules much along the lines of *Fight
Club*'s "no shirts, no shoes" interdict (FC, ch. 15). That is, as a foundation that
sets the conditions of possibility—the threshold, as well as the limits—of what
I call the "minimum content of natural *pain*." Such a primitive measure would
horrify any advocate of natural law or "social contractarian" and render even sado-
sovereigntists, such as Bentham and Austin, anxiously uncomfortable; but for me,
that's exactly what Hart's vision of the "minimum content of natural law" (CL,
p. 189) looks like: a masochistic effort to find that "just measure of pain," enabling
survival on the one hand (CL, p. 189) but on the other hand recognizing—and
reveling in—mankind's capacity to inflict injury, like Tyler's "kissburn" (FC,
ch. 19), owing to their "limited altruism," "limited resources," and "limited understanding" (CL, p. 190). Here, as in *Fight Club*, no positive morality of the rule
obtains: neither Hart nor Tyler tell us how to build a good society or fight a good
fight because, for them, the goodness (or badness for that matter) of those projects is irrelevant. Clearly, Hart is no Plato, imagining a "new republic" of norms;
and Tyler, certainly no Marquess of Queensbury, dignifying the "manly art" with
a code. Which is why Hart and Tyler, despite their differences—passive/active;
masochist/sadist—are so inextricably linked: because neither is concerned with
the law as a marker of improvement; rather, the law, in the form of rules, is there
to operate *negatively*, ensuring in both cases the preservation of what might be
called *das Spiel*, the eminently perverse game of life, be it social (Hart) or aggressive (Tyler).

What in fact seals the identification between Hart and Tyler as perverts-in-
arms is one final and shared jurisprudential attribute: that the rule, for each, is
"split" in two. Here the rule mimics the psychoanalytic subject, "perverse" in his
or her simultaneous "acceptance" and "disavowal" of two contradictory psychic
states (CILP, pp. 167–69), whose inner *spaltung* Lacan generalized from the Freudian fetishist and who is able to maintain, "I know such-and-such to be true, but
nonetheless I still believe . . . "[14] This allows, as it were, the pervert to "have" his
phallus and "be" it too (CILP, p. 175), because his rejection of castration is contingent upon its psychic introjection, its internalization. So, too, it is with the rule
insofar as, like that of the fetishist, its perverse split is occasioned by and a function
of internalization and of the egoic doubling—acceptance and disavowal—that
occurs through *Verleungnung*.[15] That internal split is spectacularly dramatized in
Fight Club, where the rules are at once exposed (as delusion) and embraced (as

binding) as the phantasmatic *vorstellung* (representation) of a pathological mind, Tyler-as-Jack, Jack-as-Tyler (FC, chs. 30, 31). Similarly, Hart installs the same kind of "pathological" dualism in his concept of law, especially when he interiorizes rules, investing them with, as noted before, an "internal aspect" (CL, p. 86). For according to Hart, what characterizes rules—setting them apart from, say, habits—is the fact that they have an inner life. That is, one *thinks* about rules, ponders their aim and ambit, and puzzles through their perplexities, inconsistencies, and exceptions; and in so doing derives conclusions about how to act. For Hart, rules are consciously *reflective*; habits, *reflexive* (CL, p. 55). The latter are unquestioning to the extent that one doesn't challenge or even attempt to work out just why one is behaving as such; while the former are profoundly interrogative, soliciting, even demanding what Hart calls a "critical" attitude (CL, p. 56).

This inward turn on Hart's part, however, reproduces in his rule system the same perverse split of *Fight Club*: that is, a situation in which two mutually contradictory conditions—the phantasmatic and the factual, the delusional and the real—coexist, despite (and because of) their ongoing tension. After all, by Hart's own admission, rules are always/already doubled as habits, at least from the point of view of the general population who must "obey" them, as opposed to that of "the officials," who enjoy the full interpretive invitation of the "internal point of view" and are required only to "accept" the rules (CL, p. 114). Thus a kind of rupture obtains right from the start in the Hartian rule between what looks like consciousness (the officials, acceptance, reflection) and the unconscious (habits, obedience, reflexiveness). But the critical reflective attitude does more than just introduce into Hart's rule the split of now garden-variety, neurotic repression; rather, it installs one that is more truly perverse by embedding, at its core, the perplexity of judgment itself in the divide between the rule's "core of certainty" and its penumbra of ambiguity (CL, p. 119). For if rules solicit, even demand critique—that is, reflection, thought, judgment—it must be because ambiguity is inscribed in and at their very meaningful core. This incongruity might be said to take the form, on the part of the official, of an implied admission and its demurral: "I know that the rules are essentially ambiguous, but nonetheless I continue to judge on the basis that their meaning is certain." This fractious paradox not only splits the rule down the middle, it also splinters it into a dozen shards. For the effect of the core-penumbra binary—conflicted as it is consented to—is that it renders rules hopelessly indeterminate, euphemized by Hart as an "open texture" (CL, p. 120). Any code of conduct, any system of norms—etiquette, games, religious observance, but especially morals—can lay claim to being rules, and rules of likely "legal" validity, since the usual positivist mark of such validity—physical force or sanction—has been dissolved by Hart into an inner compulsion to be obeyed (CL, p. 88). For this dissolution has the effect of rendering *all* obligation-imposing rules—moral and otherwise—potentially, law (and vice versa).

Hart himself is more than aware of this problem, desiring precisely what psychoanalysis teaches that all perverts want more than anything else: namely, certainty (CILP, p. 194).[16] Accordingly, he sets out a basic criterion for such certainty, sifting out the rules of etiquette, games, and the like on the grounds that they lack the necessary gravitas or "seriousness" of law (CL, p. 84). But even if one accepts this exceedingly vague standard for the other rule systems, then what of morality? Certainly, its obligations are no less "serious" than those of law. Indeed, for Hart, moral rules imposed obligations that were far more important than legal rules. So the question returns with added force: How does one tell the difference between these two types of rule systems, when both evince the same internal point of view, critical reflective attitude, obligatory nature, and so on? That is: When is a rule real law, and when a ruse of morality? Or to return to the dramatis personae of this chapter: How is one to distinguish between Hart (and his concept of law) and Tyler (and his fantasy of fights)—especially when these two figures have begun to bleed into each other, even to the point of indistinction? Is there a standard or measure that will adjudicate the indeterminacy between legal faction and legal fiction? Between the highly uncertain line separating—if at all—law from lunacy?

"Gotta Get Off, Gonna Get Out of This Merry-Go-Round": Round and Round the Rule of (Mis)recognition

The answer for Hart lies in the act of looking, a kind of voyeurism. But this perverse gaze is embedded in another set of largely adjectival rules designed to forestall this descent into metajuridical madness, and (mis)labeled as "secondary" (CL, p. 91)—ostensibly, because they supplement the "primary rules" (CL, p. 89) of civil and criminal obligation. "Ostensibly" because there is nothing supplementary in their significance, or secondary in their importance. In fact, in point of priority, they—not the ones so designated—are the primary rules regulating entry into law's empire in the first place, policing and patrolling what Alain Pottage has called its "cadastres."[17] But more than that, they try to test the claims of any and all obligations as valid law, as well as ensure the ongoing functionality of the legal system. To that latter, functional end, two of the triad of secondary rules are properly operational, as their brief is what might be called system maintenance: "adjudication" (CL, p. 94) and "change" (CL, p. 93). These two rules are allied and go to the corrective powers of the system's officialdom; that is, its judicial umpires. According to Hart, for example, the rule of change remedies "inefficiency" by empowering officials "to question whether, on a particular occasion, a primary rule has been broken" (CL, p. 94). While the rule of adjudication cures, again so Hart claims, the system's potentially "static" nature by empowering those same officials "to introduce new primary (rules) . . . and to eliminate old rules" (CL, p. 93).

So far, *so what?*—this might be the glib retort of the unimpressed Austinian positivist. For where is the rule that will not only oil the workings of the legal system but also defend its very perimeter from the onslaught of morality and other obligations, *loi manque-à-être*? Which rule enables one to draw the distinction between legal ally and moral foe? What is the *passe-partout* that will bar one and admit the other to the redoubt of law? That magic word, that open sesame is none other than what Hart calls, quite appropriately, "the rule of recognition" (CL, p. 92). So called because this rule is intensely scopic, even scopophilic in its nature, which in its capacity as the guardian of law's citadel voyeuristically examines, indeed strip-searches any and all candidates for admission, identifying law's body from its pretenders by its distinguishing marks. But what does this body of law look like in fact? Can its physiology be detailed explicitly? Legal systems are coy—at least according to Hart—about this sort of probing examination, resisting any kind of invasive (peeping Tom?) close-up, because for them, according to Hart, the rule of recognition is a chastely formal rather than an explicitly substantive measure, analogous to the meter bar in Paris, that is, the metric system's standard unit of measurement (CL, p. 106). "In the day-to-day life of a legal system," states Hart, "the rule of recognition is very seldom expressly formulated as a rule" (CL, p. 98) and could take any number of incarnations: "customary practice," "judicial decision," or "enacted by a specific body" (CL, p. 92). Hart, however, has no such scruples about attributing a very specific, substantive content to this "formal" rule. He repeats time and again throughout *The Concept of Law*—by my count, eight times (pp. 25, 36, 63, 72, 99, 104, 145, 178)—that, as far as the United Kingdom is concerned, "they recognize as law . . . what the Queen-in-Parliament enacts" (CL, p. 99).

All of which sounds suspiciously like our old friend (and bondage master), the Austinian sovereign. After all, the formulation of "Queen-in-Parliament" neatly captures Austin's own blending, in his definition of sovereignty, of the legislative and executive functions, and echoes his strictures "that the king and the lords, with members of the commons' house, form a tripartite body which is sovereign or supreme."[18] Which again prompts the query: Why all the palaver on Hart's part? That is, why all the Sturm und Drang from him about, inter alia, the rule of recognition—not to mention the nature of obligation, the internal point of view, and the concept of law—when it all boils down to the same kernel as Austin's command theory did: a parliament possessed of sovereignty? Why bother then to change the theory—rules rather than sanctions, umpires rather than enforcers—if the praxis remains the same? Context looms here, and may assist in accounting for this seemingly pointless (re)symptomization. Consider the occasion of *The Concept of Law*: published in 1961, the 1950s and height of the Cold War provide the backdrop to its composition. One interesting aspect of the Cold War, at least for students of legal theory, is the remarkable jurisprudential transference (and countertransference) that it witnessed between the totalitarian East and the bourgeois-liberal West. For in this period, the Communist bloc entrenched, like the Nazis did before them, something closely resembling the Austinian command theory as their politico-legal basis.[19] Not surprisingly, mid-twentieth-century totalitarian regimes found a good fit in Austinian-style legal theory, each seeing their dictatorial selves in the sovereign whose commands are law: that is, the party speaking on behalf of the proletariat; or previously, the Führer, on behalf of the *Volk*.

Practically, of course, totalitarian legality is as different from Austin's jurisprudence, and its political context of nineteenth-century liberalism, as the English gaol is from the gulag or the concentration camp. But theoretically, totalitarian legality might be said to have hijacked legal positivism in this era, a "theft of enjoyment" that Hart's concept of law could have been intended to recoup. Not that Hart's relationship to totalitarianism is uncomplicated; he was, after all, married to a former Communist,[20] had flirted with the far left in his student days at Oxford,[21] and for a Jew—however secular—had been remarkably detached, as noted previously, on the issue of the validity of Nazi law. Was totalitarian legality—either socialist or fascist, Vyshinsky- or Schmitt-inspired—the Real of Hart's desire?[22] I make no claims to that effect—other than to say there may be very good political reasons for Hart to screen that Real by travestying Austin's sovereign as a gunman. In so doing, he distanced himself from the sort of legalized gangsterism that had run amok in the SS and was getting a new lease on life with the KGB—in whose pay, incidentally, Jenifer Hart was accused of being. That 1980s newspaper allegation—of Jenifer's supposed Home Office treachery, recounted by no less an august "fourth estate" institution than *The Observer*—tellingly precipitated a nervous breakdown in Hart, raising retrospective doubts about the motives underlying his oeuvre.[23] One wonders whether *The Concept of Law* was written as something of an apologia for a "God that had failed," designed to convince not only the general public of legal positivism's democratic credentials but also *Hart himself*, thereby forestalling his collapse from (masochistic) perversion into full-blown psychosis.

Thus *The Concept of Law* can be and has been read[24] as an attempt on Hart's part to redeem legal positivism, making it safe for democracy—or at least, by my lights, the cricket pitch of a good British public school. For that is the very venue—with its Etonian playing fields, its "man in white is always right"[25] ethos—that Hart seems to have at the back of his mind when he overhauls legal positivism, replacing the set of commands for the rules of the game, the sovereign for the judicial umpire, and above all, recognition for violence. But just as in the British public school, the "jolly hockey sticks" of *Tom Brown's Schooldays*[26] can often mask, as Hart knew all too well,[27] something very much like the blood sacrifice of *The Lord of the Flies*[28]; so, too, in the "concept of law," violence isn't so much replaced as *dis*placed—and nowhere more so than in the rule of recognition. For it turns out to be something more along the lines of what Lacan might call a rule of "misrecognition," the *méconnaissance*[29] of which not only gets the law wrong, but mistakes itself as a unity rather than a fractured entity, divided against, even fighting itself. Just exactly who or what is doing the fighting here will be discussed shortly; but first I want to dwell on this pugilistic point because it brings me to the heart of my reading of Hart: specifically, that there is an inner act of violence, an internal coming to blows, a psychic fight club at the very center of his concept of law. This is why, for me, Fincher's film provides such a useful analogue, such an insightful gloss on Hart's legal philosophy; as *lex populi*, it not only stages but also "outs" this fight as the pathological *psychomachia* it is, over and about law's highly contested foundations. By the end of the film, all of Jack and Tyler's fights are exposed as projections, externalizations of a nomological mental struggle, in which consciousness (Jack) "misrecognizes" its unconscious (Tyler) as both a source of law—the rules—and a site of conflict—the fights.

Thus the violent corporeality of Fincher's film and the (seemingly) bloodless conceptualism of Hart's schema ultimately come together, miming each other in a shocking act of self-transgression: in a psychological melee located either within its main character, Jack/Tyler, or within the key rule, the rule of recognition.

Initially, however, these instances of psychic collision—Hart's, Fincher's—take the form of a failed encounter, a missed connection, the one disappearing just as the other arrives on the scene, and vice versa. *Fight Club* gives a dramatic rendering of this sort of vanishing act when Jack, in the latter half of the film, is in hot pursuit, crisscrossing America—its airport lounges, highway motels, departure gates—searching for but always just a step behind, a car ride away, a flight path removed from that obscure object of desire, Tyler (FC, ch. 30). Tyler, of course, turns out to be Jack himself, an identic circularity that allegorizes and in turn is allegorized by the "revolving door" quality of Hart's rule of recognition. For that rule, as Neil MacCormick has pointed out at some length,[30] is involved in its own tail-chasing race, its very existence predicated on officials empowered by the rules of change and adjudication. But those rules, which constitute the official and empower him or her to deploy the rule of recognition, are themselves predicated on their recognition by that rule in the first place. But that rule of recognition is in turn contingent upon the official—who, likewise, is empowered by the rules of change and adjudication, themselves dependent upon recognition, and so on. And round and round it goes, as if circling Llewellyn's bramble bush or, even better, riding the merry-go-round of *Fight Club*.

How do we "get off . . . this merry-go-round"? So sings an off-key Marla as she leaves Jack's derelict squat on Paper Street (the haunted house of law?), referencing the score of that camp 1960s classic, *The Valley of the Dolls*[31] (FC, ch. 17). I'd like to suggest that the answer to the lyric's question is this: when the *psychomachia* is concretized and brought up short—indeed, to a dead halt, by an actual, embodied blow. And the blow I refer to is neither one of the feints of the fight clubs nor the scramble of the secondary rules. In each case, a phantasm is either fought (the fights between Tyler and Jack) or followed (the rule of recognition tailing the rules of change and adjudication, which are in turn shadowing the rule of recognition). Rather, the moment of impact, of contact arrives both filmically and philosophically when this blow is presented in all of it visceral vérité as violently automasochistic. Think of *Fight Club*, particularly those scenes toward its close, where Jack is caught on camera—the truth regime of video?—fighting *himself* in the parking garage, bloodying his own nose, cracking his own jaw, throwing himself down the stairs (FC, ch. 34). Intercut here toward its close are earlier scenes from the film—like the first fistfight outside Lou's—now revealed, in flashback, as bizarre and oddly funny, a reaction registered in the uncomfortably bemused faces of the spectators (FC, ch. 31). These looks have their equivalent in the quizzical readership of the second edition of *The Concept of Law*, because in the postscript[32] penned by Hart in the 1970s and 1980s but only appended by Joseph Raz in 1992, the same sort of retroactive rewriting is engaged in, producing a similar sort of audience *revisioning*. Such revisioning occurs when Hart, intending to defend his increasingly embattled position against the sustained pummeling of, inter alia, Ronald Dworkin, instead *hits himself*—and does so with a vengeance, dealing a near-fatal blow to (what else?) the rule of recognition.

This putative knockout happens when Hart writes in the postscript that "in some systems of law . . . the ultimate criteria of legal validity might explicitly incorporate, besides pedigree, principles of justice or substantive moral values" (CL, p. 247). Now, this is an astonishing boxing ring maneuver, so self-defeating that—one would think—no amount of fancy footwork will salvage it. After all, if this is (or was) so, then what is (or was) the point of the rule of recognition, now or in the first place? Wasn't its very raison d'être, from the beginning, to distinguish moral from legal obligations, justice from law? Indeed, in the absence of sanction or force as the defining feature of law, wasn't the rule of recognition the "ultimate" (CL, p. 145) measure or standard by which to differentiate law from any kind of rule, moral or otherwise? Hart, nonetheless, persists in his state of *denial:* one that, perversely, is predicated on the affirmation that "substantive moral values" and "principles of justice" have always been a potential part of his rule of recognition and rule system writ large (CL, pp. 247, 250). Accordingly, Hart blunts the effect of *Fight Club*'s reflexive blow that rouses Jack from his psychic (and physical) civil war. Instead, Hart remains locked into a kind of perpetual "war of position," one that transforms the rule of recognition from a benchmark into a *trench-mark*, the dugouts from which law and morality battle endlessly. I allude to the First World War here because its static trench warfare provides a compelling image and "trenchant" metaphor for the painful stalemate in which Hart's jurisprudence results, as a no-man's-land of the law, a wasteland of rules. Thus Hart's concept of law ultimately ends with a whimper, at variance with, indeed in bold contrast to, *Fight Club*. For despite all their shared perversity (S&M, scopophilia, fetishism, *spaltung*, and the rest), Hart's concept and Fincher's film, in the last analysis, end on diametrically opposed notes. Instead of a whimper, *Fight Club* goes out with a bang—and a "big bang" at that: a virtual *Götterdämmerung* in which Project Mayhem realizes its wildest dreams of anarchy in the detonating bombs and collapsing skyscrapers—a prolepsis of 9/11?—of the film's final scene (FC, ch. 35).

Welcome Back John Austin, but First—
Shoot the (Hartian) Positivist!

This "apocalypse now" that *Fight Club* so vividly enacts is supplemented by a postapocalyptic vision, one in which Tyler, earlier in the film, recounts to Jack, seeing him "stalking elk through the damp canyon forests around the ruins of the Rockefeller Center. You will wear leather clothes that last you the rest of your life. You will club the wrist-thick kudzu vines that wrap the Sears Tower. You will see tiny figures pounding corn and laying strips of venison on the empty carpool lane of the ruins of a superhighway" (FC, ch. 28).

This trope of retrogression, of humanity reverting to a more savage Hobbesian state, something "nasty, brutish, and short," is a pop culture staple of film (the *Planet of the Apes* series,[33] the *Mad Max* trilogy,[34] *The Postman*,[35] *Waterworld*,[36] and many others), TV (*Survivors*,[37] and *Firefly*,[38] among others), and even music (the likes of Bowie[39] and Devo[40])—that *Fight Club*, in the figure of Tyler Durden, takes up and reiterates, though with one critical difference. For devolutionary reversion to "the primitive," the "Blonde Beast" is Project Mayhem's principal objective rather than an unintended consequence (of war, science, or technology), as is usually the case in this genre. This agenda situates *Fight Club* within a specific political tradition: what the late Susan Sontag once called "fascinating fascism."[41] A whole host of critics of the film have branded it "fascist,"[42] given its rather blatant—and not so fascinating—Mussolini-like accoutrements of black-shirted paramilitaries and a charismatic leader. But what I find so fascinating about *Fight Club*'s fascism is the way in which it (dialectically?) subverts itself, giving vent to an opposing antifascism. This antifascist antithesis is implicit in Tyler's eminently fascist "shape of things to come," because here, this vision—of humanity as a tribe of survivors, *klein aber fein* (smaller yet purer)—is predicated on a radical rupture, a fundamental antagonism that *Fight Club* clearly draws our attention to and subjects to its own critical reflective attitude. That is, that fascist fantasies of "the One"—the nation, the race—are contingent upon notions of "the Two," the Schmittian friend and enemy, who turn out to be, as Jack and Tyler are, two sides of the same pathological person, endlessly fighting himself in his imaginary, Manichean projections of self and other, Nazi and Bolshevik, Aryan and Jew.

This is why, as well, *Fight Club* ultimately undoes its own fascist fantasies, an undoing induced by the "separation" (CILP, pp. 175–81) staged in the last scenes of the film. For in separating himself from Tyler, Jack exposes the Two in the

One, and the One containing the Two. Once this is divulged, the collapse of his hallucination is inevitable, ending with Jack's shooting of Tyler (and himself) (FC, ch. 36). Such an end, however, is denied Hart's "concept of law"—which remains thoroughly mired in its perverse delusions, forever split between the law and morality, on one hand, and the ongoing psychic struggle between the two, on the other hand. This is a strange and sad end to what might be called Hart's "noble dream"[43] of a new, revivified legal positivism. For in attempting to rescue legal positivism from the clutches of Austin's Sadean gunman, and the violent (il)legality to which he gives rise, Hart lands it in something far worse: what might be called a "totalitarianism of the concept," a "fascism of the mind." By internalizing the law and its obligatory force, Hart seals off any escape the legal subject hitherto had from it in other varieties of legal positivism—the sovereign couldn't be everywhere, could he?—submitting all and sundry to its relentless and omnipresent inner imperative, "Obey!" In so doing, Hart realizes his deepest masochistic fantasies of complete submission, of total surrender to superegoic command. For that, strangely, is where the masochism's passivity ultimately leads: to active and absolute control. And with the installation of that control, I contend, so goes the possibility of any sort of sustained critique that some psychic distance from the law might have provided. This is the ultimate irony for a jurisprudence trumpeting the "critical reflective attitude," because it effectively signals the end of critique. All of which illustrates Lacan's law to the letter: that you get back in *reverse* form that which you desire most.

This is why I close this chapter with a plea: Come back John Austin, all is forgiven—even if it means accepting the lawman-as-gunman into the cultural legal fold. Oddly enough, it is *his* sadism that will save us at the end of the day from Hart's masochism. Because, for all his flaws, the gunman of Austin's command theory delivers us from the sealed, phantasmatic realm of the Hart "fight clubs" (and their never-ending psychic struggle) and returns us to the "real" world: that is, to the arena of what Raz calls "the social,"[44] with its web of concrete relations and its networks of power centralized in the sovereign who commands and the subject who obeys. That obedience, however, differs from Hart's because it doesn't totally conquer the "h(e)art"—or the mind for that matter. Hearts and minds are not the sort of absolutizing allegiance that the Austinian sovereign is necessarily concerned with, or intent on securing. For his commands operate, on the whole, *externally*, leaving some inner space free—after all, even Tyler lets Raymond go to remake his life on his own. And ironically, by letting something of the legal subject and his psyche alone, Austin—like Tyler—creates the mental distance necessary for an inner dissensus, for an internal point of view that is thoroughly reflective and truly critical. Which is why I, for one, would welcome back the command theory with open arms: because it situates the law in the *somewhere* of the social rather than in the *nowhere* of the psyche, and in so doing liberates it from Hart's phantasmatic perversity, opening up, once again, the possibility of critique. So hurry back, John Austin, and bring your gunman with you. For there *is* a precondition to your reentry into *lex populi*; as your first act of legitimate (?) violence, you must do what Jack could not do to Raymond and *shoot the (Hartian) positivist!*

CHAPTER FOUR

One *Recht* to Rule Them All!

Law's Empire in the Age of Empire

Dark Lord or Law Lord? *The Lord of the Rings* as *Lex Populi*

Allegory is nothing new in Tolkien studies—despite Tolkien's own strictures against it.[1] Indeed, the temptation to allegorize Tolkien's masterpiece, *The Lord of the Rings*, seems to be almost as impossible to resist as the Ring itself.[2] For each successive generation of the text's readership has produced its own allegorical version[3] of the fellowship and its quest, alternatively emphasizing either the beginning or the end of the trilogy. Readers in the countercultural 1960s and 1970s, for example, focused on the beginning of the trilogy and its idyllic scenes set in the Shire, which stood in for the commune, with the halflings' leaf—"Old Toby," so favored by Gandalf (and Saruman!)—a code for that period's mind-expanding drugs.[4] The previous generation, the original readership of the 1950s, looked to the end of trilogy and its dramatic battle scenes, which they couldn't help but read in light of their own wartime experiences, equating the Nazgul with the Nazis, Sauron with Hitler, and Saruman with Stalin.[5]

In this chapter, I want to suggest yet another allegorical reading of Tolkien, one that stakes a claim for the law. I will argue that *The Lord of the Rings*—both the classic Tolkien trilogy and the contemporary Jackson triptych—is nothing less than an allegory of jurisprudence and an exemplary instance of *lex populi*. But instead of privileging either the beginning or the end of the tale, this jurisprudential allegory—this cultural legal reading of Tolkien-as-*lex populi*—begins with and is centered round the Ring itself. To that end, I will argue in the next section of this chapter that the Ring is a metaphor for desire and its law, and in turn, the desire *for* law. I will then connect the Ring of Power to high-positivist Hans Kelsen's central juristic concept, the *grundnorm*, itself advanced as the controlling trope and emblem of a "new world order," the eponymous empire of Hardt and Negri's justly celebrated politico-legal text, *Empire*. A prospective candidate for the imperial throne of the "Empire" will be advanced in a later section, analogizing Sauron's bid for domination as "Empire" and the Ring as the *grundnorm* legitimizing his rule. As I shall argue, however, that candidature is highly contested by the claims of Aragorn, whose return as king is made possible only by throwing the Ring away. That act—*the* central act of the narrative, I contend—is truly Kelsenian in that it dematerializes the Ring-as-*grundnorm*, which now, as a pure theory of law, ushers in a much more complex, indeed chilling version of "Empire": perpetually peaceful but always at war, multiculturally tolerant but racially segmented. That is, the *Pax Gondoria* with which Tolkien's tale ends so happily is the catastrophe in which we, according to Hardt and Negri, find ourselves living out at present: under the global aegis of a ruthlessly self-serving hyperpower, far more terrifying in its volatility than any "axis of evil" that it misrecognizes as a threat to world peace. Prescriptions for collective action against such a foe are then canvassed in *Empire* and *The Lord of the Rings* in this chapter's final section, the most efficacious of which arises from the intertext of both: that is, the forging of a new Ring of rights—not so the One can rule the many but so the many can rule through the One. Thus what this intertextual reading of Tolkien, Kelsen, and Hardt and Negri holds out is nothing less than *lex populi*'s promise of a new jurisprudence of resistance, if not emancipation.

Middle-earth's "Juriscape": The Law of Desire, the Desire for Law, and the Ring-as-*Recht*

My reading of *The Lord of the Rings* as a jurisprudential allegory—that is, as *lex populi*—neither begins in Hobbiton (as I suggested it did in the 1960s) nor ends at Barad-dur (as it did in the 1950s). Rather it opens with and provides a vista or panorama—a "bird's eye view" as if we were borne aloft by Gwaihir, the Windlord of the Eagles himself—of the entirety of Middle-earth, which could be renamed, at least by my lights, "the province of jurisprudence determined." For Tolkien's detailed topography provides nothing less, so this chapter will argue, than what might be called, with a nod to Judith Grbich, a "juriscape."[6] Here, analogies could easily be drawn, for example, between the Elves and Natural Law; their departure, after all, signals the disenchantment of their world, a metaphor if ever there was one for the secularization of our own in the wake of the *lex natura*'s retreat. Or take the Dwarves and their fetishization of mineral wealth: clearly budding bourgeois-liberal legalists in their substitution of mithril for money and their reliance on bargaining bordering on sharp practices. Or consider the Orcs: all "nasty, brutish, and short"—a rather obvious referencing of the Hobbesian "state of nature" prior to the forfeiture and amalgamation of natural rights (to kill and be killed) in the form of the Leviathanic state. Even the Steward of Gondor, Denethor, "mad, bad, and dangerous to know" as he is, seems to hold office on trust—until the king's return—a kind of Lockean sovereign who is the equitable but not legal ruler of his realm. Wending its way through this nomological space, marking and mapping its juristic cadastres—its sacred sites of natural law (Rivendell, Lothlorien), its depths of liberal legalism (the mines of Moria), its armed camps of *omnium bellum omnium* (Cirith Ungol, Minas Morgul), and its stately halls of social contract (Edoras, the Tower of Ecthelian), subsuming as it supersedes them, accreting their multiplicity into One—is none other than that adamantine talisman of the *lex talionis*, that totalizing trope of the text, the Ring of Power.

But what is the nature of the Ring's power, and how is that power connected to law, let alone jurisprudence? At first blush, there seems to be no connection, and the reverse obtains. The Ring's power seems to reside precisely in the fact that it annuls legality, enables usurpation, and facilitates illegitimate force and control. At least, that is the Actonian fantasy of absolute power that "history," "legend," and "myth"—in both the trilogy's appendices and the first film's prologue[7]—ascribe to the Ring. But consider for a moment what the reader or filmgoer is not so much told as shown: namely, *how* the Ring works its magic, that is, functionalizes its power. For the Ring does not so much invest its bearer with the possession of power as exert its power to possess over the bearer. Frodo, to name the most obvious example, cannot throw the Ring away. His will gives way, and he capitulates to the power of the Ring just as his mission is on the verge of fulfillment: "I have come," Frodo says, "but I do not choose now to do what I came to do. I will not do this deed" (LR, p. 924). Instead, it is Gollum, famously, who turns out to be the instrument of the Ring's destruction. He gnaws it off Frodo's hand, finger and all, and perishes with it in the most "fortunate fall" in all of fantasy literature, a *felix culpa* that plunges him into the fires of Mount Doom (LR, p. 925).[8] Bilbo, of course, gave the Ring away—a terrible wrench for him, though doubtless one that saved him from a Gollum-like fate (LR-FR, disc 1, ch. 6). But he still longs for it, even in the serene security of Rivendell, where, espying the Ring on Frodo's neck he undergoes a temporary shape-shift of things that *could* have come: "Frodo quickly drew back the Ring. To his distress he found that he was no longer looking at Bilbo; a shadow seemed to have fallen between them, and through it he found himself eyeing a little wrinkled creature with a hungry face and bony groping hands. He felt a desire to strike him" (LR, pp. 225–26; LR-FR, disc 2, ch. 2). And Gandalf won't even touch it, fearing to become "like the Dark Lord himself" (LR, p. 60; LR-FR, disc 1, ch. 10). "'No!,' cried Gandalf, springing to his feet. 'With that power I should have power too great and terrible. And over me the Ring would gain a power still greater and more deadly'" (LR, p. 60). Boromir, of course, is the first of the fellowship to fall under the spell of the Ring (LR, pp. 389–90; LR-FR, disc 2, ch. 16), and even Sam hears its siren call.[9]

But it is Galadriel—Lady of the Wood, queen of Lorien's Elves, and surely *the* incorruptible presence in the text—who is most sorely tempted by the Ring, a temptation that points us in the direction of its jurisprudential significance. Consider Jackson's filmic representation of the last temptation of Galadriel, herself changed—nay, transmogrified—into something rich and strange, at once tantalizing and terrible, by the mere possibility of possessing the Ring. "In place of a Dark Lord you would have a Queen," roars a stentorian Galadriel. "Not dark, but beautiful as the dawn! Treacherous as the sea! Stronger than the foundations of the Earth! All shall love me and despair!" (LR-FR, disc 2, ch. 12). The film's dialogue is for the most part faithful to Tolkien's tale (LR, p. 356), but the cinematic representation of this scene, when compared to its textual sources, is much more dramatic, even overheated. Galadriel is left breathless from her fantasy of power, panting like some pagan St. Theresa, pierced by erotic ecstasy, saturated by *jouissance*. All of which suggests that if the Ring activates anything, it is *desire* and desire's *law*. What's more, this Law of Desire that the Ring not only initiates but also instantiates is itself driven by a desire: a desire for law.

This is announced right from the start of the narrative by its celebrated poetic epigraph, which Gandalf intones for Frodo while both are still in Hobbiton (LR, p. 49):

> Three Rings for the Elven-Kings under the sky,
> Seven for the Dwarf-lords in their halls of stone,
> Nine for Mortal Men doomed to die,
> One for the Dark Lord on his dark throne
> In the Land of Mordor where the Shadows lie.

> One Ring to rule them all, One Ring to find them,
> One Ring to bring them all and in the darkness bind them
> In the Land of Mordor where the Shadows lie.[10]

The reference to the Ring's "rule" (line 6) is suggestive of Hartian prescription—the law as a system of rules—as much as Austinian command. And even more curiously, the Ring's "binding" nature (line 7) evokes the stare decisis of judge-made law. Thus the desire for law is woven into the very fabric of the text's language, the epigraph's subtextual "legalese" turning its paean to the Ring's power into something like a restatement of the philosophy of right. And Tolkien's verse could conceivably conclude not with the exclamatory refrain, "One Ring to rule them all" but rather with the titular cod-Hegel (*Philosophy of Right*) that entitles this chapter, "One *Recht* to Rule Them All."

The Evil Empire of Law's Empire: Isildur's Bane as *Grundnorm*

Nonetheless, a rule-skeptic could easily object to this reading of the Ring-as-*recht*, arguing that *recht*—or right—is the last thing on anyone's mind when wearing or wishing for the One Ring. Consider the two most driven and desiring of the Ring's seekers: Sauron and Saruman. Neither is concerned with legitimacy, let alone law; indeed, if any one thing is the object of their opposition, it is the restoration of legitimacy, that is, the return of the king and his just law that will smite the wicked and reward the faithful. Then why would they, of all beings, need to possess the Ring-as-*recht*? It is precisely this paradox—of the lawless searching for the law, the illegitimate looking for legitimacy—I will argue, that drives the narrative and contextualizes my jurisprudential reading of *The Lord of the Rings* as very much one of the millennium. For this is an epoch that has been characterized by a particular *point d'ancrage* with strong juridico-political resonances: Empire.

"Empire" is emerging, much as "*eeevil* is stirring in Mordor" (LR-FR, disc 1, ch. 10), as the sign of our very interesting times, deriving of course from the tome of the same name by Italian anarchist Antonio Negri and American literary critic Michael Hardt.[11] As every (theoretically *au fait*) schoolchild knows, *Empire* is currently as much a cult hit among hip, happening global theorists, especially those of a critical legal or cultural persuasion, as Tolkien's trilogy was and *is* among the anorak-wearing, "dungeons 'n dragons"–playing trainspotters, ever too irony deficient to be, as *National Lampoon* would have it, "Bored of the Rings."[12] In fact, the readership may be one and the same, the Tolkien text an adolescent version of the Hardt and Negri text, attracting as readers our younger selves, now adult and mature and "all growed up" but still looking for the same story. Which brings me to my central point of comparison: that *Empire* and *The Lord of the Rings* tell similar if not identical tales. In *Empire*, for example, Hardt and Negri herald the emergence of a "new world order" to be as menacing as the "Darkness," which—warns Galadriel's ominous voice-over in the prologue to the film—has "crept back into the forests."[13] But this "nameless fear," this "Shadow" of whispered rumor comes not, according to Hardt and Negri, from "the East" (the Arab littoral, the ex-Soviet Eurasian landmass) but rather from the West (Caucasian, Christian, Capitalist). And it takes the form not of the dark lord of despotism (either the imam or the apparatchik) but of the demos of consensual sovereignty (whether it be Westminster, Washington, or other power center), conquering under the letter of the law rather than the jackboot of power.[14] What is this law? And more to the point, what is the juristic spirit driving its letter? Hardt and Negri identify it as hybridized in origin, the mutated progeny of an unholy coupling, much like Saruman's "fighting Uruk-hai," half-orc, half-goblin (LR-FR, disc 2, ch. 13). Deriving from a source just as diabolic as it is dual, this spirit of the law issues from two forces. On the one hand, the transcendent and centrifugal force of globalization, forever transgressing borders, always crossing lines of demarcation[15]; and on the other hand, the immanent and implosive logic of Capital, relentlessly producing, distributing, and consuming, subjecting everyone and everything to its processes of pricing, profit, and commodification.[16]

Working increasingly in tandem throughout the postwar period, and triumphant all but everywhere since the fin de siècle, this "double trouble" of Capital and globalization is nonetheless missing one vital item to complete its agenda for world domination—a remainder, a supplement, an indefinable "X." Or not so indefinable, as this missing piece turns out to be. For Hardt and Negri name this lack. And this singular nomination is what distinguishes *Empire* from all the standard-issue sociological analyses of global Capital—dumbed-down versions of Ulrich Beck,[17] Arjun Appadurai,[18] David Held[19]—that have appeared with numbing regularity since the fall of the Berlin Wall.[20] What is absent from these accounts[21]—an omission that Hardt and Negri draw our attention to and seek to rectify—is Global Capital's lack of and desire for nothing less than the Law itself. "This is really the point of departure for our study of Empire," they write, "a new notion of right . . . and a new design of the production of norms and legal instruments."[22] So it is that most superstructural of forces—law—which is the component necessary to ensure that the Global Capital infrastructural machine is fully operational. This is a dramatic reversal, of course, of the instrumentalist view of the law in the Marxist theory often inflecting "globalization studies."[23] Hardt and Negri go well beyond this view, past even the postmodernization of Marx—even his "Derrideanization"—in the work of, for example, Ernesto Laclau and Chantal Mouffe.[24] Indeed, *Empire* may very well mark the *post*-postmodernization of the theory of Global Capital in that it announces not the end of the juridical metanarrative (asserted, especially, by Jean Baudrillard),[25] but rather its return. Nowhere is this return more striking than when Hardt and Negri proclaim "Empire's" jurisprude du jour ("that utopian and thus involuntary discoverer of the soul of imperial right")[26] to be none other than that *echt*-positivist, the bane of legal theory examinees everywhere, Hans Kelsen.

Kelsen is a peculiar choice of jurisprude for a pair of critical legal theorists tracking the sociolegal phenomenon of globalization, especially given the hostility of the Kelsenian "pure theory of law"[27] to "legal sociology."[28] But it is precisely Kelsen's claims to "purity"[29]—however specious and impure they may turn out to be—that recommends his normative account of law to Hardt and Negri and renders it, according to them, so necessary for the project of "Empire." This is because Kelsen's well-known hierarchy of norms—the lower ones (local or domestic law) being validated by the higher ones (constitutions, international law), until reaching the overarching and all-inclusive ur-norm, the (in)famous *grundnorm* (or "basic norm")[30]—effectively dematerializes the law. Dematerialization would seem at first glance to be an odd jurisprudential maneuver for the leading Continental advocate of positivism, not the least because it appears to depositivize the posited law, abstracting its apex—the *grundnorm*—as a "presupposition" of "consciousness."[31] But far from depositivizing positivism, Kelsen strengthens it, even secures it through the very dematerialization of the *grundnorm*. For this dematerializing move renders the posited law, hitherto localized by command or rule, omnipresent in its normativity. But here normativity lacks any of the moral baggage of its competing legal universal—natural—law because Kelsen's "legal science" of norms is firmly located in the secular, not the sacred[32]; the "consciousness" of the "jurist"[33] rather than the mind of God.

No wonder then that Hardt and Negri hail Kelsen's "legal science" as such a harbinger. Because its notion of an absolutizing "juristic consciousness"—itself "quilted" around the *point de capiton*, the basic norm from which all other legal norms derive their legitimacy—is the very mind of "Empire." A mind that is systemic, connected and thinking as One—akin to the Borg Queen in the *Star Trek* series.[34] The Borg are apropos any discussion of "Empire" and its juridical order because, against such an enclosed, self-validating system, resistance is futile. For where is there a space to protest, what counterhegemonic strategies are available, and how are norms to be transvalued within and against "Empire's" all-embracing, hermetically sealed "pure theory of law"? It is precisely because the "pure theory" is so thoroughly stifling of dissent, so absolutely silencing of critique that protoimperial Global Capital is "seeking . . . seeking" (LR, p. 61; LR-FR, disc 1, ch. 10) its *grundnorm*, much like Sauron and Saruman are searching for Isildur's Bane, the One Ring. Kelsenian law, as much as the lore of the Ring, thus promises a system so total that it makes alternatives not only unmanageable but also unthinkable.

The Two Towers as Twin Towers: The Shadow of Globalization

This set of analogies I am drawing here—the Ring as the *grundnorm*, Sauron and Saruman as "Empire" *manque-à-être*—may explain Tolkien's current appeal, even vogue, among the youth of the Left. This appeal is of course all the more bizarre given Tolkien's own High Table Toryism, Little Englandism, and Tridentine Roman Catholicism.[35] But just as Milton was of the devil's party without knowing it, so too Tolkien may very well be on the side of today's romantic overreachers, the antiglobalization movement, whose tatted and pierced, dreadlocked and vegan shock troops reference in their appearance and reproduce in their practices, *The Hobbit*.[36] Think of mid-1990s British activist, Swampy,[37] burrowed into his own version of Bag End, literally a hole in the ground blocking the expansion of a Midlands motorway. So here is a generation not only raised on the Tolkien corpus, but who also enact it, becoming their own walking, talking allegories of Middle-earth and seeing the world through its typology of Dark Lords and White Wizards, ecofriendly Ents and tree-destroying Orcs. Is it any wonder that this new New Left taps into the imagination of the Old Right of organic (even Heideggerian) conservatism—clearly Tolkien's politics, however incoherent he was on the topic—because it provides such rich iconic fodder by which to demonize Global Capital as both Sauronic and Sarumanic?

Here the film is even more central than the text, because it literalizes the figurative significance of Sauron and Saruman, throwing the trilogy's subtext of political economy into bold relief and representing in its mise-en-scène the emergence of proto-Empire in the form of Global Capital. Capital is most vividly dramatized in the scenes set at Isengard, Saruman's domain, and its transformation from what might be called, in an inversion of Durkheim, "the organic" to "the mechanical."[38] While the text merely reports this movement through Gandalf's vocalization at the Council of Elrond, the film revels in the *focalization* of this metamorphic process. The camera swoops and soars vertiginously from the digitally generated heights of the Tower of Orthanc (where Gandalf is held in captivity, frantically dispatching distress signals to and through Nature's Kingdom—butterflies, birds, and their brethren) to the infernal depths of Saruman's subterranean "dark, satanic mills" (LR-FR, disc 1, ch. 20). There, tunnels and mines are endlessly dug by orcs; forges and fires tirelessly tended by goblins, rendering this scene a site of frenzied and frantic production: in short, the domain of Capital.[39] And an advanced form of Capital at that, one that pushes its reifying logic to the limit, reproducing by the most literal of means its own productive relations in the creation of the Franken-stein-like Thing of the Uruk-hai, a monstrous figure spawned in the poisonous industrial ooze of Isengard (LR-FR, disc 1, ch. 20).

What these scenes at Isengard realize—or better yet, *materialize* in the most Marxist sense of the word—is the objective of both Saruman's *and* Sauron's agenda, the bondsman disclosing the design of the lord. For Sauron's project has been, until now, disconcertingly vague in its expansionism. Why is he expanding, and what is he expanding? Or to rephrase the question slightly: What is the ulti-mate goal of Sauron's will-to-power? It doesn't seem to be, at least at first blush, ex-change—globalization's privileged modality—because that is exactly what Sauron does not do. He takes but he does not give. "There is only one Lord of the Rings," thunders Gandalf at Saruman, just before his dramatic eagle-engineered escape from Isengard, "and he does not share power."[40] Thus Sauron seemingly defies the "give and take" logic of exchange and in so doing looks back, in his "smash 'n grab" expansionism, to nineteenth-century social theories of "the primitive" (Weberian charisma?[41] Marx's Asiatic mode of production?[42]) instead of to the twenty-first-century notion of the postmodern market. Indeed, Sauron is coded by the film, even more than the text, as an archaic figure. In a kind of Second Age "prequel," telescoping the history of Middle-earth prior to the War of the Ring, the film's prologue gives its audience what the text insistently denies its readers. That is, we are vouchsafed the obscene sight of Sauron incarnate, the embodiment of *mala fides*. Ensconced in his fastness of Barad-dur, he stands invincibly immense, impenetrably armored and wearing on one steely glove, the Ring of Power, the

"One . . . to rule them all . . . and to find them / One to bring them all and, in the darkness, bind them" (LR, p. 49; LR-FR, disc 1, chs. 1, 10).

Curiously enough, the filmic emphasis on Sauron's premodern primitivism doesn't so much as atavise him as an archaic figure of the past, as propel him forward to contemporaneity. There he joins the current popular culture as well as the high-politics pantheon of "radical evil": from Harry Potter's Voldemort[43] to "Dubya's" malign axis of North Korea, Afghanistan, and Iraq. This is why the representation of Sauron here must be read in conjunction with the film's noncanonic interpolations, especially the scenes set at Saruman's Isengard lair, Orthanc. Otherwise, Sauron might end up just another filmic "phantom menace" on temporary loan from Dreamworks or Lucasfilm. Instead, the Orthanc scenes with Saruman supply a specific *economic* content to the Shadow's global form, thereby foreclosing any right-wing "culturist" readings, à la Samuel Huntingdon, of Sauron as "the Enemy" in the "clash of civilizations"—as either the Islamic or Orthodox East against the Latin West.[44] For, at Orthanc, Saruman is revealed as something more than just the White Council's most notorious quisling, because he is a comprador as much as collaborator, Mordor's economic agent as well as its favored "sorcerer's apprentice" administering the logic of Global Capital and the triumphalist march of the Sauronic market (LR-FR, disc 1, ch. 18).

Thus Middle-earth and its "free peoples"[45] stand poised to fall under the sway of Sauron's Barad-dur and Saruman's Orthanc, the two towers—or rather, twin towers—of world trade, linked by the communicative network of the *palantiri*, or "seeing stones." Circling these structures are the Ringwraiths, as airborne on their winged mounts as al-Qaeda was in its hijacked jets, only here they function as the praetorians of, or rather kamikazes launched at Global Capital. Thus "Empire" looms and indeed has arrived at Tolkien's "imagined community"[46] fifty years earlier, but with a remarkable prescience of our *own* era's "postmodern condition"[47] with all its talk of *ends*—the end of history, the end of ideology—and the changes introduced by the likes of digitality and the information economy. Jackson's *The Lord of the Rings* foregrounds this mood of change, citing a speech of Treebeard's in the text (LR, p. 1017), which it then (mis)attributes to Galadriel and her opening voice-over as the first bit of English (rather than elvish) dialogue in the film: "The world is changed. I feel it in the air. I feel it in the earth. I taste it in the water" (LR-FR, disc 1, ch. 1).

Or has it? Has the world changed at all? After all, Sauron's bid for global domination is not so much a change, even less, for that matter, an end or a beginning. Rather it is part of a pattern of cyclic recurrence: "Always after a defeat and a respite" warns Gandalf in the text: "The Shadow takes another shape and grows again" (LR, p. 50). But what recurs with Sauron is neither the premodern primitive (autocracy or autarky) nor the postmodern "plague of fantasies" (religious strife, ethnic conflict) but rather modernity itself, and its metanarrative of governance and "discipline and punish."[48] Consider the form Sauron takes in the text and, for the most part, in the film. "A great Eye," intones Saruman, "lidless and wreathed in flames" (LR-FR, disc 1, ch. 12) that violates psychic as much as physical boundaries, its gaze penetrating the "I" of consciousness ("You cannot hide. I see you!" threatens the filmic voice of Sauron when Frodo inadvertently dons the Ring at "The Prancing Pony" in Bree [LR-FR, disc 1, ch. 15] at the very moment its armies are pressing upon the borders of Rohan and Gondor, even Lothlorien and Thranduil's realm.)

Now consider the literary representation of the Eye of Sauron getting an eyeful of Frodo while atop, appropriately enough, Amon Hen's Seat of Seeing:

> At first he could see little. He seemed in a world of mist in which there were only shadows: The Ring was upon him. Then here and there the mist gave way and he saw many visions . . . everywhere he looked he saw signs of war. The Misty Mountains were crawling like anthills; orcs were issuing out of a thousand holes. Under the boughs of Mirkwood there was deadly strife of Elves and Men and fell beasts. The land of the Beornings was aflame; a cloud was over Moria; and smoke rose on the borders of Lorien . . . All the power of the Dark Lord was in motion . . . Thither, eastward, unwilling [Frodo's] eye was drawn. It passed the ruined bridges of Osgiliath, the grinning gates of Minas Morgul, and the haunted Mountains, and it looked upon Gorgoroth, the valley of terror in the Land of Mordor . . . Then at last his gaze was held: wall upon wall, battlement upon battlement, black, immeasurably strong, mountain of iron, gate of steel, tower of adamant, he saw it: Barad-dur, Fortress of Sauron . . . And suddenly he felt the Eye. There was an eye in the Dark Tower that did not sleep. He knew that it had become aware of his gaze. A fierce eager will was there. It leaped towards him; almost like a finger he felt it, searching for him (LR, pp. 391–92; see LR-FR, disc 2, ch. 16).

The passage is interesting for a number of reasons, not the least of which is stylistic, form reinforcing content here. The brevity of the opening sentence conveys just how little Frodo can see—and then, as the mist lifts, explodes into a series of independent clauses and sentences ("orcs were issuing out of a thousand holes; "there was deadly strife of Elves and Men and fell beasts"; "the land of the Beornings was aflame"), punctuated periodically or semicolonically, suggestive of a landscape alive with activity, "crawling like anthills." As the Dark Tower comes into focus, however, the sentence structure shifts to short, sharp phrases, tracking

Frodo's field of vision as it crosses the ruined landscape ("the ruined bridges of Osgiliath"; "the grinning gates of Minas Morgul") and then ascends through an almost steplike (the Winding Stair?) series of repetitions ("wall upon wall, battlement upon battlement") arriving, linguistically, at a set of forbidding epithets, "mountain of iron, gate of steel, tower of adamant" that announce Barad-dur like some grammatical court chamberlain, and within it, "the Eye." The passage's final and very disturbing ophthalmic image—of an eye, situated within a tower, its "gaze" subjecting all and sundry to its ever-widening, quasi-digital reach ("It leaped towards him; almost like a finger he felt it")—cannot help but recall (and may very well instantiate) that infamous, nineteenth-century blueprint for 24/7 surveillance; namely, Jeremy Bentham's Panopticon.[49] The Panopticon is more than just a failed design proposal; according to a certain historicist moment in poststructuralist thought, it is a metaphor for as much as a model of the regime of discipline and punish, and its strategies of "governmentality."[50]

Thus Sauron's eternal recurrence does not look forward to "Empire" and its dispersed network logic as much as it looks immediately backwards to its condition precedent. Specifically, the centered disciplinary society (of scrutiny, of observation) that is in turn subsumptive of the previous order of punishment (of spectacle, of display), as well as proleptic of "governmentality's" policing of "security, territory, population."[51] Take, for example, the grim vistas briefly opened up by Tolkien's text of the Sauronic realm, mobilizing for war, well beyond the immediate field of vision of Frodo and Sam. "Neither knew anything," interjects the text's omniscient narrator, "of the great slave-worked fields away south . . . beyond the fumes of the mountain, by the sad waters of Lake Nurnen; nor of the great roads that ran away east and west to tributary lands from which the soldiers of the Tower brought long waggon-trains of goods and booty and fresh slaves" (LR, p. 902).

Is there a more chilling vision in fantasy, or for that matter, mainstream literature, of biopolitics—what Agamben might call "bare life"[52]—and its "governmentalization" through the all-seeing agency of the panoptic sovereign? I would say no, most emphatically. This suggests that if *The Lord of the Rings* is a juridico-political allegory, then it allegorizes the oeuvre of the late, great Michel Foucault rather than Hardt and Negri's *Empire*.

Gondor as Schmittian Superpower: Policing Middle-earth's Crisis

That said, I would like to advance, in this chapter, the allegorical claims of another candidate for the throne of "Empire," the missing heir of which is none other than that prince-as-pauper, Strider, a.k.a. Aragorn, a.k.a. Elfstone, a.k.a. Elessar, whose return as king, by the grace of God and Gandalf, will dominate and designate the last third of the trilogy. My argument here is, simply, that Aragorn's restoration is Hardt and Negri's "Empire" brought to textual life and represented in the reconfigured Middle-earth—the Fourth Age, the Age of Men—that emerges at the end of the trilogy. I stress "emerges" because this representation of renewal—the White City as a kind of Celestial City—exists pretty much solely in the text's interstices: in select asides in the concluding chapters[53] and in remarks scattered throughout the appendices (LR, pp. 1020, 1032, 1053). These asides take us well beyond the end of the narrative's diegetic reality, namely, the departure of Frodo, Gandalf, and the High Elves from the Grey Havens for the Undying Lands in the West (LR, pp. 1006–7). In fact, the reader travels in time several hundred years into the future of Middle-earth: after the death of King Aragorn (LR, p. 1072), the sailing of Legolas and Gimli (LR, pp. 1055, 1072) and most poignantly of all, the twilight years of Gondor's queen mother, Arwen Evenstar, in a now deserted Lorien (LR, p. 1038).

Indeed, one of the considerable pleasures of Tolkien's trilogy is that it has a future as much as a past. This rich historical imagination is as functional as it is fun, not only tying up loose narrative threads (Who did Pippin marry?[54] How many children did Sam and Rosie have?[55] Whatever happened to the Red Book?[56]) but also performing a significant structural role; principally, by supplying an overarching thematic continuity for Middle-earth's conditions as well as characters. And the future condition of Middle-earth that emerges in these various postscripts is something very much like a vision of "Empire." That is, a network[57] of semiautonomous states—Ithilien, Dol Amroth, Rohan, the Shire—linked together by and under the benign governance of Middle-earth's global hegemon, Gondor, itself peaceful, consensual, *and totally oppressive.*[58] Oppressive? Gondor? Many of Tolkien's readers might well look askance at such an inference and the seemingly scant evidence giving rise to it. This is especially so when the text goes out of its way to hymn the praises of good King Elessar's reign, "of which many songs have told." After all, Aragorn's first act of sovereignty is one of amnesty granted to "the Easterlings that had given themselves up." Treaties and emancipation follow closely upon this: he "made peace with the peoples of Harad"; and as for the slaves of Mordor, "he released and gave to them all the lands about Lake Nurnen to be their own" (LR, p. 947).

But "crises" remain on the borders of "Empire," as much in Aragorn's Gondor as in Hardt and Negri's imperium; in fact, the state of "Empire" is one of ongoing crisis, of the naturalization and normalization of crisis, all of which calls for the perpetual policing of crisis.[59] Gandalf has warned, in text, of trouble to come: "the fall of Sauron," he cautions, "will only remove one, admittedly great evil among many. Other evils there are that may come; for Sauron is himself but a servant or emissary" (LR, p. 861). The appendices confirm this state of affairs, especially those regarding the future of the Rohirrim and, specifically, King Eomer's reign.

> (T)hough Sauron had passed, the hatreds and evils that he had bred had not died, and the King of the West had many enemies to subdue before the White Tree could grow in peace. And wherever King Elessar went with war King Eomer went with him; and beyond the sea of Rhun and on the far fields of the South the thunder of the cavalry of the Mark was heard, and the White Horse upon Green flew in many winds until Eomer grew old (LR, p. 1045).

Thus Rohan and its patron state, Gondor, both seem to operate on a semipermanent basis in a Schmittian "state of exception,"[60] governing by emergency measures that suspend the Law indefinitely in order to manage Middle-earth's "lesser breeds without the law."[61] Kipling is cited here purposively, his jingoism linking the race hierarchies of the defunct British Empire with those of Gondor's because, interestingly, Middle-earth's "lesser breeds" are enraced along the lines of the old colonial color bar. Those "beyond the Sea of Rhun" are "Orientalized,"[62] as Edward Said might say, as either Semitic, Sinic, or Slavic "hordes"; while those to "the South" are the torrid zone's "negritude"[63] embodied. And if these fringe-dwellers of Middle-earth are being brought into line, one can well imagine what has happened to the Orcs and Uruk-hai. Here, modernity's all-too-efficacious forms of racial science loom. For doubtless these "creatures" have met the same genocidal fate confronted by all twentieth-century groups designated "subhuman": Jews, Romany, but especially the Indigenous peoples of the globe, for whom they are so clearly stand-ins. Think of their filmic representation, especially when in "hot pursuit" of the fellowship (LR-FR, disc 2, ch. 15). Kitted out in Australian Aboriginal face and body paint, much is made of their Aotearoa–New Zealand Maori warrior ethic and fighting prowess. Not for nothing is *The Lord of the Rings* a movie triptych made in the "Land of the Long White Cloud" by a *pakeha*[64] Kiwi.[65]

Thus the *Pax Gondoria* embodies all the contradictions of "Empire." Particularly in the way its federated nations yoke together the old vertical hierarchies of the colonial era—white hegemons (Gondorians, Rohirrim), subaltern subjects (Easterlings, Southrons), and protected peoples (the Hobbits)—and map them onto the new, horizontal segmentations of postcolonial difference.[66] To that end, spheres of influence and zones of autonomy[67] have been drawn up in the Fourth Age, largely along racial lines: the Shire, for example, is off-limits to men by order of the king.[68] But these vertical and horizontal coordinates are in turn subtended by the midcentury totalitarian distinction, beloved of fascist societies: Are you a friend or an enemy? Are you with us, or against us? One of the *Volk*, or a subspecies fit only for extermination?[69] So what Tolkien (and Jackson) expose here is the obscene underside of "Empire," its peacekeeping revealed as nothing more than brute force, its "mystical foundations of authority"[70] nothing more than military fiat. How then does "Empire," either Aragorn's or anyone else's, come to be as a *Rechtsstaat?* That is the key question posed by *The Lord of the Rings* and by Hardt and Negri's *Empire.* Of course, we know in point of fact that the state, whatever arguments it adduces to the contrary, is born of violence: in Gondor's case, the defeat of Sauron and the occupation of Mordor. But as a *Rechtsstaat,* a state of legitimacy—which, after all, grounds Gondor's claim as primus inter pares in Middle-earth—where is the Law and its initiating gesture of *recht?* After all, no constitution is proclaimed, let alone a bill of rights. But these declarative acts of legality's independence are, according to Hardt and Negri, as unnecessary for "Empire" in the here and now as they are for Aragorn's Gondor, because the Law—of legitimacy, of *recht*—has already been disseminated throughout the realm of right. How did this come about? Why did it? And more immediately: When?

I would like to locate the moment of the *recht*'s installation in the central narrative act of the text. What is this act other than the moment when the Ring is cast away? For what is the Ring—just to revisit, momentarily, earlier arguments in this chapter—if not a metaphor for *recht,* for the law. That law is to be understood, as I have argued, in the strictest of positivist terms: the Kelsenian dematerialization of the law into normativity. To reiterate: this "legal science" of normativity installs the law everywhere as an abstracted ideal—the *grundnorm*—located in global "juristic consciousness" because, to push Kelsen's logic, it is nowhere as an actual fact, having depositivized itself of the sovereign's command. But it is here that my argument seemingly breaks down, the analogy I have been drawing between the Ring and the *grundnorm* unraveling at this point. For while the basic norm is characterized by absence (of materiality, of the real), the Ring is presence itself, the *objet petit a,* that "little piece of the Real"[71]—something like the minimal materiality of good consideration (a peppercorn?) in contract.

This is why Sauron desires the Ring so desperately: as consideration that will seal his novation of the social contract, and impose his imperium on Middle-earth. But it is here that Sauron's panoptic sight fails him, "misrecognizing"[72] imperial right as residing in the positivity of the Ring, rather than its predication on the *grundnorm's* dematerialization of the law. So Sauron can never be anything more than an old pretender to the imperial throne, because he is incapable of transforming the Ring into the *grundnorm.* Instead of divesting the Ring of its materiality, he clings to its "Thing"-ness, searching everywhere for it. This is why the Council of Elrond is the true architect of "Empire"—a kind of proto-U.N.—because it opts for a strategy that is the opposite of Sauron's. Instead of pursuing and possessing, using and being used by the Ring, they vote to destroy it—not, as it turns out to thwart "Empire" but to facilitate its emergence through a universal *recht* that is everywhere because it is nowhere.

So when read conjointly and jurisprudentially, Tolkien's text completes Hardt and Negri's tome, and supplies the missing link between Kelsenian jurisprudence and the politics of imperial sovereignty.[73] In its riveting climax atop Mt. Doom, with Sam, Frodo, and Gollum struggling over the Ring before its final destruction, *The Lord of the Rings* provides its readers with a vivid dramatization of the "primal scene" of state construction that Hardt and Negri only suggest: how "Empire" comes into being through the law, generally, and through Kelsenian "pure theory," particularly (LR-RK, disc 2, ch. 34). Moreover, and this may be the real source of *lex populi's* power, when read jurisprudentially, *The Lord of the Rings* goes well beyond Hardt and Negri. That is, the trilogy not only stages "pure theory's" site of state construction but critiques it. For Tolkien's text exposes the "juristic consciousness," within which the *grundnorm* is embedded, as embodied, as personified. Who personifies "juristic consciousness"? Whose body is this?

Surely, it is none other than the critical intelligence of the text: that is, king maker and wizard breaker; Mithrandir to the Elves, or Gandalf to Men and the Hobbits. By the end of the narrative, Gandalf himself is revealed as a bearer of another ring—Cirdan's Narya (LR, p. 1007)—and as a great Lord from the West, dispatched by those cosmic Guardians, the Valar, to negotiate Middle-earth's transition to the Fourth Age by establishing, or rather restoring, its normative order. So behind all the mythopoeic flummery, Gandalf turns out to be someone strongly resembling the Kelsenian legal scientist, his jurisprudence "purified" by the struggle with the balrog (the bane of legal sociology?) transforming him from "Gandalf the Grey" into "Gandalf the White" (LR, p. 484; LR-TT, disc 1, ch. 15).

The "whiteness,"[74] not only of Gandalf's robes but also of Gandalf himself, is very telling here because it suggests the kind of body within which "juristic consciousness," and indeed the "pure theory of law," is enfolded: namely, the white body, the male body, the ruling-class body. No wonder then that a carefully calibrated race hierarchy (as well as those of class and gender) is the "legal sociology" that obtains in Middle-earth. Because its legal science, its normative order is itself a product of the *white mythology*[75] of Empire's positivist jurisprudence.

The Return of the Ring: Rights, Revolution, and the Fellowship of "the Multitude"

This argument is left here in something of an impasse, much like the fellowship's quest stymied by the impossible choices of Cadahras, Moria, and the Gap of Rohan (LR-FR, disc 2, ch. 4). Because if Tolkien's Middle-earth and, by extension, our own Earth of Hardt and Negri's "Empire" are subject to a pernicious, inequitable sociological order, closed off by normativity, indeed, vacuum packed by its *grundnorm*, then the possibility of internal reform, let alone revolutionary transformation is rendered impossible. For how is Law's Empire to change when all possibility of change has been foreclosed by Hardt and Negri's "Empire"? That is the paradoxical question that this chapter ultimately proposes, and for which Jackson's films may provide an answer, however provisional. I return to the scene of the fellowship's arrival, in the first film, in Lothlorien, and Galadriel's comforting words to the weary travelers, that "hope remains" (LR-FR, disc 2, ch. 11). Why does hope remain? Because, so she continues in private with Frodo: "even the smallest person can change the course of the future" (LR-FR, disc 2, ch. 12). Galadriel's point is pertinent to the discussion of "Empire." For it is precisely the "little people" or "halflings," as it were, of Global Capital—those whom *Empire* calls "the multitude"[76]—that Hardt and Negri turn to for revolutionary hope, as much as Galadriel does to the Hobbits.

That hope seems misplaced at first. Like the Hobbits, "the multitude" is as untraceable as it is insignificant. No longer an identifiable, organized industrial proletariat,[77] they are dispersed and decentered: diasporics[78] all, manning the "productive forces"; be it the McDonald's chain in the Philippines or the sweatshops in Manhattan upon which the service economy of Empire so clearly rests. Nonetheless, Hardt and Negri insist, like Galadriel does of Frodo, that it is its revolutionary potential or no one's who will make a difference. For, while "Empire" is reactive—that is, can only strike back—"the multitude" is proactive[79] and capable of initiating real change.[80] Enabling this initiative is a powerful and efficacious discourse, providing "the multitude" with a way in which to speak their needs, voice their desires, and make their demands heard. That language is, of course, *rights*.[81]

Hardt most certainly betrays not only a jurisprudential but also a national bias, tying his notion of "counter-Empire"[82] to a particular political and juridical order of rather dubious subversive potential. For it is ultimately the American Bill of Rights[83] and its peculiar constitutional history (of tolerating slavery, segregation, indigenous genocide, working-class exploitation, and gender inequity) that acts—or at least should act, as a precursor of—as the aspirational model of "the multitude." So the up-to-the-minute millennial and putatively Marxist Hardt begins to sound, here, very much like liberal American jurisprudence of the 1970s, channeling, even ventriloquizing Ronald Dworkin[84] in their mutual valorization of that nation's fetish, *rights*. But Hardt departs from Dworkin and his sort of rights chauvinism, to the extent that *Empire* acknowledges impliedly that, if rights are to have any purchase on "the multitude," if they are to have any transformative power, then they must be radically reconceived. Instead of the old autonomic rights of "negative liberty"[85] encoded in the U.S. Constitution as rights of speech, movement, privacy, and the rest, Hardt and Negri advance a model of "positive liberty,"[86] implying a system of public entitlements in its rights to a social wage[87] and the appropriation of space,[88] for example.

This sort of argument is something all critical legal scholars have heard before—especially those who cut their teeth in the 1980s on another fantasy trilogy, Roberto Unger's magnum opus and massively utopian, *Politics*.[89] In that series, Unger argued for an ambitious and radical reformulation of rights discourse as part of his "superliberal" project: market rights, destabilization rights, immunity rights, and the like.[90] How is Hardt and Negri's essentially Ungerian dream of a revivified rights discourse to be realized? *Empire* is as vague about this process of rights reform as it was about positivism's production of the state. Once again I turn to this chapter's privileged mediation of the law, the *lex populi* of *The Lord of the Rings*, to point the way to a law of and as mediation; that is, a reconfigured rights discourse. But Tolkien's text is more suggestive here than determinative, implying an answer only by way of negation, by way of what it does not say or do. For if throwing away the Ring installed a juridico-political order—the Law of "Empire" immunized from critique, let alone combustion—because it had been dematerialized, then any move to reform or change the system implies, a fortiori, the law's rematerialization. That is, in order to deconstruct and reconstruct the law, critique needs first and foremost a construction to work with, a piece of the real to act upon: namely, the *posited law*. All of which means, when retranslated back into Tolkien's metaphoric terms, the Ring of Power must be forged anew! Yet such a reforging would go well beyond the notion of "the One" and would restore, as Alain Badiou might put it, the concept of "the Multiple"[91] allowing for and indeed ensuring a multiplication of rings and, through them, a pluralization of Law. Thus instead of "One Ring"—or *recht*—"to rule them all," the many, or "the multitude" *could rule themselves* through the One of a rights discourse, itself predicated on the *différance*[92] of difference. Such a transformation of rights discourse would be disseminated across the halflings of Empire: to the "Bagginses" and "Boffins"; "Tooks" and "Brandybucks"; "Grubbs," "Chubbs," "Burrowses," "Bolgers," "Bracegirdles," and "ProudFEET" (LR, p. 29; LR-FR, disc 1, ch. 5). It is this very dissemination, this dispersal of rights that would be, as Gollum himself might say, very *precious* indeed.

CHAPTER FIVE

Precrime Never Pays!

Law and Economics in Minority Report

Preempting Prediction: *Minority Report* as *Lex Populi*

All the current talk about preemption amid the highest circles of global politics (Washington, Westminster)—and more ominously, the deployment of its tactics among the lowest (Iraq, Afghanistan)—cannot help but recall, for the student of popular culture,[1] 2002's cinematic celebration of the preemptive strike, *Minority Report*.[2] With its vivid depiction of a future in which murder is thwarted before it occurs in fact but not in thought—by the Department of PreCrime—*Minority Report* provides an eerie foretaste of the foreign policy of the Bush administration and the "coalition of the willing," intent on checking, with its gunboat diplomacy, the terrorist threat from the Islamic Middle East *before* it materializes, even in the absence of weapons of mass destruction, and all evidence to the contrary. Another tragically Wildean instance of (political) life imitating (popular) art. But my opening comments notwithstanding, the focus here is not political, rather it is legal and concerned with the ways in which the law is reflected in but also refracted by popular culture to produce what I have been calling throughout this book *lex populi*—or popular law. What makes *Minority Report* such an interesting example of *lex populi* lies not so much in its analepsis of the present-day politics of preemption, but rather in its representation of a thematic of far longer standing in the nomological tradition: law's prediction.

It is with this theme of law's prediction—in jurisprudence as well as in *Minority Report*—that this chapter is most directly concerned. In the following section

I will historicize this theme, locating *Minority Report*'s notion of "precrime" as the jurisprudential descendant of American Realism's (specifically that of Holmes) "predictive theory of the law" and as a gloss upon what this article argues is the current inheritor of its predictive aspirations: Law and Economics. I will then lay out and link the kinds of predictive scenes that inform the PreCogs' prophecies in *Minority Report* and the heuristic models of Law and Economics as equally phantasmatic *and* subject to an(O)ther law: the Law of Desire. In a later section, I identify the nature of that desire as the desire for consumption, the desire for commodities. Here I will examine the ways in which *Minority Report* graphically stages the commodity fetishism that so clearly powers the psychic life of Law and Economics. Next I explore the nature of the "forced choice" that underpins this economy of consumption in both Law and Economics and *Minority Report*, and gauge the extent to which that economy transforms the law into an instrument of coercion, and the state behind it into an authoritarian security system. A critique of that system in terms of the "politics of the law" is then proffered, and I will speculate on the way in which *Minority Report* enacts the desire of critical legal studies as well as Law and Economics. By way of conclusion, the final section turns from the critique of system to an analysis of the subject, engaging a characterological trope utilized in both *Minority Report* and Law and Economics, that of the missing child. This figure—and the anxiety, indeed trauma, it summons up—intervenes in and opens up a space for not only the critique of Law and Economics[3] but also, through *Minority Report*, a "critique of the critique." In so doing, *Minority Report* may suggest a way out of the theoretical impasses that afflict contemporary legal theory, both right (Law and Economics) and left (critical legal studies). For when it is read as *lex populi*, *Minority Report* holds out the possibility of a jurisprudence of popular culture, and a popular culture of jurisprudence that actually preempts prediction and thereby confounds preemption itself.

"Can You See?" Philip K. Dick's "Predictive Theory of the Law"

Following closely upon *A.I.*,[4] *Minority Report* is another Steven Spielberg foray into filmic futurism and bears all of his (largely) malign influences: the overproduced set of Washington in 2054 (more D.G. than D.C.; that is, more digitally generated than District of Columbia), the overheated script of exclamatory one-liners ("Everybody runs!": MR, ch. 8) and of course the lamentable overacting of Hollywood icon Tom Cruise. Nonetheless, this fifth cinematic outing[5] for a Philip K.

Dick fiction[6] is of particular interest to lawyers, especially jurisprudes—much more than either of the most recent, and very uneven, cinematic translations of Dick: 2003's passable *Paycheck*,[7] derived from his short story of the same name[8]; or 2002's bomb, *Imposter*,[9] also from a Dickian story of the same name.[10] More than mid-1990s Canadian shock horror, *Screamers*,[11] based on Dick's story "Second Variety,"[12] or early 1990s Arnie vehicle, *Total Recall*,[13] the original of which is another Dick short story, "We Can Remember It for You Wholesale."[14] Even more interesting than, with all due respect to Peter Hutchings,[15] Ridley Scott's 1980s masterpiece, *Blade Runner*,[16] taken from Dick's dazzling novel, *Do Androids Dream of Electric Sheep?*[17] This is because Dick's abiding metaforensic interests in identity and its detection,[18] in memory and its policing,[19] as well as the much-critiqued philosophical/psychoanalytic issues of sight, vision, and the unconscious[20] are yoked in *Minority Report* to an aspiration that has haunted legal thought—especially American legal thought, from the Realists on down—for the last century: namely, how to develop a foolproof "predictive theory of law."[21]

That highly suggestive sobriquet—the predictive theory of law—owes its coinage to and is of course identified with one of the "founding fathers" of American jurisprudence, the first of the Realists, that striking, walrus-mustachioed amalgam of Moses and Massachusetts, Mr. Justice Oliver Wendell Holmes, Jr.[22] Though it must be said, at first blush, Holmes makes an odd, even strange advocate for prediction, given his starchy mid-nineteenth-century Unitarian-Congregationalist upbringing[23] (a sect, then in its "high and dry" phase as the unofficial "established church" of the New England elite) and his relentless pragmatism (he was a devotee of William James's philosophy, as much as he was a friend of James's brother, Henry).[24] Such a religious background and philosophical orientation—both numbingly rationalist in outlook—might militate, one would think, against something as irrational, superstitious, even occult as prediction—with all of its pagan associations of sibyls, entrails, burnt offerings, and cryptic prophecies. But being the hardheaded (and often hard-hearted) Yankee he was (albeit "from Olympus" as one biographer has put it),[25] Holmes's "predictive theory of the law" turns not upon a sacred Pythia at Delphi but instead a very secular figure: namely, the client-litigant, the user and abuser of the legal system—or more scandalously, the "Bad Man."[26] Not for nothing is Holmes hailed as the first of the "Realists" because, by drawing attention to and refocusing on the standpoint of the Bad Man, he redirects nineteenth-century (and subsequent) American jurisprudence away from its stale preoccupation with law's posited sources—the Langdellian emphasis on the "law in books"[27]—and toward the law's processes—proleptic of Pound's "law in action."[28] For the Bad Man is not concerned with the niceties of formalist doctrine, whether conceived, variously, as command, rule, or norm. "(H)e does not care two straws for axioms . . . or deductions," declaims Holmes in a justly celebrated passage from *The Path of Law*, "but he does want to know what the Massachusetts or English courts are likely to do in fact."[29] So the Bad Man is a seer to this extent: he wants to know—and preferably, know in advance—just how far he can go in his testing of the rules, all the while avoiding (barely) their breach and the concomitant attraction of judicial sanction.

Here, then, for Holmes is the true "path of law," a road that goes ever on, in all of its never-ending peripateia. For Holmes, the best way to plot a course through it, to anticipate its manifold twists and turns, is to shadow the Bad Man because, in this latter's pushing of the rules to the limits of legality, *he*—not the judge or lawyer, let alone the rule maker–legislator—is the real force directing and shaping the future of the legal system. However, this predictive bid for law's futurity takes on, with the succeeding generation of Realists (but for one notable exception), a less rule-skeptical approach, going so far as to rehabilitate and revalorize doctrine—though now subordinate to and facilitative of "law's jobs."[30] This is precisely the wager of Karl Llewellyn, who, assuming Holmes's mantle in the 1920s, argued for a modified "predictive theory of law" that "took rules seriously." So seriously, in fact, that now regulatory instruments—such as his model Uniform Commercial Code[31]—could be aligned with, and indeed *anticipate*, a range of legal problems, issues, and pressure points. Especially those aporias and ambiguities in the realm of exchange writ large and generated by the vast social, economic, and political changes of the period. Thus the Realists, in the main—excepting of course radical skeptics of both rules and facts, like Jerome Frank[32] want to correlate rules with results.

Therein lies the difference between American Realism and our privileged text and putative legal fiction, *Minority Report*. While Realists, like Holmes, Llewellyn, and others want to be able to predict the outcome of the court's decisions, either to realize or rectify the (mis)application of the rules when measured by some standpoint (the Bad Man) or process standard (law jobs); Dick and his cinematic translator, Spielberg, want to circumvent the courts altogether in order to predict, and nip in the bud—like Dr. Hineman's all-too-clinging vines (MR, ch. 10)—the *facts* of crime, rendering the rule system supernumerary. Not that all legal channels are absent from the world of *Minority Report*. In fact, a judge is present by video linkup at the first (Howard Marks; MR, ch. 1) and second (John Anderton himself; MR, ch. 7) prescenes of the crime, to validate and authorize arrest, keeping the procedural ball rolling, as it were—literalized in the snookerlike wooden "red ball," inscribed with the names of the perpetrators and his victims. But despite this judicial imprimatur—and the fleeting digital image of Judge Pollard (MR, chs. 1, 7)—the focus in these scenes is forensic (rather than formalist), and squarely on Anderton and his conductorlike orchestration of facts (rather than the writing of writs), as he magnifies scenes, isolates details, collects and collates clues, all to the lush Romantic strains of Schubert and Tchaikovsky and, significantly, without any recourse to the rules (MR, chs. 1–2, 7). Thus Realism, as noted above, wants to correlate rules with results; *Minority Report* wants the reverse: that is, results without rules. All of which suggests that *Minority Report* may be articulating a kind of counterjurisprudence, even antijurisprudence, that writes the law—its rules, its processes—out of the picture altogether.

Such antijurisprudence is nonetheless an intensely jurisprudential move, echoic of but also forcing to their logical a-legal conclusions both Holmes's and Llewellyn's rule skepticism and Franks' fact skepticism. But this "jurisprudence of antijurisprudence" is by no means confined to the Jazz Age and indeed goes well beyond its "Jazz jurisprudence" (as one commentator has called Realism[33]), finding its fullest, most radical articulation in the here and now, in a contemporary legal movement that has dominated the last thirty years of American juristic method. The identity of that movement was hinted at by Holmes when he engaged in a bit of jurisprudential prediction himself—again in that *I Ching* of legal theory, *The Path of Law*—forecasting that the logical successor and heir apparent to the Realists would be the "man of statistics," "the master of economics" who would supplant the "black letter" lawyer and usher in a new dispensation of curial decisionism, predicated on utility calculation rather than judicial reasoning.[34] Surely, this is Holmes at what one textbook quite appropriately refers to as his most "prescient,"[35] because in his vision of judgment to come, he previews, indeed previsualizes—like one of the Precogs themselves—the reigning hegemonic discourse in late twentieth- and early twenty-first-century American jurisprudence, the "new pragmatism," though one uncluttered by and eschewing any philosophical "-ism"—like critical legal feminism, legal postmodernism, or Realism itself—and marching under the simple dyadic banner of "Law and Economics."

Law's Labor Lost: Displacing Rights in *Minority Report* and Law and Economics

The above rather lengthy historical prologue brings me to the heart of this chapter, its central and overarching argument being: that *Minority Report* and Law and Economics are animated by what might be called the same "jurisprudence of antijurisprudence." Specifically, both are committed to preempting the law through prediction, thereby enabling the address and redress of a potential legal problem before it occurs. Yet the means and modalities of the prediction differ markedly, taking on and locating these two instances of "legal fiction"[36] within what at first appear to be vastly dissimilar discursive sites (the language of numbers vs. the signs of language, for example) and representational frames (such as graphs vs. glyphs). Law and Economics, on the one hand, goes out of its way to "mathematize" (in the mode of econometrics) its predictive power, pressing into service congeries of formulas (like that of Learned Hand's $B<PL$: the burden of the cost is less than the probability of the accident times the loss[37]), concepts (Pareto optimality and superiority[38]; Kaldor-Hicks[39]), and paradigms (the "new institutionalism" of the "transaction costs" school[40]; the "free market" of the classical neoliberals[41]). And the effect of these various measures and tests is to update and breathe new life[42] into the old Benthamic dream that you can find an arithmetic of happiness, a "calculus of felicity."[43] Nowhere, though, does this reinvigorated standard of utility find a more complete expression than in what might be called the hegemonic equation of prediction, the signature sequence of Law and Economics, the (in)famous Coase Theorem.[44] As every schoolchild knows—at least those trained in the economic analysis of the law—the Coase Theorem, named after "Chicago School" economist Ronald Coase, prognosticates that, in the absence of transaction costs (a rather whopping presupposition demanding an enormous suspension of disbelief), an efficient allocation of resources will result, *irrespective of the assignment of rights.*[45] Thus efficiency and its assumption of a set of constants driving all transactions—of reasonable exchanges, mutually satisfactory outcomes, the maximization of wealth—is what enables prediction in Law and Economics.

In *Minority Report*, on the other hand, prediction is "mythicized" rather than "mathematized," and takes the occult form of the Precogs' vision of crime-to-come. The Precogs are the vatic fulcrum around which the Department of Precrime and indeed the entire narrative of *Minority Report* rotates. Simply, they are a trio—an (un)holy trinity?—of young adults: two males, twins Arthur and

Dashiell, and one female, Agatha—their names rather obviously referencing the canonic threesome of detective literature: Conan Doyle, Hammett, and Christie. Abandoned as birth-defected infants and destined for a life (or more likely, early death) on the now-derelict inner-city streets, owing to their unique capacities they have been rescued and raised by the state under experimental conditions (by that anything-but-maternal "mad scientist," Dr. Hineman). For the Precogs have been "gifted" (as a kind of "cosmic joke") with second sight, itself a result of their respective mothers' addiction to Neroin (MR, ch. 10), the drug du jour of the mid-twenty-first century and John Anderton's high of choice (MR, ch. 3). Confined to the womblike environs of the "Temple" and guarded by Precrime cops who see themselves as attendant priests or "clergy" (MR, ch. 5), the Precogs are as lacking in pigment, hair, even determinate gender as fetuses, a neonate identification that is driven home by the milky, almost amniotic-looking pool of water in which they float (MR, ch. 5). There, the Precogs experience seerlike trances as "One"—projected, indeed almost cinematically screened, in images onto the roof of the Temple–that are very much at odds with the carefully calibrated trajectories of Law and Economics (MR, chs. 1, 5).

Nonetheless, both *Minority Report* and Law and Economics, whether they mathematize or mythicize, ignite what might be called—to shift discursive registers again, this time to the psychoanalytic—the phantasmatic. For each indulges in an imaginary, even "primal" scene of fantasy—to adopt the argot of Freud.[46] These respective scenes differ as much from one another in their content as the prime numbers of mathematics do from the metaphors of myth. But both share an intensely visual sense and tap into the scopic drive itself, attracting, even arresting the gaze of the reader or viewer. In Law and Economics, that scene inevitably takes the form of a heuristic exemplifying and concretizing the theorem in question, modeling in a set of assumed and selectively sifted facts, the operation of its predictive calculations. Consider the Coase Theorem and the way in which its application is routinely illustrated in the popular literature of the economic analysis of the law, in what David Sugarman[47] would call its jurisprudential "textbook tradition." There, in text after text, a narrative is adverted to, a story is told: in short, a scene is imagined. That scene always turns out to be the same one: dreamt up by Coase explicator, Michael Polinsky,[48] and repeated ad nauseam in the literature therein afterwards.[49] Set in a bleak, industrial landscape, this scene revolves around a factory, the pollution from which has generated damage (of $375), sustained by the five neighboring householders (at $75 each). For Polinsky, the whole point of this

scene lies in cracking the mystery of: Who should purchase the requisite prophy-
lactic screen when the measure is one of economic efficiency rather than juridical right? The solution to this "whodunit" is clear to Polinsky: the factory should
install "the smokescreen because it eliminates damages of US $375.00 for an outlay
of $150.00, and it is cheaper than purchasing five dryers for US $250.00." What's
more, the neat, narrative closure effected here is unaffected by law and its con-
tingencies, as Polinsky is adamant that the most efficient outcome—the factory's
purchase of the screen—would result, regardless of whether a right to clean air was
granted to the householders, or a right to pollute, to the factory. The "measuring
rod"[50] of money prevails over law, and the "truth" of the Coase Theorem is cat-
egorically confirmed. *Quod erat demonstrandum.*

   Or was it proved? After all, the reality check proffered here is a highly unreal
one, a concocted, even artfully contrived yarn that may say more about the pleasures of fiction plotting than about the factual proof of prediction. Indeed, the
telling of the tale; that is, the formal act of narration, rather than the substantive
content of the tale told, may be the real lesson here. Instead of instantiating the
Coase Theorem, Polinsky's hypothetical becomes an occasion, indeed an outlet,
for Law and Economics' rich fantasy life, a model-building imaginary comparable,
at least in its aesthetic impulses, to the vivid scenes conjured up by the Precogs in
Minority Report. Of course, the Precogs' visions have the decided dramatic advantage of crime—and crime at its most deliciously over the top; murder most
foul—not merely the only crime rending the "metaphysical fabric" (as Anderton
rather pompously explains to former seminarian, Witwer; MR, ch. 4), but also
outdoing tortious liability for good theater, the latter (tort) being far too prosaic
and lacking the powerful dramatic possibilities of the former (crime). But whether
it is a startled and startling Agatha, and her curiously affectless but incredibly un-
nerving wail, "Can you see?" (the crime in question; MR, chs. 5, 15, 16, 20), or
Polinsky's industrial landscape (of civil wrong), in both cases—*Minority Report*
and Law and Economics—a space is visualized, a set of facts is hypothesized, and
a solution is propounded (the purchase of a screen, the incarceration of a suspect),
none of which involve rights. That is the "fundamental fantasy"[51] at work in and
underpinning the scenes that *Minority Report* and Law and Economics recursively
iterate: of a world without right, without the law because prediction has rendered
it irrelevant. Or at least "law" in the conventional jurisprudential sense, as involving some recourse to rules or norms, whether strictly posited or obtaining from a
higher justice. But the interdiction of "trad" jurisprudence here does not exclude

the possible presence in *Minority Report* and Law and Economics of other, more "rad" kinds of law, lurking on their respective margins, doubtless under erasure, but nonetheless circulating in their textual unconscious. Indeed, I will argue that, paradoxically, it is precisely this repressed form of law that supports and sustains the fundamental fantasy, present in each here, of a world without law. Because underpinning that fantasy structure, for both *Minority Report* and Law and Economics, is of course a shared *desire*—and desire, as Lacan teaches us, obeys, operates according to, and is subject to an(O)ther law, the Law of Desire.

We Can Murder for You Wholesale: *Minority Report*'s Mall of America as Law and Economics' America as Mall

In its opening scenes, *Minority Report* gives its viewer a strong and powerful indication as to the nature of that desire and its law, throwing into relief Law and Economics' Law of Desire, as well as its own. For the initial "scenes from a marriage" represent *Minority Report* as a world drenched in desire, pulsating with sexual passion, alive with erotic charge: namely, in Agatha's prevision of the adulterous couple—Sarah Marks and Donald Dubin—rudely surprised, in their midmorning tryst in the inner suburb of Georgetown, by the cuckolded husband of the errant wife: fat, forty-something Howard Marks (MR, ch. 2). Marks himself is anything but immune to desire, though the nature of his lust—his buttoned-down, bespectacled appearance to the contrary—is for blood rather than booty (think how easily he stabs Sarah to death), thereby embodying the dark, obscene, even murderous underside of what Lacanian psychoanalysis might call *jouissance*, or "enjoyment."[52] In this representation of "enjoyment"—that is, of desire run amok, psychoticized in Howard Marks' future frenzied killing spree of his wife and her lover (MR, ch. 1)—*Minority Report* provides a bold contrast to usually bloodless (excepting the aliens) and particularly sexless world of sci-fi. Think of the Roddenberry oeuvre—especially shows like "Star Trek: The Next Generation,"[53] all drip-dry bodysuits and shaved heads—where no one gets any nookie; a bland, antiseptic Habermasian world in which everyone has been "vulcanized" à la Spock with any and all passion beaten out of them.

Of course, *crime passionnel* is the first precrime we see thwarted in *Minority Report*, with Howard Marks stunned, "haloed" (MR, ch. 2), and then transported to the department's panoptic prison, where he is encased in what looks like a human-sized test tube, eerily reminiscent of *The Matrix*'s pods[54]—or worse, the cocoon of *Aliens*[55]—and condemned to a lifetime's viewing of instant replays of his attempted murders (MR, ch. 6). This might support an inference that the Department of Precrime is there to eradicate passion, to incarcerate desire. Yet nothing could be further from the truth. For what the film stages is not the replacement of desire (by, say, reason) but rather its displacement; and in so doing, *Minority Report* mimics Law and Economics' rechanneling of desire as market choice. For what everyone desires in Law and Economics—no matter how much they dress it up as stable preferences, the flow of cost and benefit, or allocative efficiency—is the choice of objects or things: in short, the purchase of commodities. *Minority Report* graphically realizes and draws attention to this "commodity fetishism," as Marx would put it.[56] After all, one of the most heart-stopping sequences in the film—John Anderton's hot pursuit by his erstwhile Precrime confrères through the flophouses and shooting galleries of D.C.'s "Sprawl"—culminates in a factory (Polinsky's?) during the full-scale production of a commodity—and a luxury one at that, the not-so-obscure object of Hollywood desire, the flash sports car (MR, ch. 9).

Naturally, the pillar-box or fire-engine red Lexus provides Anderton's means of escape and thereby functions as a kind of creaky deus ex machina, literally "driving" the plot of *Minority Report* on to the next bend in the story line's road map (MR, ch. 9). But consider for a moment what this scene shows the viewer in terms of its "deep structure," bracketing its surface parole of the foregrounded chase scene. Doesn't the real force of this scene lie in the industrial, indeed mechanical mise-en-scène? That is: of a production line and the way in which component parts, high-tech nuts and bolts, are soldered and welded, assembled and finished with a ferocious efficiency by a dizzyingly synchronized array of robotic arms, all in the service of and to produce—what else?—another machine. Of course, part of the dramatic tension generated here lies precisely in the "rage against the machine" and Anderton's near escape from being reified with and as the car. But the focus is first and foremost on the car itself and its productive output, its potential allocative circulation as a commodity, however misallocated it might end up being by Anderton's stunning (but all too convenient) escape (MR, ch. 10).

Other commodifying scenes abound throughout the film, replete with enough designer goods and other high-end for-sale labels to spark a Naomi Klein–inspired "No Logo"[57] demo. Consider the most egregious scene of the film: John Anderton's flight through one of D.C.'s skyscraper arcades, where he is literally "hailed" by the various holographic wares on display, a *salon des glaces* of simulated goods and digital adverts that, as if endowed with a prescient subjectivity of their own, peer into the "windows to his (consumer) soul"—his eyes—and interpellate him, with a nod to Althusser,[58] as the subject-as-shopper (MR, ch. 8). More than any other, this scene has achieved a certain journalistic notoriety, having been read by many reviewers when the film first came out as a crass and cynical stab at product placement—and it certainly is that. But all the flagrant "branding" here, all the global merchandising—of Bulgari, of Guinness, of Amex, of Lexus (again!)—makes a particular thematic point *about* sales in the process of making the sale: that the world of *Minority Report* (that is, the future) is the one that Law and Economics prescribes as much as describes as a shopping mall (that is, the present), the emblematic Mall of America becoming its metaphoric inversion, or America as Mall, in which a "free market" of relentless exchange prevails, in which everything and everyone—real and virtual—is up for sale, and in which we realize our all-consuming desire to consume.

Free to Choose! *Minority Report*'s Gospel of Free Will (According to Milton Friedman)

But this market "freedom"—and its concomitant desire to consume (and be consumed)—comes at quite a cost. I use the word "cost" with a very particular "term of art" precision, because as Law and Economics reminds us, despite its cost-free best-case scenarios of Pareto optimality and superiority, there are always transaction costs. "All solutions," acknowledges Coase, "involve costs."[59] So even the Coase Theorem's boilerplate waiver of rights turns out to be a ruse, soliciting the "return of the rules" in the very act of their repression, in much the same way contractual "exclusion clauses" provoke, in their very prohibition, the juridical imposition of liability. But the law doesn't merely return by means of the Coase Theorem; it returns with a vengeance—the rules becoming, oddly enough for such an antistatist principle, the dirigiste means by which to "minimize," as Polinsky affirms, "transaction costs."[60] That is, the law functions in the Coase Theorem as a modality, even an instrumentality: a stick to beat people with, as much as a carrot to facilitate market freedom. All of which imposes a cost on the law itself—a cost that *Minority Report* vividly dramatizes, of which more will be said later. This is the real contribution of the film as *lex populi*, pointing to why precrime never pays but also to how the Law and Economics' solutions, like Coase, not only cost but cost the law. The cost is incurred in this way: instead of a process of right, let alone justice, the law in Law and Economics is turned into a tool, even a weapon of executive diktat, carrying out the ukase to be "free." Free, that is, to choose anything and everything, as long as one chooses. And one must choose!

It is this paradox of the "forced choice" à la Milton Friedman[61]—one is free to choose (that is, any of the consumables that the market offers), but one must choose freedom (specifically, the precondition of Capital itself)—that *Minority Report* captures and draws attention to, in all of its theological palaver about free will and predestination, rendering its ostensible topos of prediction something of a thematic red herring. For if *Minority Report* insists on anything at all—and it does so repeatedly, compulsively, even hysterically—it is the liberal mythos that we are autonomous agents endowed with the capacity to make independent decisions. Anderton, after all, in what must be a supreme act of self-control as well as individual judgment, heeds Agatha's frantic pleas not to kill his son Sean's putative murderer, child molester Leo Crow (MR, ch. 18). Similarly, Lamarr Burgess resists, in the penultimate scene and climax of the film, the equally overwhelming urge to kill John Anderton, opting instead to commit the ne plus ultra of self-governing acts, that of suicide (MR, ch. 23). In either case, each rejects every constraint— external precognitive prediction; internal id-like drive for vengeance—upon their freedom to choose, except, of course, the threshold constraint that they *must* choose. For Anderton and Burgess, despite their contrastive functions as hero and villain—each the other's nemesis—are identical in their exercise of what might be mistakenly called, with all due respect to Isaiah Berlin, "positive liberty"[62]—or the freedom to positively choose a course of action. Yet neither one indulges in or is afforded what could be called, in a similar Berlin vein, "negative liberty"[63]: that is, the freedom *not* to choose. It is this denial of negative liberty, this incapacitation of "not choosing" in *Minority Report* that, more than anything else, reproduces and resonates with Law and Economics' vision of the "forced choice" and the "bounded rationality"[64] that underwrites it.

What bounds this rationality? What forces this choice? Surely, it is none other than the law, conceived of in the crudest, most coercive form, that limits rational boundaries and compels choice. Law and Economics, however, largely euphemizes this violence of the law—and the Coverian pain and suffering it entails[65]—as "incentives" and "disincentives."[66] *Minority Report* is far less "podsnapian" here, making no bones about representing these incentives and disincentives as weapons, or more accurately, as high-tech stun guns, all in the service of a police state that has reduced the law to the status of a security system. With this representation of the law-as-security system, *Minority Report* effects what Law and Economics would decry as a distorting, even downright wrongheaded inversion of its "jurisprudence of antijurisprudence" because the film repositions the law in a way that is the precise opposite of the movement's rhetoric. Rather than functioning, as Law and Economics would have it, as an avenue of last recourse, the dim background against which bargaining takes place (captured brilliantly by Stewart Macauley's metaphor, "the shadow of the law"),[67] the law-as-security system in *Minority Report* moves to center stage. There, it acts as a sinister, even lethal force, a "dangerous supplement"[68] omnipresent in its surveillance—not only with the PreCogs' visions, but with the roving mechanical "spyders" (MR, ch. 14)—and ham-fisted in its tactics, its officers bursting through doors, abseiling from roofs and rounding up "the usual suspects" with a senseless, Gestapo-like violence—or better yet, like the SAS-style police in Terry Gilliam's 1980s dystopia, *Brazil*.[69] But far from misrepresenting Law and Economics' legal theory, what *Minority Report* enacts here is the contradiction that lies at the movement's heart—and that of its political fellow travelers, the libertarian advocates of the "minimal state"[70]—pointing the viewer to the reality that lies beyond their rhetoric. That is, in searching for a regulation-free world, in looking for a Nozickian "nightwatchman state"[71] with token law (but, interestingly, a Precrime-like "protective association" charged with the maintenance of public order), Law and Economics produces, in fact, its reverse: an authoritarian "nightmare state." After all, what kind of state but a dictatorship would reduce the law to the level of a blunt instrument? And not just any kind of dictatorship, but a highly positivized one—in the style of John Austin—where the law is constantly adverted to and functionalized as a mechanism and means for modifying behavior, managing exchange, and mandating choice—all under the guise of utility's ever-calculating and predictive "right reason."

Critique's "Cosmic Joke": Outing the "Politics of the Law" in *Minority Report*

This "right reason" of prediction and utility is exposed, ultimately, in *Minority Report* as nothing more than a twisted and irrational "triumph of the will"—that of the baddest of "Bad Men," Lamarr Burgess, the venality and corruption of whom *predetermines* predictive outcomes. Consider how easily Burgess, as the Director of Precrime, suppresses Agatha's eponymous "minority report" in much the same way critical legal studies routinely accused courts of doing, throughout the 1980s, with respect to the law: that is, of playing fast and loose with the rules for their own partisan ends, magnifying the significance of some precedents, all the while ignoring if not censoring others in order to achieve their desired, partisan outcome. The same process is at work here in *Minority Report*. After all, the Precogs constitute a kind of courtlike tribunal, the objective of which is a consensus that, once arrived at, is as unchallengeable as it is infallible. Or at least that is the theory. But practically, the PreCogs, like courts, are just as susceptible to curial dissensus—and with it, the possibility of *per incuriam*[72] mistake—as evidenced by the twins' difference from Agatha's dissenting *and correct* judgment in one of the department's first cases: the "golden oldie," according to Gideon, of Ann Lively's murder (MR, ch. 6). Lurking behind that dissensus is that critical legal bogeyman, the consummate politician of the law, Lamarr Burgess, manipulating, even manufacturing consensus. Why? To promote the Precogs as foolproof and in so doing secure a landslide "Yes" vote in the looming referendum over the Precrime Initiative, the adverts of which shrilly proclaim, throughout the film, "It works!" (MR, ch. 3).

Or *does* Precrime work? After all, Agatha's dissenting opinion—and the visual echo of it that Anderton watches—threatens not only to upset the "politics of the law" of the Precrime campaign but also to expose the very notion of precrime itself as grounded in, literally, a jurispathology. This is because Agatha records an alternative version of events, a countermajoritarian scenario in which Ann Lively is killed not by her supposed drug dealer but by—who else?—Lamarr Burgess. Why does Burgess have her killed? Because she is none other than—as *South Park*'s Eric Cardman might put it[73]—the "crackwhore" Mum of Agatha who reappeared some years ago, off the streets, "clean" and keen on reclaiming her daughter. Of course, this mother-daughter reunion would have derailed Precrime because Agatha is the strongest and most powerful of the Precogs. Thus Burgess, in a gross caricature of utility's ethics of "the greater good,"[74] decides that only Ann Lively's elimination will save the department's nascent program and bring order to America's "mean streets." Consequently, he arranges for two attempts on Lively's "liveliness": first, a staged one with a drug dealer who is "misrecognized" and haloed for his efforts at the twins' behest; and second, Burgess's own successful commission of the offense, one that goes undetected but for Agatha's soon-to-be censored "minority report." With the report's retrieval and Burgess's spectacular revelation as Lively's murderer at a posh Washington gala in his honor—a case of the politics celebrating law being used as a platform to denounce law's politics—the "radical indeterminacy"[75] at the heart of Precrime is disclosed, and the system collapses (MR, ch. 22).

Or at least that is the *wunsch* of critique that *Minority Report* vouchsafes here. That is, to "out" law's prediction as nothing more than law's politics is to do more than just wish prediction away. It actually *does* so. Thus the film ends with the dismantling of the department, the reassignment of its officers, and the restoration of the criminal justice system with all its process imperatives and presumptions (that is, of innocence) (MR, ch. 24). One is tempted to read this denouement as an enactment, in highly coded form, of a very specific kind of wish fulfillment (as well as ressentiment) on the part of much contemporary legal theory—not only critical legal studies but also feminism, race theory, and rights activism. Namely, their desire to see Law and Economics' institutional embeddedness (in the courts, in the law schools) shifted, if not displaced; its theorists (on the bench, at the podium) sidelined or demoted from their current positions of prominence; and the return of core jurisprudential values (of justice, of rights, of ethics) to a law released from the spell of "efficiency." And all that is required for this to come about is for a united front of "crits" to "out" Law and Economics as involving neither "the legal" (after all, it reduces the law to its lowest common denominator, coercion) nor "the economic" (owing to the limited and restricted nature of the economics it employs), but rather as turning on an essentially political choice—of laissez faire over command economies. To utter this political critique in the Symbolic—so hope springs eternal here—is to effect, in the Real, a change of legal language, process, and personnel. That may be the tantalizing prospect—or cosmic joke—that *Minority Report* holds out, implicitly, to contemporary jurisprudence in its explicit critique of the politics bedeviling prediction's institutional and discursive system. Which may be why, in its closing scenes, *Minority Report* turns away from this system, that is, the public sphere of law and order, and toward the private realm of hearth and home; from the processes of precrime to the pleasures of procreation, because the work of critique—and the deconstruction of the "predictive theory of the law" as yet another instance of law's politics—is, seemingly, done here (MR, ch. 24).

Have You Seen This Child? *Minority Report*'s "Economics of the Baby Shortage"

The film thus ends with a domestically overdetermined shot of Lara Anderton—in the arms of her long-estranged but now reconciled "ex," John—heavily pregnant with another child, the imminent birth of whom will replace, presumably, the void left in their lives by the still unsolved disappearance of their son, Sean (MR, ch. 24). With this scene, *Minority Report* seems, at its close, to trumpet human values of feeling and affect as an antidote to the cognitive ones of prediction. But I would suggest that these last shots in the film—with Agatha and the twins simulating a "family romance" in a Thoreauvian retreat; with John and Lara replicating a family back in D.C.—echo and reverberate with all the ambiguities of prediction in Law and Economics. For don't these happy-family scenes suggest an endorsement of a core belief of Law and Economics: namely, the credo that everything and every*one*—a lost child, a dead mother, a shattered family—can be "substituted" and replaced? Richard Posner suggested as much when he wrote, with Elizabeth Landes in "The Economics of the Baby Shortage,"[76] advocating free-market principles as the best solution to the crisis of adoption in America. A potential rival to Swift's eighteenth-century satire on the Irish question—but for Posner's deadly earnestness—his article constituted an infamous low point of an already ethically thin jurisprudential discourse. Patricia Williams, in true Swiftian fashion, has teased out the not-so-latent race politics in Posner's argument.[77] But no such critical riposte is mounted in *Minority Report*. Instead of satire, a sweetness prevails: too sweet, to my mind, to be wholesome. Think of Agatha's tear-jerking (and sick-making) vision of Sean's life that could-have-been, forecast with a view (his high school dreams, his college romance) to wrenching every last tear from his distraught parents—and of course the audience for which they are surrogates.

So my question is this: Is Steven Spielberg a Posnerian legal economist in highly sentimental clothing? Certainly he shares Posner's interest in what might be called the theme of the missing child. Though in Spielberg's case, this interest borders on the obsessive, as evidenced by a cinematic oeuvre replete with "lost boys" (not only Sean, but also child android David in *A.I.* and everyone's favorite alien foundling, E.T.[78]). But boys aren't the only children to go on walkabout in the Spielberg universe; after all, Agatha is another abandoned child—and significantly, the last we see of her she is clasping a Perspex holographic image of her mother (MR, ch. 24), as if attempting a kind of family reunion beyond the grave (as *A.I.*'s David does by replicating his human "mother" figure, or even as E.T. does by "calling home"). Given this shared thematic of lost and found relations—or *fort-da* of parent and child[79]—the answer to my question (is Spielberg Posner? Is Posner Spielberg?) would be: possibly. But even more than answering this rather glib (and largely rhetorical) question, what these last scenes in *Minority Report* do is highlight the importance of what Terry Eagleton would call "reading against the grain."[80] That counterreading traverses and undoes not only *Minority Report*'s "happy ending" but also its critique of the jurisprudential subtext: namely, the allegory of Law and Economics. For when read "otherwise," these closing shots in the film suggest that any sustained critique of Law and Economics should and must operate on two levels—not just that of the system (the nightwatchman state becoming the nightmare state, freedom of choice curtailing choice of freedom, reason as will-to-power), but also the subject and ultimately its reconception.

Consequently, the real challenge that *Minority Report* issues is for nothing less than a reclamation, on the part of critique, of the subject-centered humanism (Marxist? secular?) that it has so long disavowed and decried. That humanism—and the jurisprudential tradition of civil liberties it stands for—is now more than ever necessary, given the recent moves in some American jurisdictions to make *Minority Report* a reality by deeming admissible, as evidence in court, the highly questionable pseudoscience of predictive "brain signatures."[81] If this challenge to human rights is to be thwarted, if *Minority Report* is to be prevented from materializing before our very eyes, not only in the United States, but elsewhere (in the form of preemptive strikes against precriminal nations), then critique must go beyond the mere combustion of the logic of prediction—and the rationality of utility that is its avatar. It must reconstruct a positive jurisprudential alternative as much as deconstruct its antijurisprudential predecessor; asserting, contra *Minority Report* and its Law and Economics subtext, the primacy of the human. Such an assertion would carry with it the correlative claims that individuals cannot be substituted, that families cannot be conjured out of the air. In short, some things—or rather, some persons (Sean Anderton, Ann Lively, Danny Witwer)—cannot be replaced. To argue otherwise risks replicating rather than rebuking the reason that underwrites prediction and authorizes efficiency; it would consign critique to its current position of merely shadowing utility's "jurisprudence of antijurisprudence," with the grim prospect of becoming mired in the same Posnerian ethical cul-de-sac that much of Law and Economics finds itself: namely, *that it knows the price of everything but the value of nothing.*

CHAPTER SIX

Critically Blonde

Law School as Training for Her*steria*

Trashing Harvard: The Law School *Lex Populi* Loves to Hate

Why does *lex populi* love law school? A constant stream of books,[1] films,[2] and television series[3] would attest—seemingly—to its abiding affection for the institution. Which is strange, if not bizarre, particularly when all the insider accounts of legal education—be they factions or fictions—are so full of bile, fear, and loathing: in short, *hate* for the place. A hate, one might say, to which *lex populi* loves to give vent. Which raises another, allied question: Why don't we love to hate other tertiary forms of professional training and their organizing discourses as much as law school and indeed the law? Where, for example, are blockbuster hits about dental faculties (*Peridontally B(l)onded?*), prime-time movies about business schools (*The Paper Audit?*), or airport novels about first-year engineering students (*One E?*)? And why always the American law school? Why not Dalhousie[4] or Osgoode,[5] ANU[6] or Melbourne?[7] UCL[8] or Edinburgh?[9] And why, over and over again, just one American law school?[10] In fact, as far as *lex populi* seems to be concerned *the only* American law school—notwithstanding Columbia, Michigan, Chicago, Stanford, and a myriad others[11]: that is, Harvard Law School. Of course, one could defend this exclusive (obsessive?) focus[12] in terms of the usual admissions brochure superlatives: Harvard as America's oldest, richest, most selective, most prestigious law school.[13] Except that these hubristic claims ring hollow with just the mere mention of a four-letter word, foul to all who wear the Crimson: *Yale*.[14]

So to repeat the question: Why Harvard Law School as *lex populi*'s idée fixe? By way of an answer, I would like to suggest another, much more ambiguous superlative: that if *lex populi*'s gaze is transfixed by and on Harvard Law School, then it is because Harvard provides, currently as well as historically, the most *spectacular* form of legal education, a veritable theater of pedagogic pain known as the "Socratic method."[15] With its classroom agon of question and answer, of call and response, the Socratic method is a highly staged, artfully contrived technique of tuition, ripe with all sorts of dramatic possibilities such as comic "misrecognition," tragic choices, and heroic *hamartia*. But underlying this "tragicomedy of errors," this very crafted and blocked performance, is a more deeply embedded explanation for why Harvard, its law school, and the Socratic method so fascinate. This is because its dialogic scene of instruction dispenses with the metaphorical proscenium arch separating audience and player, student and teacher so clearly in place in other forms of *savoir*, other "discourses of the university."[16] In doing away with this imaginary boundary, the Socratic method confronts its student-spectator in the most direct way possible, with the operations of *pouvoir/savoir*: that is, academic power and its strategies of discipline and punish. Or to reformulate this quasi-Foucauldian account in more Lacanian terms: what the Socratic method enacts is nothing less than the "discourse of the Master"[17]—with all of its hierarchical imperatives of dominance and submission, as well as its dialectic of orthodoxy and iconoclasm.

I want to interrogate this discourse, not so much to "out-Socraticize" Socrates, but to suggest a discursive alternative for legal education that goes beyond "Mastery" and the critique it has attracted. This alternative, I shall argue in this chapter, is offered by the very *lex populi* that mythologized the Master in the first place. Specifically, I want to examine two exemplary representations of law school drawn from what Les Moran, Elena Loizidou, and others would call "law's moving image."[18] The first is that ur-text of the genre, James Bridges' now classic 1970s film, *The Paper Chase*,[19] based on John Jay Osborne's 1967 novel of the same title. The second is a more recent generic outing, Aussie expat Rob Luketic's millennial hit, *Legally Blonde*,[20] a star vehicle for one of the most talented actors of twenty-something Hollywood, Reese Witherspoon. In this chapter, I want to juxtapose these two films, bringing their moving images of law school into dialogue, not only reading the films qua cinematic text but also allowing them to read each other *jurisprudentially*, because although separated by nearly thirty years, when placed side by side they tell the viewer something about the law school's discursive dialectic of "Mastery" and critique; about the challenges to, but also, as I argue in the next section, the uncanny persistence of the "training for hierarchy"[21] that critical legal studies denounced as the raison d'être (or *succès de scandale?*) of the Harvard Law School, its Socratic method, and the discourse of the Master that underpins it.

Furthermore, when taken in tandem, these two films hold out the tantalizing prospect of going beyond this dialectic, mapping a course toward a retheorization of legal education in terms other than those of 1980s critical legal studies. Instead of Duncan Kennedy's (by now) well-worn shibboleth quoted above, the cultural-legal reading propounded here by a reading of these films detects a much more serious condition of cognitive dissonance, of psychological turmoil submerged in legal education's (largely unconscious) deep structures. I will argue that law school trains not only for hierarchy but also for *hysteria*—and a whole host of symptoms, illnesses, and mental disturbances that support and sustain hierarchy. All of which are vividly realized and represented in *The Paper Chase* and *Legally Blonde*, so much so that these instances of *lex populi* amount to, in a paraphrase of Freud, "a psychopathology of (law school's) everyday life."[22] But such a "psychologization" of the law school does more than just confirm hierarchy's habitual grip on the legal academy. It holds out the possibility for a renewal of resistance against hierarchy, pointing the way not only to a different set of critical strategies but a different site of critique—a site that turns out to be that of difference itself. For that site of difference, I will argue, is nothing less than *La Femme*, "Woman" herself (as the Lacanians say, "not-all," at once inside and outside the law)[23] and the set, psychoanalytically oriented feminist strategies (of Riviere's masquerade, of post-Lacanian theorizations of the phallus noted in this chapter) that *Legally Blonde* enacts for and solicits from its audience. The effect of which is to turn this seemingly lightweight teen comedy into a transferential "talking cure" in dialogue with and diagnostic of *The Paper Chase*'s law school pathologies that haunt us to this day.

The Primal Scene of Legal Education: The First Class of the First Day of the First Year

Is there a more traumatic encounter—nay, a veritable "primal scene"—for law students than the first class of the first day of the first year? The reason being: this is the moment, so to speak, when the Socratic boom is lowered. Certainly Kennedy,[24] as well as Turow[25] and Kahlenberg,[26] document this day in lurid detail: the low-level anxiety wrought by unfamiliar subject matter, its arcane vocabulary matched only by its obscurantist themes and *topoi*; the mounting alarm, as the volley of questions begins (something akin to the opening shots of a battle); the full-scale panic attack that sets in as one is caught unprepared and exposed as such before a classroom of complete strangers, soon to be collegial rivals. Both *The Paper Chase* and *Legally Blonde* tap into and give vivid cinematic expression to this disturbingly dreamlike, even nightmarish scenario, the mise-en-scène of each being strikingly similar: the large lecture hall, its desks slowly but steadily filled with students, ordered precisely by seating chart and organized around a panoptic podium, soon to be inhabited by a grim professorial presence (PC, ch. 1; LB, ch. 9). And both films' protagonists—Elle Woods and Jonathan Hart—are judged and found wanting in their respective Langdellian cross-examinations on their first days: the former by Prof. Stromwell on "subject matter jurisdiction" in *Gordon v. Steele*[27] (LB, ch. 9); the latter by Prof. Kingsfield on the quantum of damages for the notorious "hairy hand" in *Hawkins v. McGee* (PC, ch. 2).[28] In either case, the mode of instruction is interrogative, and though Stromwell references another "dead white male" (Aristotle), her unacknowledged source—like Kingsfield's explicitly cited one—is the same: Socrates (LB, ch. 9). Or at least Socrates as filtered through Christopher Columbus Langdell,[29] Harvard's most celebrated law dean and the pioneer of what might be called the case method's "sado-Socraticism." Now the interesting thing about this filmic use and reuse (abuse?) of Langdell's version of Socrates is this: while these two representations are separated by almost thirty years, both still pay homage in that most flattering way—imitation—to an educator dead for more than a century and a philosopher dead for two-and-a-half millennia. All of which suggests that, for the American law school, *plus ça change, plus c'est la même chose*—the more things change, the more they remain the same.

Or are they so unchanged? After all, *The Paper Chase*, when compared to *Legally Blonde*'s almost cartoonlike brightness, is definitely showing its age as a 1970s period piece, a sort of counter–*Love Story*,[30] all muted camera shots and muttonchop sideboards, laconic dialogue and campus casual sex. But beneath these superficial differences in style lie much deeper social, intellectual, even *technical* changes in the law school, a vérité that both these films register. Indeed, what strikes a viewer from the vantage of today's "digital culture" is just how much of a literal "paper chase" law school was, not only for Hart but also for his real-life equivalents, the law students of the 1970s (and 1980s): of casebook highlighting and judgment briefing, of classroom note taking and library research. No wonder so much of the film finds Hart and Ford lurking in the basement stacks of Langdell Hall, because what these scenes drive home is that the world of the law school—and the law—is a text, sealed off from context, self-referential and enclosed so that one might say *il n'y a pas de hors-texte*, "there is nothing outside of the text."[31]

This virtually Derridean world of textuality that *The Paper Chase* realizes becomes in *Legally Blonde* a closed-circuit and totally wired world of virtuality. There, paper is nowhere to be seen in either of the classroom scenes—Stromwell's Con Law (LB, ch. 9) and Callahan's Crim course (LB, ch. 12), both of which are alight with student computer screens and the attendant Net surfing, e-mailing, and downloading that is a product of such hardware. But even more noticeable than *Legally Blonde*'s "technologization" of the law school is its "feminization" of that domain; in fact, the film records a kind of institutional transgendering in terms of student body composition that is a bold contrast to the oppressively male-dominated environment of *The Paper Chase*. Consider the latter film: there, just one woman, Miss (certainly not Ms.) Ferranti is given a classroom voice as well as a presence. And quite a "different voice"[32] at that, as if literalizing Carol Gilligan's central metaphor: a thick (and doubtless "hick") Southern-accented voice, the voice of Arkansas, Tennessee, or West Virginia (PC, ch. 10). In short, the voice of the outsider (and the "outsider jurisprudence"[33] it vocalizes). Compare this singular feminine instance of what Australian critical race feminist Aileen Moreton-Robinson would call "talkin' up"[34] to the classroom contributions of Ford's study group, all of whom are called upon repeatedly, and each of whom is unquestionably male: "Liberty" Bell, O'Conner, the "robot pimp" Anderson, the hapless Kevin, Hart, and naturally, Ford himself (PC, ch. 6).

Of course, this boy's club aspect of *The Paper Chase*, with its stark gender imbalances not only in class but also the "tree fort"–like study group—no girls allowed!—reflects all too accurately the sociolegal realities of the era and the shocking underrepresentation of women in law school student bodies at Harvard and across America. Not just black women, not just Latinas, not just lesbians, but *all women*, who Judith Resnik says in the 1970s made up less than 15 percent of the law school classroom.[35] And they were the "lucky" ones; that is, the ones fortunate enough to have secured a place, because the last law school bans on the admission of women were abolished by ABA fiat only as late as 1972[36]—the year *The Paper Chase* was released. What's more, women attending law school during this period, even among feminists as informed and alert as Deborah Rhode, for example, attest to how "accepted," even "natural" this sort of pervasive sexism was.[37] *The Paper*

Chase reproduces this misogyny, going even several steps further. First, in the ventriloquization, on the part of several characters (Anderson and Kevin's exam crammer, Moss), of a near-Freudian fear of the female: their repeated diatribes about the deleterious effects of "broads" upon (male) law students and their grades (PC, ch. 10). Second, by reducing all female characters to little more than walk-ons, either as a wife to serve coffee (the Stepford-like Asheley, Kevin's wealthy spouse; PC, ch. 26); or a wench to bed (the crammer's housecoated, smoking 1960s "bird"; PC, ch. 17); or the elegant Susan Kingsfield herself, now onto her second law school affair—each there to offer, as Hart smugly and selfishly puts it, "sustenance" to the male members (and *their* members) of law school's "boyzone" (PC, ch. 11).

Contrast this representation of Harvard Law School to that of *Legally Blonde.* Not that all troglodyte attitudes have disappeared there. Far from it—although in this film they are marginal rather than mainstream, confined to the least palatable characters (Warner, Prof. Callahan), and function as an index of these characters' villainy, in their relentless objectification of women as either social assets (Warner: "If I'm going to be a senator, I need to marry a Jackie, not a Marilyn"; LB, ch. 3) or sexual prey (Callahan: "You know what competition is really about? . . . Knowing exactly what you want and how far you'll go to get it? How far will Elle go?"; LB, ch. 26). For women occupy center stage in *Legally Blonde*, in both its classroom dynamic and its character system. From East Coast WASP Vivian (played to preppie perfection by a sour Selma Blair), to West Coast lesbian activist Enid (the forte of "indie" actress Meredith Scott), to the formidable feminine counterpart to Kingsfield, Prof. Stromwell (the star turn of TV's Holland Taylor of *The Practice* fame), *Legally Blonde* is awash in estrogen,[38] depicting Harvard Law School as something approaching a gynocracy. Of course, this female-friendly profile exaggerates the strides law schools actually have made in gender equity; think of the paucity of women in the senior ranks, the statistics of which make Stromwell more a figure of *wunsch* rather than reality.[39] Even so, the portrayal of the classroom here chimes in with the current enrollments, the law school student body at present consisting of 40 to 60 percent women.[40] Now the question this chapter poses is: Does this gender difference make a critical difference? That is: Does the change in the sexuated composition of the classroom effect change in terms of the law school's institutional and intellectual hierarchies? In short: Does sociology affect epistemology? Does the body affect the mind?

Legally Blonde suggests not, at least initially. Hierarchy—sociological, epistemic—is alive and well at Elle's Harvard, although its caste system seems to owe more to 1980s and 1990s teen films than it does to Duncan Kennedy. For the law school of *Legally Blonde* is organized along the lines of high school cliques, led by an in-crowd of popular girls (Vivian *and friends*) who seem to have wandered in off the set of *Mean Girls*,[41] followed by a "geek squad" (Enid and her posse of identity politicians), and trailing at the bottom, the abjected and excluded "Other," in this case, the "blonde joke"—Elle. This sort of adolescent hierarchization could be dismissed as just a *Heathers*,[42] or better still, *Romy & Michele's High School Reunion*[43] rip-off but for the fact that Kennedy himself analogizes law school to high school, and then affirms the minutely calibrated layerings of the law school classroom in terms almost identical to *lex populi*, such as *Broken Contract*,[44] *One L*,[45] and especially, *The Paper Chase*. In the last, the law school "class struggle" turns, as much for Hart as it does for Kennedy, on the possession of symbolic capital, as gauged by performance in lecture hall discussion. There are those on top, the *crème de la crème*, who confidently volunteer (analytic capitalists like Anderton, Ford, and Bell); then those lost souls at the back, diffidently floundering (proletariats like Kevin, fit only for the most mechanical of memory tasks); finally, there are those, as Hart says of himself to Susan, somewhere "in between" (petits bourgeois strivers?), conflicted by the desire to speak out and/or to remain silent (PC, ch. 9).

Whatever way the classroom is divided, be it along the lines of preparation (the voice) or popularity (the gaze), both *The Paper Chase* and *Legally Blonde* make the same point: that law school still trains for hierarchy, be it the precritical phallocracy under Kingsfield or the postcritical gynocracy under Stromwell. This is because the two governmentalities turn out to be one and the same, Stromwell having assimilated the epistemic hierarchies of Harvard Law School so well that one suspects that she was taught by Kingsfield himself—and he, in turn, by Williston; and Williston, by Langdell, so that the "New Order" and its current feminine exemplar are just an extension of and variation on the patrilineal ancien régime. Certainly, like Kingsfield and all those distingué formalists before him, Stromwell cultivates a tough cognitive style that neutralizes and nullifies her gender difference, all the while replicating, in her teaching, the Socratic focus on the case to the exclusion of its history, politics, or economy. No wonder, then, that her classroom, as well as Kingsfield's, produces a broadly similar set of psychological effects and affects among its students: that is, it *pathologizes* them. Think of the "walking symptoms" that figure among the casts of characters in both *Legally Blonde* and *The Paper Chase*, a veritable psychoanalytic checklist of neuroses and psychoses: aggression (O'Conner), ressentiment (Vivian), paranoia (Bell), satyrism (Callahan), automatism (Anderson), not to mention the most symptomatic—namely, Elle and Hart.

Enjoy Your Law School! The Psychopathology of Legal Education

The nature of these symptoms and the respective pathologies they symptomatize for Elle and Hart, however, differ markedly and, interestingly, invert the usual gender *doxa* of psychiatry by reassigning a classically "masculine" condition to the female, and vice versa. Thus Hart is gradually *hystericized* throughout *The Paper Chase*, a neurotic state that, with its nervous tics, paralyses, and "acting out"—tears, shouting, and so on—is most often associated with "the feminine" (Charcot's swooning patients,[46] for example, or Freud's "Dora"[47]) and that, for Lacan, poses the question of gender identity: "Am I a man or a woman?"[48] That ambiguity of *masculin/féminin* is the key issue for the hysteric, a confusion that seems at first to be in sharp contrast to the very "cocky" Hart with which the film opens. Think of the hypermasculine arrogance so clearly on display in the dorm-room scene when he tells Ford—himself having made the highly obnoxious faux "confession" to being a genius—that he "outgeniuses genius" in his parable of the three University of Minnesota applicants to Harvard, only one of whom—himself—got in (PC, ch. 4). And this from someone whom you might expect to be chastened by the humiliating events earlier that same day when, bruised and battered from his first classroom run-in with Kingsfield, Hart, as the dorm proctor puts it, "lost his breakfast" (PC, ch. 3). But then that scene can be read as a kind of purge of the self, Hart literally vomiting up his "Midwestern charm"—as Susan puts it—to clear a space for a more competitive, indeed testosterone-driven cockiness. Yet as the term progresses, this cockiness "detumesces" and goes limp, as Hart becomes less and less certain of himself in the classroom hierarchy of active speakers and passive listeners. This signals, of course, the onset of Hart's hysteria, because it is here that he begins to sexualize the world of the law school in terms of "tops" and "bottoms," or "doms" and "subs," and cannot decide where he fits.

Not surprisingly, the film oscillates from then on between the rather lifeless heteronormative bedroom scenes with Susan (PC, chs. 9, 10, 11, 13) and what a "queer" reading might take to be a clue as to the story's real erotic core; that is, the highly homosocial—if not out-and-out homosexual—locker-room scenes of Hart showering, inter alia, with the effete Ford (PC, ch. 28). Not that Ford is Hart's true object of desire; like Susan, he is but a substitute figure for Hart's real partner in juristic joy. That source and site of law school *jouissance* is, I claim, none other than that rather unlikely love object, the jowly Professor Charles W. Kingsfield, Jr. For the film is quite clear here: Hart *longs* to merge with Kingsfield. Think of him in Kingsfield's study, gloating over the collected memorabilia—a photograph taken with Adlai Stevenson, another from Helen Keller—imagining himself as, or better yet, *with* Kingsfield (PC, ch. 15). This yearning recalls another, more famous case study of juridical perversion, that of Freud's President Schreber whose phantasmatic union with God took the form of anal penetration, the deity taking him from behind, "like a woman."[49] It is this form of intercourse that I suggest is euphemized by Hart when, in conversation with Susan at Harvard's football stadium, he proclaims that he is having a "true Socratic experience" with Kingsfield (PC, ch. 20), itself not only suggestive of the Platonic Dialogues' implicit anal-eroticism, but in its blurring of sodomy and Socrates, also indicative of Hart's deepening psychic crisis as he moves from neurosis (hysteria) to full-blown psychosis (paranoid delusion).

By way of comparison, *Legally Blonde*'s Elle Woods, at least at the film's outset, is coded—indeed, overcoded as the hysterical female "acting out" in the restaurant before subsequently succumbing to chocoholism, after being dumped by Warner for being "too blonde" (LB, chs. 3–4). But as the film progresses, it becomes increasingly clear that Elle's "blondeness"—that is, her hysterically funny, over-the-top femininity, all gold anklets, French nails, and "lucky scrunchies"—is itself, as Joan Riviere would put it, a "masquerade of womanliness."[50] According to Riviere, "womanliness" functions as a disguise to be donned (and doffed) to assuage the (castration?) anxieties of male colleagues, thereby averting the possible "retribution"[51] that clever women court under patriarchy. The complication *Legally Blonde* introduces to Riviere's thesis, however, is that Elle's "womanliness" is a *source* of such retribution—rather than an assurance or insurance against it—provoking such derisory male comments as, "Check out Malibu Barbie!" (LB, ch. 7). For in the heavily policed atmosphere of the "politically correct" campus, Elle's *uber*-femininity is read as an affront to, even a criminal assault on existing gender sensibilities. "Aren't you just a walking felony?" leers Warner, when Elle arrives at the "One L" party tricked out in—and into (by Vivian)—that most "womanly" of disguises, the Playboy Bunny costume (LB, ch. 14). Ultimately, though, Elle's case is no different from those of Riviere in that her femininity conceals—but in so doing, also reveals—a psychic condition often associated with men; the source, incidentally, of her considerable resilience and law school success: namely, obsession.

This obsession manifests itself, at least initially, in that most wily of "feminine" ways: winning back Warner. But it is only when Elle realizes that she'll never land him because she's not "good enough" that she experiences the beginnings of what might be called *clinical* obsession. For it is at this point in the film that Elle begins to pose and repose the question that, according to Lacan, all true obsessives ask: "Am I alive or dead?"[52] That is the either-or choice that troubles Elle for the rest of *Legally Blonde,* and the one she seems to be really driving at when, on the verge of dropping out, she plaintively asks Paulette whether she'll ever be taken "seriously" as a law student or if she is forever fated to be dismissed as a wannabe "Victoria's Secret model" (LB, ch. 27). Which is to say, is Elle a sentient subject or a masked imago? Or more fundamentally, is she a person or not? Paradoxically, it is precisely this question, asked over and over again throughout the film, that Elle, like all obsessives, will do just about anything to prevent the Big Other—that is, the Law to whom the query is addressed—from answering. This is because what Elle fears more than anything is the Law's mortifying touch, its letter that kills the spirit—indeed *her* spirit, affirming that she is well and truly *entre-deux-morts,* one of the law school's "living dead."

So being the good obsessive she is, Elle "ritualizes"[53]; that is, she constructs elaborate stalling devices designed to postpone her encounter with Law's nonbeing, with the Other's nothingness. This explains why Elle's cross-examination of trustafarian[54] brat (and oedipal patricide) Chutney Windham, is so compulsively repetitive, reiterating the fact of the "shower" six times (LB, ch. 29). For this strategy is intended to confound the Law, confuse the Other—until, of course, Elle can access some alternative rule system, another symbolic law by which to prove Brooks' innocence and win her case. And that is exactly what Elle does when she turns to "the rules of hair care," and for which she now speaks as its principal agent—the "*Cosmo* girl" nonpareil (LB, ch. 30). But in so doing, she undergoes a resymptomization, her obsessiveness mutating here into that of the pervert's "ethics of the Good," which substitutes its own law for that of the Other, claiming not only to know its higher commands but also to embody its imperatives.

I have lingered over these cinematic "case histories"—Elle's obsessiveness (shading into perversion), Hart's hysteria (bordering on paranoid delusions)—not only because they draw attention to the dysfunctionality of the law school as one of the most psychologically toxic of tertiary environments, but also because they throw into bold relief the even more alarming *functionality* of this dysfunctionality. That is, what Elle and Hart's pathologies convey is the way that law school can not only live with these symptoms but also, as Žižek might put it, "*enjoy*"[55] them; thriving, even flourishing on them. This is because the law school's ongoing operation is powered by these characters' nervous and neurotic energy; its processes and procedures driven by their various investments, cathexes, and psychic affects. Given this, is it any surprise that the increasingly "brunetted," almost "Vivianized" Elle and the disheartened Hart end up, by the end of both films, rehabilitated by the very hierarchy that had rejected them in the first place? And not only reintegrated into that hierarchy but in fact richly rewarded by it, each the recipient of its glittering prizes. The conferral of which, more often than not, is communicated by the interpellative means of, as Lacan might put it, *a letter that always arrives*.[56]

For Hart, that letter is a literal one; that is, the envelope containing his first-year grades that he receives by post while holidaying with Susan at the Kingsfield summer home on the Cape. Of course, Hart never actually opens the letter, instead famously dispatching it as a paper airplane into the Atlantic (PC, ch. 35)—an act that the film seems to invite the viewer to read as one of defiance, a rejection of the law school's hierarchy, and a final and fitting end to the "paper chase." But complicating that reading is the audience's knowledge from the previous scene of Kingsfield grading Hart's exam—that Hart has "aced" his Contracts final, getting an A and all that it connotes (PC, ch. 35). Hart has yet to discover this in the extradiegetic reality of the story line, no scene having been vouchsafed him. But the audience knows that whatever his (token) gestures of resistance might be here and later, Hart has been "hailed"[57] as one of Harvard's "best and brightest"—and by Kingsfield, its best and brightest ("the most expensive legal advice in the country" as Susan pricetags him; PC, ch. 24), with a law review editorship, a judicial clerkship, and a Wall Street partnership beckoning in that overdetermined career trajectory that awaits the Ivy League law school "top ten" graduate.

The law school's "hailing"[58] of Elle is even more explicit, her letter taking the form of the student ballots that have elected her, three years later at graduation, as something like "equity's darling": that is, valedictorian for the class of '04 (LB, ch. 31). *Legally Blonde* thus ends with her valedictory address, the theme of which is a postmodern plea for a "passionate jurisprudence."[59] This message is very much at odds with the markedly muted Elle, now "dressed for (corporate) success" and about to take up an associateship, so Stromwell crows, at one of Boston's Establishment firms. What's more, if the sequel, *Legally Blonde 2: Red, White and Blonde*,[60] is anything to go by—and something that can be adduced as textual evidence here—then Elle is destined for even greater things in the congressional arena of Washington, D.C.; as the legislative impetus behind "Bruiser's Bill" becoming, by the end of the film, the poster girl for American consensus politics, uniting left and right. Thus Elle, even more than Hart, will walk the corridors of power, political as much as professional. But at a terrible price: her difference has been rendered nugatory, her sparkle dimmed, and her exuberance sedated—or to rephrase, her "blondeness" virtually low-lighted out of existence. All of which suggests that any challenges to, let alone critiques of law—even ones as mild as those posed by postfeminists such as Elle—backfire, not only reproducing hierarchy but strengthening it.

Thinking Without Thought: Law School's Lobotomy and the Cut of the Master

This chapter is left asking the classic Leninist question: What is to be done? If the consequences of critical resistance—postfeminist or otherwise—are not less but *more* hierarchy, then what is the point of critique? Moreover, what is the purpose of a psychoanalytic reading that merely confirms, as hysterical, obsessive or otherwise, critique's failure? Quite simply: none. So am I arguing for the abandonment of critique, and the theoretical paradigms underpinning it—be they feminist, psychoanalytic, Marxist, postmodern, or otherwise? Nothing could be further from my intention. For my argument is this: if critique has so far failed, then its failure can be attributed to the very reason that feminist theorists—Judith Butler among others[61]—have long cautioned it about; that the critical project cannot turn solely on the identic question of *subject of law* (that is, the product of legal education; the lawyer) but must address the material question of the *structure of law* (that is, the productive means of legal education), both institutionally and discursively. This is precisely why Lacanian psychoanalysis—especially in its feminist register mapped out, for example, by Renata Salecl,[62] Jeanne Schroeder,[63] and Juliet Flower MacCannell[64]—is of assistance and indeed invaluable to the renewed critical project here. As a jumping-off point, it provides a useful taxonomy of institutional discourses—that of the hysteric, the university, the analyst, and the Master.[65]

Of course, the discourse of the Master is, in Lacan's taxonomy, the fundamental *discours*. It underpins all the others, including the prevalent discourse of our age, one that Lacan linked expressly to "the System," that is, totalized knowledge. Namely, what he called the "discourse of the university." Certainly that discourse, with its strong structural imperatives, is in all too visible evidence in the contemporary law school and legal knowledge, predicated as both are on the organizing principle of binary opposition (rights vs. duties, rules vs. norms, law vs. policy). But what indelibly marks the law school, setting it apart from other university faculties and their knowledge systems, is the persistence of that premodern presence, the Master—whose discourse is channeled through the mediating figure of the Socratic interlocutor and his or her questions. Indeed, she or he *becomes* the Master by speaking the question of the Other, the signifier of the Law: that is, "*Che vuoi?*" or "What do you want of me?"[66] a question that in turn prompts a demand from the slave, "I want an answer!" Confirming their status as respective instantiations of the Master, both Professors Kingsfield and Stromwell elicit this demand for a response—that is, for certainty, for determinacy—from their student-slaves. But that demand will never, *can* never, be met because as avatars of the Master these two figures preside over a socio-Symbolic that is incapable of meeting student-slave demands for coherence; its Law being so fractured, so inconsistent, and so internally riven as to be resistant to any kind of suture. Even resistant to the promise of closure held out by that "sublime object,"[67] by turns magnificent and monstrous: namely, the personified presence of the Master.

Yet the oppressive corporealization of the Master in the form of Kingsfield and Stromwell is highly and heavily ironic in psychological terms, because the principal objective of the discourse that each embodies is to make war on law's body and its circuits of feeling, its wiring of emotion. After all, "the law," intones Stromwell, is "reason free from passion"[68] (LB, ch. 9), an Aristotelian citation that reinscribes the split between the mind and the body, and that the Law, under the dominion of the Master, assumes as a donnée, or given. "You come here with a mind full of mush," barks Kingsfield, "and you leave thinking like lawyers" (PC, ch. 5). What does this sort of cognition entail? Does it take any particular epistemic shape? And how does it "think" the law? Kingsfield offers a clue by way of a very vivid, even vivisecting analogy by likening law school to brain surgery: "You're on an operating table; my little questions are the fingers probing your brain" (PC, ch. 5). So legal thought is conceived of here as something like a scalpel: that is, a surgical tool that *cuts*; opening the cranium, examining the frontal lobes, even lobotomizing the student-patient. In short, a kind of psychic castration is carried out by the Master and his discourse. All of which might explain why the law is not only, as Panu Minkinnen puts it, "thinking without desire"[69] but also thinking without thought, because the Master's signifying *coupure* has cut its material center of cognition—the brain—as much as its source of affect, the body.

Or has it? After all, psychoanalysis—at least in its Lacanian mode—cautions that the cut of castration is never as neat or clean as it seems; something always remains, reactivating desire, provoking enjoyment. And the Master's cut is no different. So what is his remainder? That is, what is his to keep? Namely, the *objet petit a*; and surely the clue to the *objet*'s identity lies in the very effects of desire and enjoyment that it arouses in the Master's slaves, his students. Think of Kingsfield's students; they are consumed by him, convinced he has—what? Specifically, the power/knowledge enfolded into and signified by what Lacan calls "the signifier of signifiers": the phallus. And *that* is equated here with Kingsfield's appendage, his penis. This is the not-so-"obscure object of desire" that survives, phantasmatically, the Master's cut and is appropriated by Kingsfield, sustaining his ongoing hegemonization of the Symbolic, despite its ruptured reality. No wonder Kingsfield can question everyone and everything with impunity, proclaiming, as it were, that there is no "metalanguage," no "Truth," no "Other to the Other" because the Symbolic mandate is his and his alone (PC, ch. 5). That is to say, Kingsfield most definitely has the phallus.

Lex Populi's Floating Phallus: Kingsfield, Stromwell, Callahan

Yet this phallic ascription immediately raises the implicitly feminist question: What of Stromwell? Does *she* have the phallus? Or is it the exclusive preserve, as vulgar Freudianism might have it, of penis possessors, the masculine appendage sine qua non. Lacanian psychoanalysis would hold otherwise (and is a welcome corrective to the sort of wild analysis cited above). But the phallus for Lacan, albeit the essential marker of sexual difference, is anything but *essentialist*. It is a function of culture rather than nature. For the signifier "phallus" is only the biological penis insofar as it has been "misrecognized" as such by and under the conditions of patriarchy. Thus no necessary connection obtains between the two. Which is why, oddly enough, the phallus can succeed even when patriarchy fails. Think of our own postpatriarchal era: the collapse of the paternal signifier—the *Nom-du-Père*—has not so much marginalized the phallus as multiplied it, disseminating it across all socio-Symbolic boundaries, including those of sexuation and gender. This doubtless explains why there is such a feel-good quality to *Legally Blonde*, because this quintessential "chick flick" holds out the emancipatory promise "to each and every woman a phallus" in its portrayal of that most formidable of phallic women, Prof. Stromwell.

Stromwell's phallic function, however, plays out along lines very different from those of Kingsfield. This difference is graphically dramatized in each of these characters' penultimate scenes. In *The Paper Chase*, that scene occurs in the law school lift, already occupied by Hart and into which Kingsfield enters. An awkward silence ensues, but proximity emboldens an unctuous Hart to (fawningly) congratulate Kingsfield on his tuition in Contracts. To which Kingsfield replies with an icy "thank you," followed by a loftily patrician, "And your name is?" (PC, ch. 34). Now, what's interesting about this scene is not that Kingsfield fails to recognize Hart—even though he called upon him on the first day of class, engaged and then discharged him as a research assistant, and endured his obscene public taunt, "You are a sonofabitch Kingsfield!" (PC, ch. 30). Rather, what interests me here is that Kingsfield's near autistic disconnection from his students, from their—and his— context, is completely believable. And not just because of Susan's repeated insistence that, for Kingsfield, his students have no reality apart from their classroom personae—their place in his Symbolic literalized in the seating chart assignments (PC, ch. 2). What makes Kingsfield's social myopia so credible is that it renders explicit what the film has always implied: that Kingsfield's sight is as obscured as Iustitia's, fixated as it is on law's letter, oblivious to its spirit, seeing only contracts rather than connections. For like Iustitia, Kingsfield too is blindfolded—or figuratively so; and what blinds him is none other than the very source of his power: his phallus, which he is unable to detach; his symbolic mandate that he is unable to suspend.

This failure on the part of Kingsfield is in sharp contrast to that of Stromwell, who despite her "dragon lady" mien can and *does* suspend her symbolic mandate; that is, she relinquishes, however temporarily, her phallus, transferring its power to that most unlikely of candidates, Elle Woods. Consider the scene in that veritable *salon des glaces* of femininity, Paulette's beauty parlor. Throughout *Legally Blonde*, the beauty parlor has been a kind of safe haven for Elle and other women; a place of refuge from classroom ridicule (Elle) or spousal abuse (Paulette) in which they can indulge in their fantasies, live out their dramas, and follow their hearts—"bend and snap," as it were (LB, ch. 20). Naturally enough, it is here, following Callahan's unsolicited overtures, that a distraught Elle stops for a final farewell, admitting defeat and collapsing in tears into Paulette's arms and ample bosom. It is at this point that another beauty parlor client—hitherto an anonymous head of washed 'n set hair—turns toward the camera, revealing? None other than Prof. Stromwell herself, who drops her Back Bay accent and Boston Brahmin demeanor, as well as her phallus, when she confronts Elle directly and says, "If you're going to let one stupid prick ruin your life, you're not the girl I thought you were" (LB, ch. 27). Thus Stromwell, unlike Kingsfield, can make a very decided connection with her students, expressed in terms of a sororal pact of solidarity at odds with not only Kingsfield's distance but also the illicit sort of contact that Callahan essays.

Callahan provides an intriguing counterpoint to both Stromwell and Kingsfield, tracing both and neither positions. For he embodies masculinity in the postpatriarchal law school, one that has taken "critique" on board (at least, superficially), is student-friendly and clinically oriented, but remains, at the end of the day, a complete and utter "prick." Now "prick" is a very colorful colloquialism, a vivid vulgarism, not the least because it aptly metaphorizes and metonymizes the organ with which, principally, Callahan "thinks." Even more so, what "prick" captures here, in its short consonantal sharpness, is Callahan's aspirations to *have* the phallus, a striving to reinvent patriarchy, to become the new Master. Which should serve as a warning to all those "crits" of the law—but especially those white males of the Kennedy-Unger-Tushnet ilk[70]; that in their search for a "New Order"—critical, clinical, diverse, progressive, nonhierarchical—they may end up reproducing, even exceeding the worst features of the law school's ancien régime, installing an even more malign version of the Master. "What you aspire to as (critical-legal) revolutionaries is a new Kingsfield," to misquote Lacan's celebrated riposte to the rioting *soixante-huitards*: "You will have one."[71]

There is, however, a key difference between the old (Kingsfield) and the new Master (Callahan): that of location. While the former is a lynchpin—*point de capiton*—of the Symbolic, the latter is a creature of the Real. This different positioning has consequences for their relationship to the phallus (and the Law). A relationship as it turns out, that Callahan most definitely "lacks," having only a "prick" that he has confused with the phallus. For Callahan is a father not of the phallus but another body part, an orifice rather than appendage: he is, what Slavoj Žižek would call, the "anal father."[72] That is, he is "Father-Enjoyment" who, unlike the phallic father (Kingsfield), perpetuates rather than prohibits incest, violating rather than succoring his progeny (like he does when he "hits" on Elle). In short, Callahan is the anti-Oedipus.[73] All of which means that Callahan is the obscene double, even demonic parody of the father figure; De Sade to Kingsfield's Kant.[74] And Stromwell's wager to Elle may suggest another, even more primitive paternal identification. By challenging Elle to stand up to, even supplant Callahan in court, Stromwell may equate, implicitly, Callahan with the pre-Oedipus: namely, the totemic father of "primal horde."[75] Only slaying him will end his monopoly of *jouissance* and found the Freudian social contract of what might be called "distributive enjoyment."[76]

Which returns me to my still unresolved question: if Callahan has the faux phallus, and Kingsfield the full phallus, then what of Stromwell? What sort of phallus does she possess? I suggest that what she possesses is something I will call the "prosthetic phallus," namely one that can be put on and taken off, assumed and laid aside—much like Riviere's masks. Only here, ironically, the masquerade worn in the world of postpatriarchy is manliness rather than womanliness. This is a form of artifice—a kind of drag in reverse (drag king?)—that incidentally most men seem to be blithely unaware of, still "misrecognizing" their masks of manliness as the "real thing," an identic essence that confuses masquerade with materiality, masculinity with power, and the penis with the phallus. In this world of (phallic) wonders, "*La Femme n'existe pas*," as Lacan so (in)famously put it: "The Woman does not exist"[77]—except as man's symptom. *Women*, of course, exist in law schools, as long as they have become, as Lani Guinier puts it, "gentlemen."[78] But "Woman" is positioned elsewhere, located outside the male imaginary of the Law.

As it turns out, this is not such a bad thing; in fact, it is a very good thing to have some distance from the mirages of masculinity, the lures of its phallic *salon des glaces*. For the position Woman occupies, in being "outside," is a site of *sight*; that is, a field of vision with a clear view, indeed a penetrating insight capable of shattering the masculinist "looking glass" of *méconnaissance* to disclose the "Truth" of the Law, of the Other. That "Truth" is, of course, what has been noted previously: that there is no essential connection between the phallus and the penis, sexuation and *pouvoir/savoir*. This is because all of us, both men and women—Stromwell, Callahan, even Kingsfield!—are symbolically castrated: that is, marked by signification's lack. The difference is that women, like Stromwell, *know this* while men (Callahan, Kingsfield) *do not*.

Bend and Snap! Law School as Training for *Her*steria

All of which suggests that if, in law school's moving image, there is a *sujet supposé savoir*—the "subject supposed to know"—instantiating the "discourse of the analyst," then it is Prof. Stromwell. She more than anyone is the Lacanian analyst who can solicit but also deflect (and redirect) transference by stepping in and out of the role of the Master, donning and discarding the "prosthetic" phallus of authority to an extent that goes well beyond and indeed sublates the dialectic of orthodoxy and bogus-critique of Kingsfield and Callahan. This suggests that Stromwell's referencing of Aristotle, on the first day of class, may be more truly "critical," more genuinely oppositional than was previously credited. After all, it was Aristotle who moved philosophy away from Plato's transcendent Forms, studying instead the forms of *physis* in the here and now, including the form of the human body and the "laws" regulating it. Thus Aristotle, the natural philosopher—as opposed to the Platonic metaphysician—opens up the very possibility that his citation by Stromwell seems to prohibit: that is, for a "passionate jurisprudence," a law of body's affect as much as the affective body of law. This is precisely what Stromwell's protégé, Elle, calls for in her valedictory—an effect, one can only imagine, of the older woman's affective modeling and mentorship.

It is this sort of feminine and feminist mentorship (or "[wo]mentorship," as Enid might put it) that drives home the very practical point made by countless critical legal feminists—like Deborah Rhode,[79] Margaret Thornton,[80] and Celia Wells[81]: the urgent need in the legal academy for women senior enough to mentor; that is, of professorial or decanal rank. If law schools are ever to "take gender seriously" and create an environment in which women flourish as much as men (and all other differences thrive), then there must be women in positions of authority, of influence, of (phallic) power. But I would endorse Margaret Thornton's caution[82] against an overhasty "mainstreaming" of gender called for, for example, by Catharine MacKinnon.[83] Because if feminist critique wishes to avoid becoming just another version of the "discourse of the Master," then it would be wise to take gender "satirically" as much as seriously. "Woman"—as "not-all," as the singular challenge to the universal, as both inside and outside the Law—is in a particularly privileged position to engage in and carry out this renewal of critique, feminist and otherwise. This position of privilege, of *power*, is not only a result of women's increasing involvement in the legal academy but also, paradoxically, of "Woman's" cynical distance from it.

So what might be perceived, at least initially, as a weakness—being outside the system—turns out to be a source of strength. This is because critique is grounded in detachment as much if not more than engagement; a detachment that enables it to laugh *at*, and perhaps laugh *out* of existence, Law's persistent masculinist foibles and follies as *her*sterically ludicrous. *Legally Blonde* takes up this comedic challenge and dramatizes the way in which feminist critique might proceed, in a scene that I take to be the film's paradigmatic ideological instance: once again, the exchange between Elle and Stromwell in the beauty parlor (LB, ch. 9). There, the critical moment occurs, the ideological occasion arises not in some sort of oedipal struggle (like Hart shouting at Kingsfield; PC, ch. 30) or false act of resistance (like Hart throwing the transcripts into the sea; PC, ch. 35), but when the Other—that is, the Law, *the Master*—lays down its mask, steps outside its symbolic mandate, sets aside its signifier, the phallus, and like Stromwell does to Elle, knowingly and ironically *smirks* back at us.

CHAPTER SEVEN

"It's the Vibe!"

The Common Law Imaginary Down Under

Taking *Mabo* Cinematically:
The Castle's Legal Fictions of (Dis)Possession

"It's the Constitution, it's *Mabo* . . . it's the vibe" (C, ch. 10). So goes one of the most memorable lines of dialogue from Rob Sitch's 1997 Ozfilm cult hit, *The Castle*.[1] Now a favored hook of Australian *lex populi*, this phrase has been repeated, just as feebly, by scores of flummoxed law students from Toowoomba to Tasmania grasping at constitutional straws in public law exams or essays, as it was in the film by the character of fly-by-night solicitor, Dennis DeNuto. Played here to "wog-boy" perfection by Tiriel Mora, DeNuto utters these immortal words before the federal court—with the extremely distingué Robyn Nevins cast as its presiding judge—after losing his administrative appeal challenging the federal government's "compulsory acquisition" of the modest (to say the least) Melbourne home of his truckie[2] client, Aussie Everyman, Daryl Kerrigan (a role brilliantly taken by character actor Michael Caton). DeNuto's mot (in)juste, however, is not only memorable for its catchphrase quality, though it is certainly a standout example of what semiotics would call "empty discourse," worthy to chime in along with Daryl's meaningless mantras, like "You are an ideas man" (C, ch. 1); "Tell 'im he's dreamin'" (C, ch. 1); or my personal favorite, "How's the serenity?" (C, ch. 6).

But however much this filmic reference to *Mabo* parodies, even trivializes the 1993 High Court decision declaring the Meriam people to be the owner-occupiers of Queensland's Murray Islands, DeNuto's declamation points to the very real *re*vision that case was and is for Australia. A landmark judgment in the most literal sense of that word, *Mabo and Others v. The State of Queensland*[3] instituted, for at least some of the Aboriginal peoples of the Commonwealth, a new property regime—native title[4]—thereby bringing Indigeneity into the field of vision of that *salon des glaces* of what I call, following Althusser[5] and Lacan,[6] the Anglo-Australian common law imaginary. Now focalized around the new imago of the native title holder—the land claims of Eddie Mabo, David Passi, and James Rice constituting the *objet petit a* of not just the Meriam but all Aboriginal peoples—*Mabo*[7] shattered the anamorphic "glass darkly" of *terra nullius*, the legal fiction rendering Australia a "no-man's-land" at the time of its European colonization, thereafter blinding the courts to the very presence, let alone priority of any claims to land or compensation of the Indigenous population.

Not that the Aborigines or the Torres Strait Islanders, that is, Australia's Indigenous peoples, figure very much in *The Castle*, other than by way of citation—like Daryl's en passant references to Cathy Freeman and Yvonne Goolagong (C, ch. 10). In fact, the Indigenous peoples are conspicuous by their absence here. This is a strange cinematic reinscription of *terra nullius*, particularly in a film that goes out of its way to represent postcolonial Australia's much-vaunted ethnic diversity, self-consciously showcasing, as I argue in the next section, Italian, Greek, and Arab "New Australians" as well as the native-born Kerrigans. But if the actual people referenced and represented by the *Mabo* decision are nowhere to be found here, then it is my contention that the case's core principles are everywhere felt throughout the film.[8] They power the plot, particularly its valorization, as described in this chapter, of the courts over the legislature, the common law over policy. They inflect its language, not just in its footnoting of *Mabo* but also in its historical allusions to white Australia's landgrabs and in the metaphor of the "castle" itself, with all of its resonances of conquest and settlement. They inform the theme of this chapter's final sections, with a focus on property and the legality of ownership, dispossession, and reclamation. But the film does more than just reflect *Mabo*'s *ratio decidendi*; it *reads* the decision critically, ambiguating, problematizing, even subverting it to the extent that I will claim *The Castle* puts *Mabo* on trial, becoming a signal instance of Australia's *lex populi*. In so doing, *The Castle* exposes not only *Mabo*'s—and indeed, native title's—internal contradictions, but also its own conflicted politics (activist or reactionary? Pearsonite or Howardist?) and gestures to the profound cultural, social, and particularly legal ambivalences that the decision has aroused in Australia. All of which renders this film, hitherto received in

Australia and elsewhere as a cinematic essay in ockerness,[9] as one of the bitterest of black comedies in the global *lex populi* canon, one that could be described, with a nod to Northrop Frye, as a "(tragi)comedy of jurisprudence."[10]

Ocker Oz and Working Dog's Working Class

Central to the film, and functioning something like a Lacanian *point de capiton* by "quilting"[11] together the narrative's issues of land, community, identity, politics, and especially, the law, is the eponymous "castle" of the title: 3 Highview Crescent. A "home, not just a house"—a sentiment that the script insists upon several times, the phrase having been coined by Daryl at the tribunal (C, ch. 7), commended by Farouk afterwards (C, ch. 7), and finally, repeated by Lawrie at the High Court (C, ch. 13) to that most "unhomely," or—to give the term its full Freudian spin, that most *unheimlich*[12] of families, the Kerrigans of Cooloroo, Victoria. The Kerrigans are a kind of Royle family Down Under, a sort of Simpsons of the South Pacific, although neither of these analogies does justice to the way in which Australian cinema and television of late has outpaced the Northern Hemisphere in its celluloid and video representations of domestic dysfunction. Think of P. J. Hogan's disturbing depiction of the maladjusted Hislop brood of Porpoise Spit in *Muriel's Wedding*,[13] or Baz Luhrmann's discomforting portrayal of the almost equally bizarre Hastings mob of Sydney in *Strictly Ballroom*[14]—not to mention the small-screen household grotesqueries of the Shanes and Charlenes, Pippas and Toms of, respectively, TV's *Neighbours* (the Robinsons of Ramsey Street, for example),[15] and *Home and Away* (such as the Fletchers of Summer Bay),[16] to name just two.

But even gauged by these productions' exceedingly broad standards of farce, *The Castle* presents, in the Kerrigan clan, a picture of working-class, suburban Australian life that borders on the satirically sour, glibly patronizing, at the very same moment it purports to gently rib this very "ocker"[17] world of mullet haircuts and daggy trainers, of dodgy do-it-yourself home "improvements" and stodgy *Women's Weekly* cookery, of daft cosmetology TAFE (technical and further education) diplomas, and naff poolrooms full of kitsch memorabilia and tourist tat. What with Dad Daryl's greyhounds (not only Coco, but also Son of Coco; C, ch. 14), Mum Sal's handicrafts (the bedazzled jean jacket and stenciled serving tray, for example, all rapturously greeted by her husband with "You could sell that!"; C, ch. 1), daughter Tracey's beauty salon quiff ("Now *that* is a head of hair!," enthuses her father; C, ch. 8), and their sons' respective foibles—Wayne's incarceration for armed robbery of the local petrol station, Steve's incessant "Trading Post" call and response (C, ch. 1), and narrator Dale's questioning overkill (C, ch. 5)—the Kerrigans are designed to send a collective shudder of self-recognition (as much as a frisson of relief, owing to one's ironic distance from them) down the spines of all antipodean viewers. Particularly targeted are those urban, uni-educated, media-savvy "chattering class" trendies of the Glebe–St. Kilda axis—just like, in fact, the quartet of writer-director-producers of Working Dog[18] itself: Tom Gleisner, Santo Cilauri, and Jane Kennedy as well as Rob Sitch—whose sentimental fantasy and worst nightmare this tribe of bogans[19] extraordinaire embodies.

What prevents this cinematic essay in Aussie Grand Guignol—by turns witty and sneering about the heavily overdetermined "worker's paradise" it posits— from degenerating into the kind of prole-bashing rife in American sitcoms (like *Roseanne*) is the timely arrival of Airlink's letter "compulsorily acquiring" the Kerrigan house. This narrative turn shifts the rather ham-fisted irony away from the taste-challenged dystopia (at least, from a yuppie perspective) of sponge cake, car culture, and endless reruns of *Hey, Hey, It's Saturday* (C, ch. 2) to a more acceptable object of critique: namely, Big Government. Though privately funded, Airlink is a state-sanctioned and -fronted consortium (C, ch. 8), intent on leveling all of Highview Crescent—Jack's, Farouk's, and Evonne's "castles," as well as Daryl's (C, chs. 3, 10)—so as to make way for the expansion of the freight facilities of Melbourne's airport, soon to be "the largest in the southern hemisphere" (C, ch. 3). Now, there is nothing illegal about what Airlink wants to do here. In fact, the consortium is acting well within its statutory authority, as a simpering city official full of faux sympathy (C, ch. 3) is at pains to point out to Daryl: specifically, that Airlink's expropriative power is conferred by and exercised lawfully under the Airport Commission, itself warranted by "iron-clad" agreements between federal, state, and municipal governments (C, ch. 3). An argument, moreover, that is endorsed and upheld by two tiers of adjudication: at the Administrative Appeals Tribunal (C, ch. 7) and the federal court (C, ch. 10). Thus Airlink appears to be holding all the legal cards here and may even occupy, as its lawyers argue at court, the high moral ground because it is acting in the public interest as measured by the utilitarian yardstick of the "greatest good for the greatest number."

Of course, the referencing of the utility principle by Airlink's counsel here works in precisely the same cynical way that Marx[20] said all Benthamism did: that its calculations of felicity, maximizing pleasure and minimizing pain across the broadest possible spectrum, really amount to nothing more than an ideological smokescreen, masking the private interest (the desire of the ruling few) under the guise of public welfare (and the needs of the laboring many). Certainly it is the intensely private motive of profit driving Airlink's intention to bulldoze Highview Crescent. Landfilling the neighboring quarry might prove too expensive, upping costs and thereby cutting into returns. So Airlink is acting on behalf of the public only incidentally—if at all. Just consider who they really are: government fronted, yes; but funded—and, principally, controlled—by the Barlow Group (C, ch. 8), a mysterious triumverate of financiers who, as Dennis warns Daryl, not only "write the rules" (C, ch. 8) through their traveling claque of legal counsel (think of the smooth menace of Establishment solicitor Ron Graham, popping up at DeNuto's office with his bribe of AU$25,000, and the not-so-veiled threat strongly "advising against further action"; C, ch. 9), but also enforce these semisovereign commands through their gang of "hired thugs" (remember the leather-jacketed hood "just passing on a message" at the Kerrigan's doorstep one night, to "take the offer"; C, ch. 9). Sequestered behind their security systems, and never more than a dis-embodied voice over the tannoy, or intercom (C, ch. 9), the Barlow Group rep-resents a new stage of Capital for the "lucky country" that exceeds, in its unseen malignancy, even the corrupt cronyism of the 1980s (at least, Alan Bond and his ilk were identifiable[21]) because it is so decontextualized, invading but also evading the state, here today and gone tomorrow. So what *The Castle* dramatizes here are the massive inroads this globalizing form of anarcho-capitalism—acting both within and outside the law—is making into the hitherto tightly protectionist and highly unionized economy of Australia under the guise of "privatization" (C, ch. 8). Airlink embodies the monstrous hybridity created by that policy which, like all other unholy alliances of state and market (those extractive industries operating through lease, for example), are intent on demolishing, as much at Jabiluka[22] as at Highview Crescent, all that the nation holds dear—ecosystems, beauty spots, even sacred sites—in order to carry out their "development" projects.

Is There an Aborigine in This Text? Daryl Kerrigan as Indigene *Manque-à-être*

It is at this point in the narrative that the film comes closest to articulating a critical legal, even Marxist analysis, aligning the Kerrigans' plight with the class struggles that beset contemporary Australia's "politics of the law."[23] But class is not the only basis for critique here. Race—in particular Indigeneity—is alluded to and cited directly by the film's script and scenery, analogizing and equating the situation of the whiter-than-white, Irish Catholic Kerrigans with the fortunes of Australia's enraced "Other"—its Aboriginal peoples. Consider, for example, the physical site of 3 Highview Crescent: wedged between power lines, lead dumping, and one of the airport's busiest runways, this no-man's-land at once lampoons real estate agent*ese* ("location, location, location," as Dale says at the opening of his narration; C, ch. 1) all the while literalizing the doctrine of *terra nullius*, thereby evoking the pre-*Mabo* juristic fantasy, or more properly, *delusion*—(dis)articulated, most notably, in *Milirrpum v. Nabalco*[24]— of Australia as a historical vacuity, uninhabited at the time of colonial contact, and ripe for the imperialist picking. No wonder then that Airlink has opted to "kick out" as Steve phrases it, the occupants of Highview Crescent, because to the powers that be they, like the Aboriginal people, *were never really there in the first place*—a presence which is really an absence, the erasure of which merits only the most minimal recompense as a form of largesse.

To which Daryl responds with true bevan[25] bluffness: "get stuffed!" (C, ch. 9). Because his "castle" is not something reducible to Airlink's exchange values, a point that the Aborigines, as the traditional custodians of Australia, have been arguing for years: that their land is not a commodity—that is, mere "real estate," as activist Noel Pearson puts it[26]—but rather their community's context, saturated with and the source of spiritual, psychic, and aesthetic meaning that in turn defines their collective and individual identity. Consider the "strong relationship,"[27] as Moynihan J. put it in *Mabo* at the Queensland Supreme Court, between the Meriam people and their "garden lands," significant not only "from the point of view of subsistence" but also for "the various rituals associated with different aspects of community life"—marriage, adoption, rite of passage, and so on—as well as "prestige" and "cohesion."[28] *Sittlichkeit*[29] or "ethical substance": that is what the land constructs and contains for the Meriam people, as much as "the castle" does for the Kerrigans; each space being imbued with the very ethical substance of Hegelian sociality, to which Lawrie Hammill refers at High Court when he talks, in his closing argument, of the "love," "care," and "memories" (C, ch. 13) that Highview Crescent holds for its owner-occupants. It is no surprise then when Daryl exclaims to Sal while packing up the poolroom after losing at the federal court, "I'm beginning to understand how the Aborigines feel," because the Kerrigan's home is "like their [the Aborigines'] land" (C, ch. 11), adding—like an Outback black fella[30] "talking up" to the white man, to crib from Aileen Moreton-Robinson:[31] "This country has to stop stealing other peoples' land" (C, ch. 11).

But Indigene *manque-à-être* is precisely what Daryl Kerrigan is not. The threat-ened dispossession of his home was not and never will be as far-reaching and final as what in fact happened to Aboriginal Australia because his owner-occupancy was always recognized as such at law, giving rise to a right of compensation that, however unsatisfactory, was *never, ever* offered to the Indigenous peoples (even by the majority in *Mabo*[32]). Nor is Daryl the class warrior he may appear to be, prima facie. The neighborhood committee he convenes remains just that: not a Leninist cell raising revolutionary consciousness, but a special interest group of property holders that he heads up by virtue of his race and gender power (C, ch. 10). As the white male patriarch, who better to lead a group consisting of a pensioner, a single woman, and a "New Australian"? Farouk underscores this point by addressing Kerrigan as "Mr. Daryl," who in turn might just as well have said "Call me bwana" as "Call me Daryl," because the Anglo-Celtic monoculture represented by Daryl Kerrigan remains, despite twenty years of official multiculturalism, the hegemonic dominant here. It prevails over and purports to speak on behalf of Australia's "pol-itics of difference," imaged not only in Farouk but in Tracey's Greek husband, Con and his parents, the Petropoulouses.

All of which situates Daryl and his struggle against the corporate "Goliath," as the Channel 9 newscast puts it (C, ch. 13), within a particular political tradi-tion as much as cinematic convention, which, if Marxist, owes more to Groucho than it does to Karl: specifically, that old Hollywood chestnut, pitting a motley group of outsiders—whose ethnic, class, gender, and age group variety reflects America's ideological amour propre as the great "melting pot"—led by a small-*l* liberal and rugged individualist, reveling in his autonomy and doing battle against some pernicious system of political economy. But in Capra's films,[33] whose stock-in-trade this kind of narrative is, the point is never to actually change the system (substituting, say, socialism for capitalism) but rather to restore it, by delivering the system from the corrupt aberration distorting its original imperatives (for ex-ample, defeating the monopoly and allowing the "free market" to be truly free). By invoking this genre, *The Castle* reveals Daryl to be anything but a threat to the established order; indeed, he is its staunchest supporter, seeking not so much a departure as a return to the Australia of the 1950s, where "every man's home is his castle," flashy financial types are unheard of, and sheilas and wogs know their place. In light of these politics and aesthetics of nostalgia, one could even go so far as to suggest that *The Castle* might be retitled *Mr. Kerrigan Goes to Canberra* or *It's a Wonderful Barbie*.

This longing to return to a past—that may only have existed on celluloid—extends as much to the law as the politics and aesthetics of *The Castle*. Consider, for example, the film's narrative and juristic climax: the hearing before the High Court of Australia. There, a kind of jurisprudential nostalgia suffuses the proceedings, harkening back to a very traditional kind of legal argument, even a particular type of "Establishment" practitioner. Gone are the references to *Mabo*, a silence suggestive of its dubious status as a cause célèbre within the common law canon rather than a sound authority, to be trotted out only as an eleventh-hour, "Hail Mary" defense by no-hopers like Dennis DeNuto. Who, incidentally, has been relegated to the judicial sidelines as a water boy (filling glasses, or passing notes like "Fucking brilliant"; C, ch. 13) as the magisterial Lawrence Hammill, Q.C. (played with patrician ease by Charles "Bud" Tingwell) takes to the curial centerfield, kicking off his case, and indeed carrying the day by adducing solid, "black letter" law, be it legislative (s. 51 of the Constitution; C, ch. 12) or judicial (the *Tasmanian Dams* decision[34]; C, ch. 12). Even when Lawrie departs from the rules and turns, as Ronald Dworkin[35] might say, to the realm of principle, he positivizes it in terms of the Constitutional framers' original intentions, arguing that the "just terms" (C, chs. 12, 13) qualifying the federal expropriative power could never have been intended to justify dispossessing a family of their "home." Why? Presumably because the framers were themselves common lawyers for whom the time-honored, traditional maxims of the common law, like "An Englishman's home is his castle" of the 1604 *Semayne's Case*,[36] were bred in the bone.

"Ruling Us from the Grave": Native Title, *Terra Nullius*, and Property Law as the Undead

Thus *The Castle* looks back to what Isaiah Berlin would call the classic common law tradition of "negative liberty,"[37] and its most hallowed right—the right to be left alone, free from interference especially by the state—all the while skirting, at the very moment it raises in its references to *Mabo*, express and implied, the prospects afforded by a new, post-*Mabo* era of judicial activism, one taking its cue from the regime of international human rights, and its more "positive"[38] conception of liberty authorizing state intervention for resource redistribution. But what is truly striking about the double movement enacted by the film—of one step forward (in the citations of *Mabo*'s positive liberty), two steps backwards (by applying the negative liberty of *Semayne's Case*)—is that it repeats the very "skeletal fracture,"[39] to deploy the judgment's most vivid metaphor against itself, which rends the structural morphology of *Mabo*, thereby throwing into bold relief the jurisprudential and political cross-purposes at work in the decision, at once regressive and progressive, proactive and conservative.

Consider the most "Whiggish" of the judgments and the source of the striking skull 'n bones similitude—that of Mr. Justice Brennan—who repeats the eighteenth-century's characteristic platitude of "progress," ironic in an era (postmodernity?) that has proclaimed the end of all such metanarratives. Brennan J. impliedly treats the common law as a dynamic force, evolving in response to the nation's economic, political, and social changes. He does this by repudiating *terra nullius* on the grounds that it is "imperative in today's world that the common law should neither be, *not* be, seen to be frozen in an age of racial discrimination,"[40] one that treats the "indigenous inhabitants . . . as [so] 'low in the scale of social organisation,' [that] they and their occupancy . . . were ignored."[41] Given this, one would expect public policy, hitherto a largely American judicial heresy, to loom large in a decision that, in its antiracism, rights consciousness, and social justice concerns, is redolent of what Karl Llewellyn would call the "grand style of adjudication,"[42] concerned more with the law's results rather than rules; its "spirit" instead of "letter," even when this means, as Brennan acknowledges "overruling . . . cases which have held the contrary."[43]

But the bench's nascent proactivity is contested and complicated (deconstructed?) by the very rhetoric of the decision itself, which invokes the ghost of Blackstone and his declaratory theory when Brennan J. holds: "In discharging its duty to declare the common law of Australia, this court is not free to adopt rules that accord with contemporary notions of justice and human rights if their adoption would fracture the skeleton of principle which gives the body of our law its shape and consistency."[44] Now the interesting thing about this tropological appeal to tradition's "bare bones"—that judges declare, rather than find the law—is that it enables Brennan J. to do exactly the *reverse*: to manipulate precedent's frame, like some sort of juridical chiropractor, realigning the lumbar of a long line of disjointed authorities, cracking the spine of domestic (*Administration of Papua and New Guinea v. Daera Guba*[45]), imperial (see *Amodu Tijani v. Secretary, Southern Nigeria*[46]), British Commonwealth (see *Calder v. Attorney-General of British Columbia*[47]), and international (see *Advisory Opinion on Western Sahara*[48]) sources, so they uphold, at common law, the coexistence and compatibility of native title with the Crown's "radical title."[49] Which is about as radical as this judgment gets because its standard interpretive move is one of infinite regress, going as far back as the early seventeenth-century cases of *The Case of Tanistry*[50] (concerning the survival at common law of "tanistry," a form of property inherited from Irish Brehon law) and *Witrong and Blany*[51] (affirming the continuity of Welsh propertarial interests predating the introduction of the common law). Given this sort of legal-historical anachronism, one might suspect that what the first British colonists to the Murray Islands—the police, the London Missionary Society, and the sort—would have found nothing less than the dry bones of the common law itself, marking since time immemorial the cadastres of native title. All of which suggests another inflection of and to Brennan's skeletal analogy: that of the common law as a corpus delicti whose dead hand, the touch of which is mortified and mortifying, continues to "rule us from the grave,"[52] as Maitland once said of the forms of action that control policy, contain activism, and ensure that every political progression is a regression to common law origins.

The "mythos of return" staged here is precisely why Indigenous activist and politico Noel Pearson, among others, dismissed *Mabo* as a profoundly "conservative"[53] decision, regardless of all the triumphalist self-congratulation with which liberals greeted the ruling when it was handed down. Despite its "reformist" agenda—or perhaps precisely because of it—the judgment largely ignored but for the few token gestures touched on above, activist claims that the recognition of native title went to the heart of the human rights debate in Australia, "presenting an opportunity to radically reassess the relationship between Indigenous and non-Indigenous Australians."[54] Yet that opportunity was lost because the court elected to take rights *less* seriously, reading native title restrictively. Although recognized as a proprietarial interest of the "indigenous inhabitants in land, whether communal, group or individual, possessed under the traditional laws acknowledged by . . . traditional customs,"[55] that interest was reduced by the judgment to something less than a "common law tenure"—like that of an "estate in fee simple" or an "estate in freehold."[56] Even when deemed "good against the State"[57] and so to approximate ownership, native title was undercut by a rather pejorative characterization: as a "burden"[58] on sovereignty.

The problem with this sort of description is that burdens can and often are laid down. Thus *Mabo* goes on to elaborate in great detail how sovereignty can relieve itself of native title's weary load, a final about-face in a judgment marked by a peripatetic doubling back. But not much interpretive to-ing and fro-ing is required here on the part of Mr. Justice Brennan *et al.*, because native title is so internally conflicted that it might well be said to carry "the seeds of its own destruction": that is, it sets up the conditions for the disavowal of Indigenous land claims at the very moment it purports to acknowledge them, repealing but also reviving a kind of *terra nullius* at one and the same time. How does native title pull off this legal legerdemain--now you see the property interest, now you don't? None other than by means of the concept of "extinguishment,"[59] and its corollary "inconsistency," as qualifying all land claims made pursuant to native title. For native title was never intended to secure in perpetuity Indigenous land claims, but rather to accommodate them, temporarily, with those of the colonizer's white settlers, envisaging their eventual obliteration by extinguishment—as the American native peoples (and later, the Canadian "First Nations" peoples) discovered to their detriment in the germinal judgment *Johnson v. McIntosh*.[60] There, Chief Justice Marshall articulated the extinguishing doctrine that Brennan succinctly summarizes in his judgment in *Mabo*: native title is "extinguished" if land claimed under it is subject to any "valid exercise of sovereign power inconsistent with the continued right to enjoy"[61] said land, whether that inconsistency takes, for example, the form of "alienation"[62] to private interests or "appropriation"[63] for the public benefit.

Wik, White Backlash, and *The Castle*'s Squattocrats

It is precisely this doctrinal delimitation that has become the source and site of curial controversy post-*Mabo*, particularly following the 1993 enactment of the *Native Title Act*,[64] which codified, inter alia, the "past acts"[65] requisite for extinguishment. *Wik Peoples v. The State of Queensland*[66] is the most prominent of these sorts of native title "test cases," which included *Fejo v. Northern Territory*,[67] and *Western Australia v. the Commonwealth* (the *Native Title Act* case).[68] In *Wik*,[69] a determination was sought regarding the status of pastoral leases and whether they, like freehold tenure, evinced—to use the common law formula developed in *Mabo*—a "clear and plain intention"[70] to extinguish native title. Even though the High Court upheld the legality of the pastoral leases, the judgment set off another wave of "*Mabo* madness"[71] because it overturned the Queensland Supreme Court's ruling extinguishing native title, finding instead that native title survived but was subordinated to the pastoral leases. The ruling, of course, stopped far short of recognizing the *coexistence* of native title and the pastoral leases, let alone the priority of native title. Nevertheless, even as cautious a decision as this was enough to rattle the national psyche, raising anxieties bordering on hysteria about dispossession in a land of householders already insecure—both financially and psychically—because of the economic and social dislocations wrought by globalization's relentlessly laissez-faire initiatives.

Following the High Court's judgment in *Wik* late in 1996 and with a national cinema release in 1997, *The Castle* taps into and gives expression to the panic, moral or otherwise, generated by the case. In its story of a family threatened with the loss of its home, the film's narrative reiterates visually the curially sanctioned, Capital-driven "plague of fantasies"[72] haunting suburban Australia for the last decade, shattering its "dreamtime" of quarter-acre lots, Hills-hoisted gardens (washing-lines), and detached bungalows. It does so by driving home the point that there are no tenurial fixities in the new Australia, and that any usufruct they enjoyed yesterday could disappear tomorrow. By suggesting through its plotline this sort of (not so) quiet desperation, *The Castle* shifts the identification of the Kerrigans and the rest of Highview Crescent away from Indigeneity—never a strong connection, given that even Jack, positioned by Daryl as the ur-resident of the district, has lived there for "only three years." No wonder, then, that there are no Aboriginal characters in *The Castle* because, not only aren't they there, as suggested earlier, but more to the point, there is no such thing as Indigeneity in Australia, everyone being an "import" from somewhere else, "squatting" on land that is unencumbered by prior proprietarial interests—though now threatened by malign, even foreign forces. All of which suggests another identification for the Kerrigans, one more consonant with their claims as much as their color: far from being stand-ins for Aboriginality that the film seems to want them to be, Daryl, Sal and their kids come to resemble no group more than those representative figures of the post-*Mabo* "white backlash"—the squattocratic[73] pastoralists of, and mobilized by *Wik*.

Yet nothing would appear to be, at first blush, further apart in class terms than the (sub)urban lumpenproletariat of Highview Crescent and *Wik*'s rural squattocrats—Australia's historic answer, for all its self-proclaimed egalitarianism, to the landed gentry of the Mother Country, though here the "broad acres" of Gloucestershire have been transmuted into the even vaster stations of the Outback. Now more than ever commercially viable because of rich mineral deposits, these huge tracts of leased land often lure corporate interest, thereby rendering the pastoralists anything but "pastoral," especially when intent on strip-mining their bucolic idylls. But whether landed or commercial, the so-called pastoralists duplicate the strategies of self-presentation of their natural class antagonists, the Kerrigans, by portraying themselves, just like the residents of Highview Crescent do in the film, as underdogs battling an inequitable system. For example, throughout the controversies triggered by *Wik*, and before that the *Native Title Act* and *Mabo*, the pastoralists struck a deep populist chord by repeatedly sentimentalizing themselves in the media as modest stakeholders, on the verge of being driven out of their homes and off their land, callously, even viciously—like the Joads of *The Grapes of Wrath*, or for that matter, the Kerrigans of *The Castle*.

Now this sort of mimicry might be dismissed as just that—a sham, with the ruling class wolf slumming in the sheep's clothes of the working man—but for the fact that both the pastoralists and the Kerrigans support their respective claims on eerily analogous grounds: by insisting upon a proprietarial interest, preeminent over and dispositive of any public or collective interest. Consider the pastoralists, who successfully maintained at the federal court that their individual statutory leases extinguished any previous native title claims to land that the Aboriginal people, as a group, argued they enjoyed, according to the 1842 Land Sales Act, by any "Contract, Promise or Engagement" preceding the statute.[74] Daryl himself counters the legalism of the city official's defense of their expropriative, public power with the sharply personal comeback about his own particular lack of privity of contract, "Where's the agreement with Daryl John Kerrigan?" (C, ch. 3). The question arises here: why this shared rhetoric of anticollectivism, cast in terms of countercontractualism? I would like to suggest that it is because both the pastoralists and the Kerrigans are positioned against the rewriting of the nation's social contract as this kind of public novation—whether Airlink-driven or *Mabo*-inspired—puts on notice, if not ousts white Australia from its "castle," be it grand (like the pastoralists of *Wik*) or grunge (the Kerrigans of Highview Crescent).

It is here that *The Castle*'s many frustrating, even maddening inconsistencies—its wavering attitudes toward native title (satirical or serious? critical or celebratory?), its shifting characterizations (Indigenes or pastoralists? heroes or villains?), its uncertain narrative tone (contemptuous or sentimental? feel-good or ironic?)—begin to exhibit a particular logic, a method to the madness, ushering the viewer into the film's ideological core, the traumatic kernel of which is *La Patrie en danger*. Threatened from outside (by the incursions of global Capital, instantiated in Airlink) and from the inside (by the redistributions of native title, allegorized in the expropriation of Highview Crescent), the film portrays Australia as a land divided against itself, split into two nations of haves and have-nots, owners and dispossessed. What, then—or more precisely, *who*—will suture this split and heal the divisions of the country, restoring Australia as One Nation? That is *the* question that the film, as *lex populi*, seems to pose—and answer—raising in its representation of working-class ressentiment the specter of Pauline Hanson's One Nation Party, the loose cannon of federal politics, which in its *Ausländer, raus!* and, especially, antireconciliation stances, threatens a return of the fascist repressed and the worst of the "white Australia" policy.[75] But a working-class hero—or its demonic parody, as the Ipswich fish 'n chip shop owner certainly is—is not the salvific figure *The Castle* vouchsafes. Instead deliverance comes from top down, in the very aristocratic shape of Lawrence Hammill, Q.C., retired Victorian barrister and constitutional law authority who lends his considerable expertise, as well as stately courtroom presence, to the case—and all for gratis, willingly dispensing with payment in order to see justice done. Now there's a real case of filmic wish fulfillment that would make even Capra arch a brow: a lawyer prepared to forego a fee, *pro bono publico*!

All of which plays into a politics of "One Nation" which is more Disraelian Tory than dizzy Queensland because it turns on the fantasy of a benevolent ruling class, acting on behalf of the lower orders—though his noblesse oblige is ultimately intended to restore the status quo, keeping us all in our "proper stations." This scenario that *The Castle* fully realizes in the deus ex machina of Lawrie's improbably timely intervention would be laughable but for the fact that it stages the kind of fantasy which features so prominently in the "politics of nostalgia" of Prime Minister John Howard, the leader of Australia's Conservatives—the misnomered Liberal Party—whose intolerant illiberalism is made all the more transparent by his rhetoric of "mateship." In the run-up to the 2000 referendum on the republic, the crypto-monarchist Howard promoted this expression as an addition to the proposed constitutional preamble, presumably as an inclusive move. But given mateship's bloke-y,[76] cobberish[77] overtones, one that was hardly fair dinkum,[78] it looks more like a code for the new alliance the prime minister was forging in Australian politics: one between the traditional Liberal constituency of the professional-managerial classes and the erstwhile Labor-voting, now disaffected white working class, realigned here and acting in tandem so as to roll back the inroads made by cultural diversity in the new Australia, of which, of course, native title was the most prominent symbol—and most reviled target.

Surely there is no better imaging of the strange bedfellows made by Liberal Party politics than the mateship that develops across class lines between Daryl and Lawrie, who by the film's finish are photographed crawfishing together in that ironic island of serenity, Bonnie Doone, the Kerrigans' holiday home. Moreover, this friendship proves strategic as well as satisfying: it is Lawrie who represents the Kerrigan's son Wayne at his parole board hearing, securing his release from prison and thus enabling a partnership with his father—Kerrigan and Son Towing—which will not only rehabilitate him ("Dad's prouder of him now than he was when he was in prison," says Dale) but also bourgeoisify the family (now with eight tow trucks, and prospects of further expansion—though "Mum reckons eleven" is enough, adds Dale). So the film ends with a vision of consensus politics—or at least the Liberal Party's version of it: with Farouk, Evonne, Jack, and the Petropoulouses as no more than walk-ons at that showcase of what Stanley Fish would call "boutique multiculturalism"[79]—namely, the party scene, where the real foci are the Hammills, *père et fils*, modeling their very middle-class values that the now fiscally and physically fecund Kerrigans all too easily mimic. With the closing snapshot epilogue of Sal and her mugs, Daryl on his new patio contemplating the power lines, and the kids with *their* kids—not just Trace and Con, but Steve and his girlfriend, all with babies—*The Castle* concludes with the Kerrigans firmly, even dynastically in situ, barricaded behind their "castle's" wrought iron gates (C, ch. 14).

Gothic Jurisprudence: The Castle of the Overlord

The last image—of the portcullis, nicked by Daryl and Steve (C, ch. 14)—bespeaks a mentality more of siege than of security and raises all the ambiguities with which the trope of "the castle" resonates. For the symbol of the castle connotes *conquest*, no matter how cozy the film wants this figure of speech to be: like a Norman redoubt, rising above and ruling over Britain's first colonial subjects, the Anglo-Saxons. Except that under common law, a conquered people like the Anglo-Saxons—and later the Welsh, the Irish, and the *Québécois*—*retained* rather than forfeited their prior rights to, and claims over land. Given that legal history, what the analogy of "the castle" conveys when recontextualized as a metaphor for Australia—which is indeed what 3 Highview Crescent, Cooloroo, really is—is that its settlement was in fact what many activists[80] have long claimed: an *invasion*, and as such, the image impliedly acknowledges, given the doctrine of conquest, native title. Thus *The Castle*'s overarching and controlling emblem might suggest a new era for Australia, one of coexistence in which everyone is secure in their castellated retreats, be they Anglo-Celt or Aboriginal. But the problem with this optimistic

(naïve?) reading is that it falsifies the way in which the common law actually operates, treating some properties as less equal than others, subordinating and even
extinguishing particular interests. That these sidelined and suppressed interests
always turn out to be those of native title should come as no surprise because they
never quite fit, in the first place, into the feudal tenurial categories of the common
law's conception of property.[81] So *The Castle*, when read as *lex populi*, might serve
as a warning to those who would put their faith in the common law—with its private, individualizing, and ultimately retrograde imperatives—as a vehicle for the
very public and political issues of social change, and the construction of a better,
fairer world. This is because the imaginary of the common law is fundamentally
"Gothic,"[82] as Les Moran would put it, being organized around and informed by
to this day, as much as in Blackstone's day[83] and earlier, the castle of the overlord
in all his guises: colonizer, patriarch, capitalist. It is in this figure that the common law vests a form of property that will trump all other antecedent and future
interests, however valid, however equitable, however just. And all property—as
Proudhon and the French socialists said a hundred and fifty years ago, and much
as Noel Pearson and the Aboriginal peoples know today—*all property is theft.*[84]

CHAPTER EIGHT

Million Dollar Terri

"The Culture of Life" and the Right to Die

"Now and at the Hour of Our Death":
Lex Populi's Last Rites (or Was That Last Rights?)

Out of the surfeit of images issuing from the American media's overexposed coverage of the medico-legal spectacle of Terry Schiavo, one stands out—or it should, at least for Catholics, either practicing or lapsed. That is: a photograph of the late Ms. Schiavo's distraught parents, the Schindlers. Both of them elderly retirees, Mary and Rob Schindler stand outside one of the many courthouses they had petitioned on behalf of their comatose daughter throughout her postseizure "life": for motions, stays, leaves to appeal, appeals, overrulings, and other legal maneuvers. Looking frail in the Florida twilight, they are accompanied not by their lawyer but by their "spiritual advisor." Now, given the Schindlers' devout Catholicism, this clerical companion should come as no surprise. Unless, of course, one is—as I am—a cradle Catholic reared in the post–Vatican II period and conditioned to expect a certain sacerdotal restraint, if not in matters theological then at least in those of garb. For the spiritual advisor attending the Schindlers, Br. Paul O'Donnell,[1] was avowedly, even ostentatiously Roman Catholic. Not for him the ecumenical "dog collar" of the workaday parish priest, so easily confused with the likes of an Anglican vicar or a Presbyterian minister. Instead, Br. Paul always appeared kitted out in a cassock and sandals, a crucifix hanging from his neck and a rosary belted around his waist. For Br. Paul is a member of an ancient (and distinctively attired) monastic order, the Franciscans; indeed, he is the guardian of their recently established, Minneapolis-based branch, the Brothers of Peace.[2] The Franciscan Brothers of Peace are committed to issues of social justice, largely pertaining to refugees; but with their superior's media splash as the Shindlers' confessor, a shift has occurred in their vocation, reorienting them toward issues organized around what the Vatican has called, particularly under the pontificate of the late John Paul II, the "culture of life."[3]

That culture, sponsored as it is by one of the most tradition-bound institutions on earth, expresses its core value—the sanctity of human life, from conception until natural death—in, astonishingly, one of the most potent and powerful discourses of modernity: namely, rights, and especially the "right to life." That right—that is, for a life protected from artificial termination, either at its beginning (abortion) or its end (euthanasia)—has become the rallying cry in America and elsewhere for a "pro-life" movement, attracting the support of a number of religious denominations: Southern Baptists, Orthodox Jews, High Anglicans, and Evangelicals across the Protestant spectrum. But spearheading the movement, providing its organizational impetus is the one Holy, Apostolic, and Catholic Church; that is, the See of Peter, the Church of Rome. Indeed, for better or worse, the pro-life movement has reenergized the Roman Catholic Church, not only politically but also spiritually, lifting it out of the torpor into which it had sunk subsequent to the stalemate of reform in the late 1960s. Since then, its hierarchy has been riven by the executive stop-go of "renewal" (aggiornamento) and "return" (ressourcement); its clergy beset by sex-abuse scandals; and its loyal congregations—always Catholicism's strength compared to the empty-pew syndrome of mainline Protestantism[4]—if not voting with their feet, then turning a deaf ear to the pulpit, or at least listening selectively ("cafeteria Catholicism"). This picture of decline, Freud's inevitable "future of an illusion,"[5] is overshadowed by the snapshot of the Schindlers with Br. Paul, in full Franciscan regalia; because in a single Kodak moment that shot captures one of the great comebacks of our postsecular era: the return of the Church militant.

Yet the success of that return (of the religious repressed?) and its attendant (symptomatic?) pro-life campaign is difficult to gauge. This is because, even in historically Catholic jurisdictions—like the Canadian province of Quebec, for example: until a generation ago *plus Catholique que le Pape*—rights to die have been asserted successfully in local courts, even promoted as ripe for entrenchment in constitutional reform.[6] So *if* it is to carry the day in the court of conscience as much as law, the Catholic *counter*reformation in matters of "life" most definitely has its work cut out for it. Not only in the Catholic fold in Quebec (and Belgium, France, and elsewhere), but also in other societies that are more evenly divided along sectarian lines (Australia, The Netherlands, Switzerland), or different in national confession altogether (the United Kingdom, Scandinavia). For the "right to life" is one of the most contested moral, legal, and medical issues in the global public sphere, impinging upon and unsettling its ethico-political imaginary, and reshaping its very notion of the symbolic Law. Given this situation, is it any wonder that the global mediations of *lex populi* have recently provided yet another forum, another venue for airing debate over "life" and its termination, both pro and con? Nowhere is the cultural legal contribution to this debate staged more vividly than in 2005's two "Best Picture" Oscar winners—one domestic, the other foreign, and *both* directly concerned with termination.

I refer first, of course, to Clint Eastwood's *Million Dollar Baby*,[7] adapted from the late F. X. Toole's collection of boxing stories, *Rope Burns*,[8] and starring Hilary Swank as the severely injured and incapacitated female boxer Maggie Fitzgerald, who wants nothing more than to die—with the assistance of her manager, "cut" man, Frankie (played by Eastwood himself). Second, I refer to Alejandro Amenábar's *The Sea Inside*[9] (*Mar adentro*), starring Javier Bardem and recounting the life story of Spanish quadriplegic and "death with dignity" activist Ramon Sampedro, right up to and including his videotaped assisted suicide in 1998, the televised broadcast of which electrified Spain. In each of these filmic representations of the right to die, the bias of the directors is clearly on the side of termination. Despite or perhaps because of this bias, both movies nonetheless give if not equal then *some* time to the "culture of life," allowing it to state its case: in the characterological form of—what else?—two Catholic priests. One of these priests is fictional, the other factual; but neither is sentimentalized, like the religious often are cinematically, in any kind of glib *Sister Act*[10] or saccharine *The Sound of Music*[11] way. Both are taken very seriously indeed, as are their theological positions. Thus for the *lex populi* of the millennium—as much as that of the last century (think of Hitchcock, Chesterton, and Conan Doyle, Catholics every one of them)—all spiritual roads still lead to Rome, a *Via Appia* along which, incidentally, another strange pilgrim can be found making his way. That lone figure would be no less a transnational legal theorist of rights than Ronald Dworkin, now a *converso* to the cause of the "sanctity of life." For Dworkin's penultimate book, *Life's Dominion: An Argument About Abortion, Euthanasia, and Individual Freedom*,[12] is at once an endorsement of and a departure from both the "culture of life" and the right to die, in terms that could very easily have underwritten the scripts of this chapter's filmic instances of *lex populi*.

So here, at the book's last substantive chapter, I want to terminate on the topic of termination—not of the beginning of life but of the end of life—call it what you may: voluntary, nonvoluntary, or involuntary euthanasia; assisted suicide; mercy killing; or murder most foul. I propose to cut my way through this semantic knot, disentangling its web of arguments—its pro-and-con binaries of freedom and faith, choice and submission, autonomy and connection—by close readings of *lex populi*'s screen representations of termination. I will compare and contrast in the next two sections the interesting inversion of theological, legal, and political positions that these two films construct and ultimately *deconstruct*. I want to extend, passim, this deconstructive operation, situating both films within the context of Dworkin's jurisprudence principally because they both instantiate and interrogate it, articulating a cultural legal critique of *Life's Dominion* and its valiant (though doomed?) efforts to reconcile the irreconcilable, that is, combining sacrality and autonomy, religious faith and *recht*. Finally, I want to return in the final section of this chapter to the "primal scene of trauma": that of Terri Schiavo's hospice bedroom in Largo, Florida. There, to look once again upon her unnervingly empty smile, to return her reflexively flickering gaze, all the while asking how *lex populi* might help us understand, even read the signs of life and death in Terri's brain-damaged and immobilized body, now the "sublime object of (legal) ideology."

"Forgive Me Father, for I Have Sinned": Screening Anti-Clericalism, Left and Right

That two of 2005's global cinema runaway hits—both commercial and critical successes—should thematize termination is a striking instance, even if coincidental, of synchronicity. That these same two films, separated by physical distance as much as linguistic and cultural differences, should feature Catholic priests in key roles is no coincidence, however, given the worldwide sweep of the *katholikos*, and especially the leading role the Church has assumed in this debate. "The Roman Catholic Church," acknowledges Ronald Dworkin in *Life's Dominion* with the kind of grudging respect one accords a formidable opponent, "is the sternest, most vigilant, and no doubt most effective opponent of euthanasia" (LD, p. 195). This primacy can be largely attributed to the extraordinary theological efforts of the late Petrine Primate, John Paul II. I say "extraordinary" because, for the most part, this preeminently postmodern pope was as short on theology as he was long on media savvy, charisma, and the common touch. While his pontificate witnessed a renewal of popular piety, particularly in the welcomed revival of many traditional Catholic practices fallen into desuetude—pilgrimage, Marian devotion, canonization—little *positive* theological headway was made under John Paul, the prevailing tone of the Vatican being an emphatic "No!"—to liberation theology (the Latin Americans, Fr. Gustavo Gutiérrez, Fr. Leonardo Boff, and most famously, the publicly scolded Nicaraguan Sandinista, Fr. Ernesto Cardenal); to inculturation (principally, Sri Lankan Fr. Tissa Balasuriya and his Buddhist-inspired makeover of Mary); and to critique (that modern-day Erasmus, Swiss born and Tubingen based, Fr. Hans Küng).

Yet this "negative theology" has a very notable phraseological exception that seems destined to outlive John Paul's papacy, in the powerful and potent phrase, "culture of life." For better or worse, this phrase may become its greatest legacy to global public discourse, not only theological but political—especially the political rhetoric of an unlikely disciple, Protestant Evangelical President George "Dubya" Bush. This expression—or something very much like it—was first used by the Pope on a visit to (where else?) the United States in 1993. While attending the Eighth World Youth Day in Denver, he decried the "culture of death," threatening, inter alia, the unborn, the handicapped, and the sick.[13] Culpable here, and executing its death sentences, is a "rights" discourse that, "without any reference to objective truth,"[14] endorses abortion and euthanasia. Instead of these rights-cloaked "works of darkness,"[15] the Pope urged the assembled to walk in the "path of life,"[16] affirming its "sacred character." But by 1995's encyclical, *Evangelium Vitae*,[17] that sacrality was couched squarely within the language of rights. There, the "first of the fundamental rights,"[18] trumping all others and exposing putative abortion and euthanasia rights as "perverse,"[19] even "evil,"[20] is none other than the right to life itself. In light of the Pope's prior critique, his embrace of rights here is an interesting, to say the least, development—a clever political about-face because it beats the "liberal" pro-choice lobby at their own game, using their very language—rights—against them. In so doing, John Paul installed the Christian Right instead of the critical left as the champions of "positive" liberty, a radical reorientation that continued apace when, upon a return visit to the United States in 1998, the Holy Father congratulated the pro-life movement as "one of the most positive aspects of American public life."[21] Although involved at the time in aggressive nationwide campaigns of intimidation, harassment, and in some cases, open attack on abortion clinics and their staff, pro-lifers were encouraged by the Pontiff to "defend life" and its "inalienable right."[22]

No wonder that Fr. Horvak—Frankie's parish priest in *Million Dollar Baby*—is so implacable, so emphatic when Frankie, still reeling from Maggie's heavily coded request for termination ("'member Axel" is all she says, alluding to an earlier conversation about an infirm family pet euthanized years before by her hillbilly dad; MDB, ch. 16), seeks him out for his counsel. Given the film's context, would one expect anything from him other than a resolute interdiction (an all-out ban?). For not only is God on Fr. Horvak's side, but the deity also now speaks—as the Pope's various *pronunciamenti* make clear—the same language as Horvak's polity: that is, the "rights talk" of its "secular scripture," the U.S. Constitution. So Fr. Horvak's zeal is emboldened twice over, a doubling occasioned by the temporal as much as the spiritual, because in the America of the millennium—of "just wars," of "crusades" against terror, of "raptures" of final reckoning—they are one and the same thing, the "right to life" infusing the life of rights. Far from being some cinematic throwback, a ludicrous echo of those Hollywood priests of the 1940s and 1950s (Bing Crosby? Spencer Tracey? Paddy Fitzgerald?), Fr. Horvak is thus very much a man of the theocratic moment, nowhere more so than when his injunction swells to a rhetorical pitch that is John-Pauline in its metaphorics of the soul's path, of spiritual *fort-da*: "If you do this thing," he cautions, "you'll be lost somewhere so deep, you'll never find yourself" (MDB, ch. 17).

This clerical warning is reiterated in *The Sea Inside* when the character of Fr. Francisco appears on the scene, ready and all-too-willing to preach the "culture of life" to Ramon. The exchange between the two, a highlight of the film and a main focus of its central "life vs. death" agon, is based, with some artistic license, on a true encounter in Ramon Sampedro's life. For Fr. Francisco is modeled upon, unlike the fictional Fr. Horvak, an identifiably real person: namely, the quadriplegic priest, Fr. Luis de Moya, a well-known activist on behalf of the differently abled and a powerful media spokesman in Spain for the "culture of life." De Moya's celebrity status is acknowledged in *The Sea Inside*, with Fr. Francisco popping up first as an interviewee on a news clip (the film within the film?), screened on Ramon's television, where he beseeches the Sampedros—and Ramon especially—for a chance to spread his message of "love." That love turns out to be the toughest of "tough love," because when he arrives in Galicia at the Sampedro farmhouse, Fr. Francisco does anything but mince the words of his loving message, calling a spade a spade ("Why don't you stop with the euphemisms and tell it like it is, as blunt as it may sound, "I'm gonna end my life," and be done with it?"), all the while putting his case for life forward, à la John Paul, on the very grounds that liberals would do so in favor of assisted suicide: namely, "freedom." "A freedom that ends life," he insists in response to Ramon's autonomic claims for freedom to choose, "is no freedom at all" (SI, ch. 9).

So here we have, in these films, two Catholic priests, identical in their John Paul*esque* ventriloquism as much as in their priestly vocation. Admittedly, they are depicted in very different characterological terms: one North American, and the other European; one young and able-bodied, and the other elderly and differently abled; one an ethnic, working-class parish priest, and the other a theologian of the Establishment. But they both speak the *same language*—despite the English of one and the Spanish of the other—articulating, at the level of deep structure, the "culture of life" in terms reminiscent of, if not directly referencing the Pope's tropes as much as text. Given the disparate contexts of each of these films, one might expect that these filtered, though still recognizably papal ukases might have very dissimilar auditory effects on addressees, either within their respective diegetic frames (that is, the characters in their narrative), or outside of it (in their audiences). For example, one might assume that in a film as thoroughly American as *Million Dollar Baby*—originating, as it does, from the land of constitutionally entrenched disestablishmentarianism—Fr. Horvak's prohibition would fall on deaf ears, a "wall of separation" springing up between him, Frankie, and the audience, much like that curially celebrated Jeffersonian one between Church and State.[23] Whereas in a film like *The Sea Inside* that makes so much of its Spanish regional location, one might well imagine its characters—and local audiences—situated as they are in the land of Loyola, to be all ears when the Jesuit Fr. Francisco speaks, even if only from a wheelchair, ex cathedra.

Nothing, of course, could be further from the filmic truth. For, if anything, *The Sea Inside* is militantly anticlerical; Ramon attacking the Church in the grand old tradition of the European Left. He targets its wealth; when Fr. Francisco, for example, reprimands Ramon that his body belongs to God and is not the object of private property, his reply is: "But the Church was always the first to secularize private property, man." He references, predictably, the Church's intolerance, all too evident in Spain's sorry history of "burning heretics." Finally, he chides its hypocrisy, apparent to this day in the Spanish Church's acceptance "of nothing else than the death penalty" at the very moment it evangelizes on behalf of "life" (SI, ch. 9). All of which makes the Protestant imaginary's polemics against the "Scarlet Woman"—and for that matter, the Spain of the Inquisition, of the autoda-fé—seem tame by comparison (SI, ch. 9). For Ramon's anti-Romanism owes its critical edge to the Enlightenment's secularism, and its Voltairean rallying cry of *écrasez l'infâme*, rather than the Reformers and their call to "salvation by faith alone." Indeed, faith itself—Catholic, Calvinist, New Age, whatever—is under attack in *The Sea Inside*, withering under the glare of Ramon's skeptical gaze. Even when his willing accomplice, Rosa, the young factory worker and single mother, asks him for a "sign" from beyond the grave (SI, ch. 15), signaling if there is an afterlife, Ramon's reply is customarily clear-eyed: "Between you and I, I think that after we're dead, there isn't anything" (SI, ch. 15). He admits that his "feeling" is only a "hunch," of which he is not entirely "sure" (SI, ch. 15); but certainly he does nothing here to humor Rosa in any maudlin supernaturalism (think how Spielberg would have played this scene!), maintaining that his "hunch" is grounded in common sense, like a sailor predicting the following day's weather, on the basis of the skies ("Red sky at night, sailor's delight").

Thus a strong rationalist project prevails in *The Sea Inside*. The film demystifies contemporary (Rosa) as well as clerical obscurantism (Fr. Francisco). Rosa's "spirituality" is treated gingerly, however, if not sidestepped altogether, with a very secular promise of an afterlife visitation, in nothing less than the unconscious: "I'm going to be," says a thankful Ramon, "in your dreams" (SI, ch. 15). No such respite is afforded Fr. Francisco, against whom the film's satire takes on a bitterly, even cruelly physical edge. For much is made of the priest's wheelchair-bound girth and the futile heave-hoing by Javi, Jose, et al. that confines him to the first floor of the Sampedro farmhouse, necessitating the dispatch of the hapless Fr. Andre—a sort of Sancho Panza–like sidekick—as a luckless intermediary between himself and the bedridden Ramon upstairs. I invoke Sancho Panza because this literary analogue identifies not only Fr. Andre but also Fr. Francisco as a Cervantes character, revealed now as a kind of disabled Don Quixote, on the same sort of "quixotic" fool's mission, "tilting at windmills" in his belief that Ramon can be talked out of his determination to die. But in this case, the deluded "Knight of the Sad Countenance," Fr. Francisco, gets his comeuppance from Dulcinea in the form of Manuela, Ramon's devoted sister-in-law and Spanish Everywoman. She says, quite bluntly—as I'm sure many Catholic women have longed to say to their opinionated parish priests (with their patriarchal homilies about contraception, marriage, child rearing, and other rites): "You have a very big mouth" (SI, ch. 9).

Interestingly, a much gentler kind of humor is directed at *Million Dollar Baby*'s Fr. Horvak. In its Python*esque* (à la *Life of Brian*) blending of the sacred and the profane, his exasperated response to Frankie after Mass one Sunday at St. Mark's,

"There are no demigods, you fuckin' pagan!" (MDB, ch. 1), is the funniest moment in a film seriously short of laughs. But the object of ridicule here is, unlike *The Sea Inside*, most definitely *not* the priest—or for that matter, the Church. Indeed, the audience may even identify with them, sharing Fr. Horvak's frustration with Frankie's theological nit-picking, a pointless scholastic exercise of the "angels dancing on the head of the pin" variety. This sort of needling—to indulge in a bad pun—is all too familiar to any ex-parochial schoolchild because it is precisely the kind of cynicism that characterizes the clever Catholic adolescent, interrogating every and all *doxa* (the nature of the Trinity, the doctrine of the Immaculate Conception, the Real Presence at the Mass), pushing them to their (il)logical conclusions. Ultimately, this sort of underdeveloped disbelief—to which Frankie gives vent—unlike Ramon's fully matured, more sustained critique, is no real threat to or concern of the Church, being instead the mark of the "true believer," the "holy Joe" tricked out, temporarily, as the "village atheist." This is precisely the dual role Frankie—being a conservative, even phantasmatic Irish American (reading Yeats, learning Gaelic)—plays here: his "doubting Thomas" performance but a mere way station to sincere and simple credence. For as any Catholic teacher worth his or her Baltimore catechism knows, you must question first in order to have faith.

These two discrepant comic registers, and the opposing ends of the politico-theological spectrum they represent—one satirically critical and coming from the Left (Ramon); the other amusingly conciliatory and coming from the Right (Frankie)—are significant, indeed crucial to my argument. This is because, as I shall argue in the next section, they point to the very different bases—theologically, politically, but especially jurisprudentially—upon which termination is grounded in these two films, even when the outcome is the same. For I want to stress here, before moving onto those differences, that the outcome *is* the same in each film. Both *The Sea Inside* and *Million Dollar Baby* end with "death and transfiguration": that is, either in the assisted suicide (Ramon) or the mercy killing (Maggie) of their respective protagonists. Sampedro, of course, (in)famously enlisted twelve friends (apostles?) to orchestrate and organize his poisoning, each with an assigned task: one to pour the poison into a glass, another to insert a straw, yet another to position it within the tilt of Ramon's head, and so on. This division of labor confounded the legal determination of any kind of causal link—who, after all, committed the *actus reus*?—thereby thwarting criminal proceedings by the state. Of which, incidentally there have been none, the Spanish authorities remaining reluctant to prosecute, even when one person—Romona Maneiro, a possible model for

Rosa—has come forward, claiming involvement as one of the twelve. No such admission of participation, however, is made in *Million Dollar Baby*, Frankie having realized Fr. Horvak's worst fears by becoming, after removing Maggie's respirator and injecting her with a lethal overdose of adrenalin, so "lost" that he is neither seen nor heard from again. Indeed, the narrative voice heard throughout the film is not even his to begin with, but that of his former fighter, janitorial assistant and friend, Eddy "Scrap-Iron" Dupris (played to his usual standard of perfection by Morgan Freeman). We, the audience, merely overhear Scrap-Iron's interior monologue, recounting this story, in a final effort to redeem his ex-trainer's tarnished reputation (and past sins?), as the last scenes of the film reveal in a letter to Frankie's long-estranged daughter, Katie (MDB, ch. 19).

"I Once Was Lost But Now Am Found": The Amazing Grace of Assisted Suicide

Or is Frankie so lost? The closing shots of the film, intercut as they are between L.A. and Missouri, suggest otherwise, implying that Frankie is more found than lost. And found at some place more believably prosaic than his previous poetic dream of escape, a "Celtic Twilight" cottage inspired by Yeats' celebrated poem, "Innisfree." Rather, his refuge here is a truck-stop diner, somewhere near the trailer park "bend in the road" that Maggie called home (MDB, ch. 19). Less whimsical than Yeats, assuredly, but doubtless better provisioned in Frankie's dessert of choice, lemon meringue pie (the meringue "homemade" in the best tradition of "white trash" cookery; MDB, ch. 11). That refuge, the viewer imagines, is as much spiritual as it is physical for Frankie, providing him with a hideaway from the police (notably absent in what is, after all, a "C.S.I." story), as well as a home where he can find, at long last, some inner peace, having redeemed himself through Maggie's death. Scrap-Iron confirms this when he writes in his letter to Katie, approvingly, indeed quietly proud of what Frankie has done: "I thought you should know what kind of man your father really was" (MDB, ch. 19). My question here is: How can this be? That is: How can a practicing Catholic like Frankie—not only Mass-going, but nightly prayer–saying (MDB, ch. 1)—be more at ease *now* than at any other time in the film proper, when after all is said and done he has premeditatedly *killed* somebody, albeit anything but cold-bloodedly? How can killing amount to, even be considered some kind of act of contrition, absolving anyone of whatever unnamed sins he or she has committed: sins so seriously "mortal" that they drive Frankie to Church every day of the week (a compulsive obsessiveness even Fr. Horvak comments on; MDB, ch. 17), and which are hinted at (sexual abuse?) in the piles of his returned, unopened letters from a long-absent Katie (MDB, ch. 16). How can grace—indeed, *amazing* grace if ever there was an instance of it—abound here, owing to the murder and mayhem of the plot?

Of course, Maggie's death is depicted as a blessed *release*, rescuing her from something far worse: a death-in-life, as her paralyzed and contracting body (think of her leg, amputated at the knee owing to ulcers) atrophies her desire, excising what Ronald Dworkin would call her "critical interests" (LD, pp. 211–23); that is, those things that make a person uniquely *that person*. In Maggie's case, her memories of triumph in the ring, of which she says, "People chanted my name" and "I was in magazines," adding, desperately, "Don't let them keep taking it away from me" (MDB, ch. 16). Usurping, in fact blotting out those memories of past gains is a future of loss: life as a breathless, limbless torso, oxygenated only because of a respirator, ambulatory merely because of a motorized wheelchair. So one might say that Frankie makes a classic Calabresi-style "tragic choice"[24]; he weighs the pleasures and the pains of Maggie's situation, opting for termination (rather than college as a differently abled student?) as the lesser of two evils. Only that such a "utility calculus,"[25] however benign, ignores the film's depiction of Frankie's act as *ethical* rather than as efficient. For *Million Dollar Baby* is quite clear, a point that I want to emphasize: the film portrays Frankie's act as intensely ethical, indeed a response to what Levinas,[26] Douzinas,[27] Minson,[28] et al. would nominate as the supreme ethical demand, the "call of the Other."

That call, however, is difficult to decipher, complicated by the fact that, like the Levinasian "Other," it is indeterminate, a matter of supposition, of inference. "*Che vuoi?*"—or "what do you want of me?" Frankie impliedly inquires. "Kill me" is precisely what Maggie does *not* answer. She may imply it by way of anecdote (mentioning Axel; MDB, ch. 16), suggest it by veiled entreaties (about preserving her memories; MDB, ch. 16), even attempt it by crude, self-mutilating methods herself (biting her tongue in the hopes of bleeding to death; MDB, ch. 17); but Maggie never comes out and says it, let alone suggest that there is any sort of *right* to die. Nor, interestingly, does anyone else in the film mention rights—or for that matter, the law, it appearing only in the venal form of the attorney for Maggie's rapacious, hillbilly family (MDB, ch. 15). That extremely negative representation is very telling, suggesting that not only is the law compromised here, but that rights themselves are, at worst, inimical to Maggie; at best, irrelevant, even moot. For the film, in making so much of the severity of Maggie's condition—all intravenous tubing, bed pulleys, and screen monitors—drives home the incapacitation of her autonomy, the core value behind rights. Thus what *Million Dollar Baby* depicts is the limit of rights discourse, a limit reached in its story of a young woman too disabled to exercise any autonomic right to terminate. For Maggie doesn't just *desire* a good death, like some bedridden Antigone; she *needs* an(O)ther to assist and abet that desire's realization if indeed she is to die with dignity. Which is why the filmic center of attention—its real protagonist—is Frankie, not Maggie; and further, why rights are so conspicuous by their absence in the plot, because the real jurisprudential basis of *lex populi* here is duty.

Duty, rather than right, is the ground upon which Frankie acts here: a duty that initially offends his personal morality. "Don't even think about that," is his horrified response to Maggie's first, coded plea for help (MDB, ch. 16). This is precisely how the "ethics of the Good" operates, its call to duty usually entailing some conflict with a deeply held conviction that the respondent must rise above, subordinating the self's beliefs, even sacrificing them for a better, more exalted purpose, here a quasi-divine *caritas*. For in killing Maggie, Frankie performs, so the film suggests, the ultimate act of love for his *"mo cuishla,"* his "darling" (MDB, chs. 10, 19). To do otherwise—that is, not to kill Maggie—is portrayed as one of the most "selfish" of acts, her life protracted to satisfy his egotistical needs. "I just want to keep her with me" (MDB, ch. 17), confesses a distraught Frankie to Fr. Horvak, but "by keeping her alive, I know I'm killing her" (MDB, ch. 17). Now, this confession raises an interesting theological wrinkle, for if keeping Maggie alive *kills* her, then, a fortiori, killing Maggie may be the very means of allowing her to *live again*. This is a startling suggestion, especially in light of the religious opposition to euthanasia, because it effectively "Christianizes" mercy killing as not just a *release from* something (pain or paralysis), but also as a *delivery to* somewhere else, a higher state, perhaps an afterlife in which one's name, accomplishments, memories—that is, "critical interests"—live on, forever immortal. So euthanasia, far from animalizing human life—reducing it the level of the Fitzgeralds' Axel, "put down" because his hind legs had given out—in fact, *supports* what Ronald Dworkin calls, in *Life's Dominion*, its "sacrality," its "inviolability" (LD, pp. 73, 81–84, 117, 237–38).

This is—or so it seems—a clever ploy on the part of Dworkin and, indeed, the makers of *Million Dollar Baby*. Because it bests the sectarians on their own spiritual ground, inverting the theopolitical and legal maneuvers of the Catholic Church and its leadership of a "popular front" of conservative Christian denominations (from the Assemblies of God to the Zion Baptists, and all the letters in between). For if the churches have colonized secularism's privileged discourse—rights—trumping the "right to die" with its logical corollary and binary opposite, the "right to live," then the pro-choice lobby (to which Dworkin and, one imagines, Eastwood belong), hitherto secular, will shift the debate back to its theological roots, arguing on behalf of a higher duty to terminate as not only consistent with, but stemming from a sacred, inviolable respect for life. However appealing this strategy may be—and is there anything more satisfying than beating an enemy at their own game?—it must be resisted, its appeal quickly becoming abhorrent. "Abhorrent" because this tactic threatens to transform termination into something much more menacing than what it purports to outmaneuver; something darker, even fiendish. Dworkin himself lays the groundwork for this sort of demonization when he begins to talk in Manichean terms about termination—initially, in the context of environmentalism (LD, pp. 75, 79) but, later, in terms of abortion (LD, pp. 84–89, 217)—as a universal affront, a source of "cosmic shame" (LD, p. 75). This "cosmic shame" is a diabolizing move, exceeding any of the Christian Right's rhetoric of guilt: now, women who elect to terminate have the cosmos, as well as their partners, parents, and own misgivings to worry about! In *Million Dollar Baby*, this shame, as well as guilt over termination takes a psychological turn. By uncoupling it from rights, from *recht*—the Law—and by (re)grounding it in a duty spoken singly to Frankie, *and from a higher power* (God? the categorical imperative? the Son of Sam?), the film "psychotizes" termination.

Or at least comes close to it. Think how easily, with a tweak here and a twist there, the film's plot could be transformed from an act of supreme goodness into one of "radical evil." Consider the narrative's facts: a man surreptitiously enters a hospital and, with FDA-restricted pharmaceuticals, kills a defenseless and seriously infirm young woman, claiming that he acted in her best interests, even at her behest. That could just as well be a story line for a "serial killer" murder mystery, penned by Val McDermid,[29] Thomas Harris,[30] or Christopher Nyst[31]—or for that matter, a newspaper feature on one of the many "angels of death" recently in the global news: the notorious Dr. Shipman in the United Kingdom,[32] his elderly victims numbering in the hundreds; the less ambitious but no less deadly Dr. Patel in Outback Queensland, now sought by Interpol as well as the Australian authorities for killing one, and permanently injuring several, of his rural patients during largely unnecessary, grandstanding, and incompetently performed surgery.[33] In this international rogue's gallery of medical infamy, Frankie bears the distinct (dis)honor of being the only red-blooded "American Psycho"[34] because not only does he hear an inner voice telling him to kill Maggie, he acts and is entirely alone.

That loneliness, in fact, is Frankie's defining feature. After all, he is long alienated from his daughter, and he has no friends—aside from one (Scrap Iron), for whose partial blindness he blames himself, and one other (Maggie), whom he kills (which might prompt one to think, with a friend like Frankie, who needs . . .). Frankie is thus very much a figure without connection, detached from the contextual ties that bind. In short, he is the autonomous agent of this story. This autonomy—and the singular acts it sustains here, like the killing of Maggie—might be said to be the distinctively American virtue, the national trait. It is as celebrated in America's public mythos (the dissenting Puritan following his individual conscience, the sturdy pioneer taming the frontier on his own) as in its *lex populi* (the "Man with No Name" gunslinger of the old West, the maverick cop who bucks the system—both, incidentally, Eastwood specialities) and stands at the very center of the U.S. Constitution in that curious curial invention, the "right to privacy,"[35] or as it has been described, "the right to be left alone."[36] This privacy right and its underlying value—autonomy or aloneness—is also the principal legal basis in any number of American termination cases (*Cruzan*[37] and *Glucksburg*,[38] for example), justifying the decision to turn off someone's "life support": that is, in denying the terminally ill or "the vegetative" (*sic*) their food, water, blood, even air, hospital and hospice staff consistently have been found by courts to have been securing, indeed safeguarding their patients' "autonomy," leaving them, in the most literal way possible, legally, rightfully alone.

Of course, that autonomy is very much presumed here, a legal fiction of the most mendacious kind, steadfastly maintained (a kind of "noble lie"?)[39] in the face of the overwhelming facts that a terminal (let alone vegetative) patient is anything but alone, and is heavily dependent upon a network of aid and assistance, human and mechanical, as well as medical, emotional, and spiritual. *Million Dollar Baby* both sustains and subverts termination's legal fiction of autonomy—or the right to be left alone. It sustains this autonomic fiction by disconnecting Maggie from "the social," driving home, in the most *unheimlich* of ways, just how homeless she is in the grotesque "trailer trash" caricature of her family. Dole bludgers / lazy bums, tatted bikies, slatternly single mums—the Fitzgeralds are, certainly, not of the stuff that makes living worthwhile. Who in their right mind wouldn't want to be free of them? No wonder Maggie says to Frankie, earlier in the film, "I got nobody but you Frankie" (MDB, ch. 11). And that, to adopt the Fitzgerald patois, ain't much. For here the film subverts termination's fiction of autonomy by rendering Frankie, her unofficial guardian *ad litem*, just as pathetically lonely as Maggie, thereby exposing the potential pathology in any sort of life-and-death decision he may make for her. For such a decision would issue from a similar state of sorry solitude, a life of not-so-quiet desperation, vulnerable, even susceptible in its seclusion to the delusions of an "inner voice," a "higher power," imposing a *duty* to kill on one (Frankie) and investing a *right* to be killed in another (Maggie). So that "ol' time religion," Roman as much as Revivalist—of duty, of the good, of the sanctity of life—is not the only subject of critique here; for liberal legalism is revealed, by implication, as equally hallucinatory, even psychotic, its rights "misrecognizing" the lonely despair of sickness as the desire for death, its controlling value of autonomy mistaking an isolated, dependent reliance for an independent resolve. Behind all of which may lurk—in the form of duty—a singular, murderous *jouissance* "killing" in the "Name of the Other," as Stephen Burton might put it; that is, in the name of a deranged and deranging "Law."[40]

It is this crazy Law and its funhouse Imaginary, all distorting mirrors, as refracting as they are reflecting, that *The Sea Inside* sidesteps. That may seem, initially, to be a curious interpretive claim. For if anything, *The Sea Inside* is a very lawful(l) film; that is, it is saturated with appeals to *recht*, to rights. The protagonist, after all, demands his termination in terms of his autonomic "choice," "decision," "freedom"; arguing, much as Ronald Dworkin would, that they are implicit in the public law of any jurisdiction that takes rights seriously. "Any genuine constitution of principle will guarantee that right" (LD, p. 239), proclaims Dworkin in *Life's Dominion*—but it could just as easily be Marc, arguing before the court for Ramon's "right" to dignity, which, on the analogy of the right to be free from torture, includes the right not to be "degraded by his condition." This legalism extends as much to the film's dramatis personae as to its scripted dialogue. Most of *The Sea Inside*'s characters—outside, of course, the Sampedro family circle—are lawyers (Marc, Julia) or rights activists (Gené). Finally, the film's scenic focus, at least when it leaves the Sampedro homestead, shuttles back and forth between legal venues, from barristerial chambers in faraway Barcelona to the federal courthouse in Galicia's La Coruna.

Now this sort of sociolegal detail is appropriate given that, if Amenábar had been so inclined, *The Sea Inside* easily could have been turned into a courtroom drama of the most vérité kind. After all, actions to legally terminate Ramon's life were launched by him or on his behalf (by his sister-in-law, Manuela Sanles) right up until and even after his death in, for example, the Court of First Instance in Noia, the Provincial High Court in La Coruna, the Constitutional Court in Madrid, and the European Union Human Rights Commission in Strasbourg.[41] All of which, incidentally, were dismissed, some on very technical, even de minimis grounds—doubtless a source of enormous frustration to the Sampedro camp. *The Sea Inside* gives vent to that frustration in Gené's exasperated cry, "As if justice were so speedy in this country" (SI, ch. 7). In Spain—and elsewhere; for example, in the case of the United Kingdom's Diane Pretty[42] or that of the Australian Northern Territory's terminally ill,[43] justice was thwarted or never arrived, the European Court of Human Rights rejecting Pretty's appeal and the Australian Commonwealth Parliament rendering inoperative—effectively repealing—the territory's *Rights of the Terminally Ill Act 1995* (NT).[44] Like the applicants in these instances, worn out by the wait for their suicides' judicial and/or legislative imprimatur, Ramon Sampedro took his own life in the hiatus between the dismissal of his action in La Coruna, and his petition for *amparo*—that is, judicial consideration—by the Constitutional Court of a possible infringement of his rights.[45] In so doing, Sampedro sent a clear message to Spain's courts; he was giving up on the law.

This is why *The Sea Inside*, despite its constant referencing of rights, is so deeply cynical about the law, articulating what jurisprudes would recognize as a "critical legal reading." For the law, and its curial processes, are portrayed in the film as excessively and emptily procedural, a pettifoggery used not only to silence Sampedro (think how he is refused any opportunity to address the court) but also to sideline the substantive issue, the right to die. By allowing procedure to trump substance here, the courts themselves are involved in a "politics of the law" in that they are forestalling a political crisis; that is, a constitutional imbroglio involving State, Church, and other public stakeholders. No wonder, then, that the "villain of the piece" in this cinematic critique of the courts is not really Fr. Francisco, not even José, Ramon's disapproving and devoutly Catholic brother, but *the lawyer*: the lovely and fragile Julia, Ramon's principal legal counsel and herself suffering from a degenerative condition that inevitably will paralyze her motor skills and incapacitate her cognitive processes. Despite this condition, and the considerable empathy she has for—as well as professional commitment to—Ramon, Julia does the unforgivable. She gives Ramon hope, securing his trust, reliance, and expectation, *only to betray it*—thereby repeating, on a personal and private level, what the law does publicly to Ramon by holding out a substantive promise (in the form of rights) that it subsequently withdraws on procedural grounds (jurisdiction, or any number of other technicalities).

For Julia, like the courts, both makes and breaks a promise to Ramon, pledging to assist him upon the publication of *Letters from Hell*, the collection of his verse that she was instrumental in bringing to press—before committing suicide herself. But when the copy of the first edition arrives at the Sampedros' and Julia fails to show up—having been talked out of suicide (by her husband?) (SI, ch. 12)—the despair in Ramon's voice as much as his face is palpable, his plaintive cry to Manuela, the most wrenching line in the film, "Why do I want to die? Why can't I make do with this life?" (SI, ch. 16). This moment, as affecting as it is, is not a patch, for sheer chilling horror, on the fate that awaits the hapless Julia. The film returns to her at its close, when the kindly Gené, her husband Marc, and their child in tow visit Julia at her seaside home; now she is not only confined to a wheelchair but also so befuddled—a prelude, doubtless, to a Terri Schiavo–like vegetative state—that she is unable to recall her former client and friend, Ramon (SI, ch. 16). Such is one's fate, so the film suggests, under the letter of the Law, ultimately rendering one neither living nor dead but, as Lacan might put it, *entre-deux-morts*[46]—or one of the "living dead."

So, in the end, *The Sea Inside* turns to another law, one that goes beyond its letter to its spirit. That "spirit" is summoned up, and materialized by a communal process—like a house party assembled round a Ouija board—that shows the audience how much *more* is involved in the right to die than individual choice or autonomic "freedom." In so doing, *The Sea Inside* offers a cinematic riposte to liberal legalism and its valorization of autonomy: a riposte aimed not just at its American *lex populi* equivalent, *Million Dollar Baby*, but impliedly, at the jurisprudence of Ronald Dworkin, especially when he writes in *Life's Dominion*: "Decisions about life and death are the most important [and] crucial to make them in character and for ourselves" (LD, 239). *The Sea Inside*, in contrast, makes the opposite point: that is, such decisions are anything *but* those of one person. For Ramon's is not the only decision in the film; Rosa's decision is just as, if not more important, constituting as it does the last of the twelve and thereby closing the circle of neighborly love that will fulfill Ramon's desire. So the filmic message is clear here: Ramon's very singular desire to die needs not just another, but others—that is, a *socius* upon which it depends for its realization.

The jurisprudential bottom line of *The Sea Inside* is ultimately one that is much adverted to and anticipated in the literature of critical legal studies, as well as critical race theory and critical legal feminism: namely, individual rights are embedded in group practices, in collective acts. That is, some modicum of social assistance, even state aid—what Isaiah Berlin nominates as "positive liberty"[47]—is absolutely necessary for the free exercise of liberal legalism's most negative of "negative liberties," the right to be left alone.[48] "Negative" so called because that right's privacy, and its autonomy, negate the material context—of social support, of state backing—upon which it so clearly depends. That sense of context, moreover, is annulled so entirely, absented so utterly—either in Dworkin's text or *Million Dollar Baby*—because for liberal legalism, especially in its American version, "the social," let alone "the state," does not exist. *The Sea Inside*, however, insists upon society—and by logical extension, the state—going so far as to suggest that it is only through "the Many" (the twelve) that Ramon can experience "the One," the mystical feeling of what Freud called "the oceanic,"[49] *the sea inside*. No wonder so many sequences, in a film as militantly secular as this, are literally so fantastic, with dreams of flight across limitless seas. Because what the group act of termination does is bring about the highest form of individual autonomy, collectively releasing Ramon from the prison house of the body, and allowing him to fly free, enabling his soul to transmigrate.

There is a downside to this film—or rather an *upside*-downside; that is, another tale lurking on its borders, skulking around its story line, capable of, as in *Million Dollar Baby*, turning the narrative on its head, revealing its pathological underside. That pathology is not to be confused, in this instance, with Frankie's psychosis, predicated as that condition is on the "foreclosure"—or *verwerfung*—of the Law. Far from expelling the Law, everyone in *The Sea Inside* is all too aware of it. Each and every character in the film—as well as every participant in Ramon's "reality TV" suicide—knew that they were contravening articles 138 and 139 of the Spanish Criminal Code.[50] These provisions make it a criminal offense, punishable by two to ten years imprisonment, to induce or assist "another person to commit suicide."[51] This legal (fore)knowledge suggests another psychic structure, one that, contra the lawlessness of psychosis, acknowledges the Law in order to disavow it, and which can say "Yes, I know this is against the Law, but all the same . . ."[52] That structure is inherently perverse, a kind of Lacanian version of *Little Britain's* Vicki Pollard and her doubletalk ("yah-but-no-but-yah . . .").[53] And that perversity is as susceptible to delusions of "best interests" as psychosis—or, even worse, to cold-and-calculated "self interests" such as scheming to dispose of high-needs patients, burdens on society, and unwanted relations.

No wonder then that postcolonial critics of the right to die, like Delhi University's eminent legal philosopher, B. B. Pande, have argued just how site-specific euthanasia debates are, alerting Western audiences to the very real difference between, for example, the Dutch experience (where an individual's decision to terminate is paramount), and Pande's home jurisdiction, India (where a much more complex and involved group dynamic—like the extended family—would be involved in these decisions).[54] Pande turns, for example, to the spate of family-perpetrated bride burnings throughout India in the 1980s and 1990s, arguing that any resilement from that nation's constitutionally entrenched "right to life"[55] might serve only to inflame an already volatile situation, putting even more women at risk and reviving the Orientalist specter of suttee. So there is a very real danger in the kind of universal prescriptions of *The Sea Inside*, in its own way just as decontextualized as Dworkin—which of course means overcontextualized—as Occidentalist, or Euro-Americanocentric. All of which is to say, what may work for one culture may spell disaster for another. In the West, the right to die may set a willing Ramon free from his life of confinement; but in the East, it may just as easily consign to a funeral pyre a very unwilling Indian bride whose dowry has come up short.

My intention here is not to "exoticise" the debate over termination, nor am I arguing that some cultures are too "unevolved" to take the "right to death" seriously. The West has its own version of bride burnings. In fact, it doesn't take much imagination to recast *The Sea Inside* as a Christie-style mystery, the twelve (*Twelve Little Indians*?) becoming something like the conspirators of *Murder on the Orient Express*. Only here the victim, instead of being a fugitive criminal—the ringleader of a Lindbergh Baby–style kidnapping—is instead a cantankerous, overbearing, and demanding quadriplegic, dispatched either for convenience (to shut him up?) or base material motives (his insurance settlement?), rather than reasons of justice. That could easily have been Ramon's fate. Or more mundanely—but no less chilling—his termination might have been the result of a medical judgment call; that is, Ramon's doctors may have decided that the sum total of his life, when measured both quantitatively and qualitatively, wasn't worth the expended effort—in either human or technical resources—necessary to keep him alive. Already, the elderly in The Netherlands are said to live in fear of these sorts of "expert" decisions, dreading lengthy hospital stays. With the expansion of the "right to die" (now legislatively guaranteed in Belgium, Oregon, and soon, California), many of the infirm and the terminally ill could potentially find themselves facing a *Brave New World*[56] of premature, involuntary terminations, precisely the kind of science fiction fantasy (think of *Logan's Run*[57] or *Soylent Green*[58]) becoming the scientific fact of "medical routine" that Dworkin cautions against at the close of *Life's Dominion.*

"O Death Where Is Thy Sting?": The Trouble With Terri

Thus both *Million Dollar Baby* and *The Sea Inside* undo their very premises, each undermining the cases they mount for termination; that is, by exposing the apologias they press on behalf of duty (instead of rights) or private right (rather than public law) as potentially pregnant with a psychopathology of the law, ready to spring into life and wreak havoc (like a 1970s or 1980s slasher film maniac—Michael, Jason—running amok). Thus, *Million Dollar Baby*'s substitution of a higher "duty" for positivized *recht*, or rights, can be read as a "psychotization" of the "right to die," the "call of the Other" turning out to be the delusional voice of a deranged superego. Equally, *The Sea Inside*'s turn from legality's public realm (of courts and legislatures) to its private sphere (of inherent right, of *recht*) can become, just as easily, a kind of perverse sort of "vigilantism" in which the Law is disavowed, so that one (or the few) may become it, taking it into one's own hands. Neither film's position on termination is free of taint; both are "stained" with the pathological, as Žižek might put it, either psychotic or perverse.[59]

Each of these pathological conditions is played out—indeed performed to the hilt, in the case of Terri Schiavo—on both sides of the case's divide, between her husband and her parents. There, for example, Michael Schiavo embodies "the perverse" in all of its ambiguity, all its doubleness. On the one hand, he appears to be Terri's devoted and long-suffering spouse, a characterization confirmed by many reports, who is intent only on securing her "last wishes" and thereby safeguarding her "best interests." On the other hand, a cloud of suspicion hangs over the repartnered Michael, his parents-in-law, a former *guardian ad litem*, and a number of media pundits having accused him of—aside from wanting to be rid of her—the basest venality, motivated by and angling for what's left of Terri's medical settlement. The Schindlers, by way of contrast, resemble nothing less than Frankie—though in reverse: because their voice of conscience, of faith, imposes a duty not to dispatch but to keep Terri alive at all costs. And at what a cost—the time, effort, and money involved, now a public as much as a private expense. Witness their ongoing battle through the courts, the state legislature, U.S. Congress and Senate, up to and including an appeal to an extremely sympathetic President Bush, an unstoppable politico-legal juggernaut driven by what cannot be anything other than obsession bordering on, if not under the sway of, the psychotic.

So the two sides of the Schiavo case—the Schindlers and Michael—repeat the very inversion, the core chiasmus at the center of both *lex populi* films discussed in this chapter: in the former (the Schindlers representing *Million Dollar Baby*), faith shades into a delusional, indeed psychotic higher duty; while in the latter (Michael representing *The Sea Inside*), positivized law is set aside for a perverse belief in one's right to choose. Either way—be it an unwavering commitment to a "higher duty" or an unshakeable "belief in rights"—what the two sides of the Schiavo case (and the films that dramatize its polarities) demonstrate is the difficulty of drawing any determinate line between matters of law and morality, religion and *recht*. Neither can be detached so clearly from the other without—so I will argue by way of conclusion—producing the very pathology (psychosis, perversion) outlined above.

Now a critic could very well object here that this pathology is a direct effect of the attempt to blur the sacred and the secular, *theos* and *nomos*; and that any effort to prolong this (unholy?) alliance of faith and forensics will reproduce rather than resolve the impasse, the deadlock so spectacularly dramatized in the Schiavo case. There is much to credit in this kind of argument. After all, a range of religious groups, a kind of fundamentalist "coalition of the willing" was in the forefront of pressurizing the Florida legislature to pass "Terri's Law" empowering Gov. Jeb Bush, himself a devout Catholic convert, to override any kind of curially sanctioned disconnection of Terri's life support. When this political pressure increased, extending as it did to the federal level, the principal congressman to take up the issue was Christian Evangelical (Baptist) Tom DeLay,[60] who spoke on its behalf with as much if not more fervor than the Rev. Jesse Jackson—or Br. Paul O'Donnell (neither of whom, like DeLay, threatened the courts with reprisals in this life or what comes after).

The mention of Br. Paul here brings this chapter full circle, back to where it started, and its key issue: the role of faith in public life—or morality, whether credal or by personal conviction, in the law. That uneasy relationship continues to vex many polities, especially America, where the debate rages over not only euthanasia but also abortion and school prayer, because, as Ronald Dworkin admits, the United States is "among the most religious of modern western countries . . . and by far the most fundamentalist." The irony, of course, is that this intense religiosity—often of the most politically proselytizing kind—takes place against a constitutional backdrop in which Church and State are notionally "separate" but everywhere, it would appear, mutually implicated: from public buildings' sculpted Ten Commandments to town commons' Christmas crèche scenes. One wonders, then, if that very constitutional separation—and the repeated curial insistence upon it—is not so much the bar to, as *the precondition of* American confessionalism and its fanatical *jouissance*. All of which proves the truth of the Lacanian adage that what is foreclosed from the Law of the Symbolic (confession, faith, *Ecclesia*) reappears in the Real of delusion—the fundamentalist "plague of fantasies."[61] Think of the eruptions of religious enjoyment—"Great Awakenings," "Revivals," and calls to be "born again"—that punctuate American history: a history that begins, in the first place, with militantly Protestant "purifiers" of established Anglican ritual, safely "high and dry." To which now, of course, the Roman Catholic Church—once the scourge of these very purifiers—now adds its considerable historical luster, global reach, and theological gravitas, weighing in with its clarion call of a "culture of life."

For some liberals, the Catholic concordat on "life" with its hitherto antagonistic, "happy clappy" Protestant partners, may spell the end (assisted suicide?) of the secular state, evangelical zeal now joining with papal absolutism in an unbeatable combination. But I would like to argue that this alliance is as fragile as it is (seemingly) ferocious, and in the end, its internal fissures may open up, in its fault lines, a space for public debate over the "culture of life" and the right to die that is truly catholic in the original sense of that word: that is, universal, ecumenical, and representative of faith communities across the denominational board. *Contra*, standard American "liberal" *doxa*: Why shouldn't religious advisors, as well as ethicists, counselors, doctors, and other health care professionals join the chorus of voices, debating over generally, indeed specifically deciding upon—in hospital ethics committees—cases of termination? Surely they too have a right to be heard and, if persuasive, to have their opinions acted upon. Of course, their voice is just one of many and is by no means dispositive of the issue—nor for that matter is the ethicist's, or the doctor's. Rather, that dispositive voice, that determinative decision—the final court of conscience, as it were—belongs to one person, the applicant for assistance, be it Ramon Sampedro, Maggie Fitzgerald, even Terri Schindler Schiavo.

Not that these persons and their cases are commensurate. After all, the trouble with Terri lies precisely in the fact that, unlike Ramon's explicit demand or Maggie's implied request, her wishes are ultimately unknown and unknowable. For in the absence of a "living will" or some other express form of communication, Terri

Schiavo went to her death under a question mark—or several question marks. Not just, "Would she have opted for termination?" but: "Could she have recovered?" "What was the cause of her condition?" and probably the most vexing question of all, "Was she in pain during the fortnight it took her to die of dehydration and starvation?" This is precisely why a legally empaneled and authorized group decision is called for here, one that includes not only Michael and the Schindlers, not only Br. Paul and Terri's doctors, but independent assessors who include lawyers, health care professionals, counselors, ethicists, *and clergy*. Such clerical delegates would themselves be representative of a "Broad Church"; that is, a latitudinarianism that gives voice to a range of theological, ethical, and moral perspectives that are truly reflective of the *katholikos*. More than talk, however, these confessors would perform their age-old function of listening, attempting to hear a voice, distant and obscured, but still audible; one that has resonated and resounded throughout the ages—in myth, legend, and history—of those blessed (or cursed?) with eternal life, from Tithonus to Tiresias, from the Cumaean Sibyl to Terri Schiavo, a voice that says: "I want to die."

Conclusion

Whither Lex Populi*? A Law by and for the People*

Two parallel lines of analyses, running in tandem, have emerged in the course of this book's argument, bifurcating the text and its constituent chapters. One line might be called "the legal" and turns on the representation of questions of doctrine (the right to die, native title), procedure (courtroom strategies, policing initiatives), and principle (the state's founding legitimacy, its telos of *recht* and justice). The other might be called "the cultural" and issues from sometimes recognizable juridical contexts (a law school classroom, a High Court hearing, a murder trial), but in the main remains remote from the concerns of the nomological and revolves around the a-legal quotidian: settings like a boarding school or a suburban house; characters like a missing child or a seriously injured young woman; even gestures like tossing a ring away, a punch, or the act of staking. Nothing here really announces or marks these structural, characterological, or narrative features as *lex populi*. After all, where is the law in them? That sort of puzzled question is valid, however, only if one is content to understand these features descriptively, staying on the level of what narratology might call their content's surface parole. But if one shifts position here, plumbing the depths of deep structure, then a different sort of scene of interpretation appears, one that connects, for example, vampire slaying with the semiosis of legal language; a boxing match with the perversity of legal positivism's rule system; a quest romance with the search for a new law; a disabled patient with the medico-legal conundrums over termination; a lost boy with marginal utility's substitution hypothesis; a family's home with *terra nullius* dispossession; a very special prep school with notions of access to justice.

Mediating between these two types of inquiry—the legal and the cultural—bringing them into dialogue with each other, and creating a cultural legal intersection is nothing less than a mode of theorizing and method of explication that I call "reading jurisprudentially." For what this sort of reading does is tap into and extract the thought of one of the great unmined intellectual resources of the twenty-first-century academy—jurisprudence—attempting to realize its tremendous hermeneutical potential and reclaim much of its (now somewhat tarnished) intellectual prestige, making it a worthy rival, indeed alternative, to the array of interpretive paradigms available in the humanities and the social sciences: psychoanalytic, new historicist, deconstructive, feminist, queer, postcolonial, and so on. Such a jurisprudential reading is valuable not only because it yields mutually illuminating understandings of "the legal" and "the cultural," but also because it proffers an alternative intertext—or rather, *intertexts*—all of which synthesize, sublate, and go beyond both our pop cultural texts (Tolkien and *Buffy*) and legal topoi (the *grundnorm* and divine justice), enabling one to look at "the legal" and "the cultural" *otherwise*—as a site of discursive difference rather than binary stasis, of theoretical inquiry rather than sociolegal representation.

This intertextual space not only provides a venue to read jurisprudentially, but also conduces to *jurisprudence's (re)reading*, allowing the reader to repose and rethink its core issues, its persistent dilemmas: for example, the renewal of the promise of liberal legalism; the postmodern reformation of natural law; the tension between law-as-rule and law-as-command; the redeployment of positivism under the conditions of "Empire"; the irrationality of Law and Economics' rationality; the "critique of the critique" of critical legal studies; the pervasive whiteness of the law; the battle for life and death in contemporary rights discourse. All these highly contested juristic "fact(ion)s" are reflected and refracted in pop culture's legal fictions. This forging of legal fiction and faction thus produces a renewed jurisprudence, recuperative of its full range of canonical and contemporary questions and answers. But this forging not only renews, it *revives*, recalling jurisprudence to life, as vibrant and relevant as well as open and accessible to all. Now liberated from the closed "interpretive community" of lawyers, judges, and jurists (and their increasingly narrow economic/sociological issues), jurisprudence is free to disseminate throughout the community at large, once more assuming a central position on the social agenda through popular culture's various media of pulp fiction, TV series, blockbuster films, and cult fantasies.

All of which suggests that popular culture, despite its uneasy alliance with and co-optation by Capital (networks, publishers, and sponsors, for example), could and should play a signal part, indeed a profoundly democratizing role in the ongoing battles over the "politics of the law" and the law in and of politics. That is, by delivering jurisprudence from the "classes" (the Posners or Dworkins, for example) to the "masses," popular culture's *lex populi* holds out the prospect of effecting social change by soliciting broad comment and input into the juridico-political issues of our day. After all, think of how general opinion on a range of gender issues (single parenthood, gay sexuality, a woman's right to choose) has been affected significantly by TV shows such as *Murphy Brown*,[1] *Queer as Folk*,[2] and *Sex and the City*.[3] Why not jurisprudential issues? Why shouldn't such issues as the law's morality, the nature of rights, and the notion of a "higher justice"—each of urgent (and abiding) interest to us all—be subject to the same kind of open questioning, the same type of public debate? This book is an attempt to provoke precisely this sort of debate, to generate this line of questioning by examining the way in which popular culture overtly and impliedly addresses jurisprudence. Indeed, it is the author's hope that any and all discussion that this book might stir up about the jurisprudence of popular culture will take us a step closer to the construction—but also deconstruction and reconstruction—of a truly people's law, a *lex populi* by and for the people.

Reference Matter

Notes

Introduction

1. J. K. Rowling, *Harry Potter and the Goblet of Fire* (London: Bloomsbury, 2000). (Hereafter cited as HP&GF.)

2. Joss Whedon, *Buffy the Vampire Slayer* (Mutant Enemy, 20th Century Fox, 1998–2003). (Hereafter cited as BtVS.)

3. *Fight Club* (DVD), directed by David Fincher (Moore Park, Australia: 20th Century Fox Home Entertainment South Pacific, 1999). (Hereafter cited as FC.)

4. *The Lord of the Rings: The Fellowship of the Ring* (2001; New Line Home Entertainment, 2002); *The Lord of the Rings: The Two Towers* (2002; New Line Home Entertainment, 2003); *The Lord of the Rings: The Return of the King* (2003; New Line Home Entertainment, 2004); all directed by Peter Jackson (special extended DVDs). (Hereafter cited as LR-FR, LR-TT, and LR-RK.)

5. J.R.R. Tolkien, *The Lord of the Rings* (Boston: Houghton Mifflin, 1994). (Hereafter cited as LR.)

6. Michael Hardt and Antonio Negri, *Empire* (Cambridge, Mass.: Harvard University Press, 2000).

7. *Minority Report* (DVD), directed by Steven Spielberg (2002; 20th Century Fox Home Entertainment, 2003).

8. *Legally Blonde* (DVD), directed by Robert Luketic (Metro Goldwyn Mayer Pictures, 2001; MGM Home Entertainment, 2001).

9. *The Castle* (DVD), directed by Rob Sitch (Village Roadshow, 1997).

10. *Mabo v. The State of Queensland* (no. 2) (1992) 175 CLR 1.

11. *Million Dollar Baby* (DVD), directed by Clint Eastwood (Warner Brothers, 2004; Lakeshore Entertainment, 2005).

12. *The Sea Inside* (DVD), directed by Alejandro Amenábar (2004; Sogepaq and Fine Line Features, 2005).

13. Alison Young, *Judging the Image: Art, Value, Law* (London: Routledge, 2005).

14. Desmond Manderson, *Songs Without Music: Aesthetic Dimensions of Law and Justice* (Berkeley: University of California Press, 2000).

15. Judith Grbich, "Language as the 'Pretty Woman' of the Law: Properties of Longing and Desire in Legal Interpretation and Popular Culture" in *Romancing the Tomes: Popular Culture, Law and Feminism*, M. Thornton, ed. (London: Cavendish, 2002, 131–46).

16. Mary Farquhar and C. Berry, *China on Screen: Cinema and Nation* (New York: Columbia University Press, in press).

17. Suzanne Christie, "Judge Judy: The Courtroom as Classroom" (*Australian Feminist Law Journal* 13, Sept. 1999, 86–97).

18. Jenni Milbank, "It's About *This*: Lesbians, Prison, Desire" (*Current Legal Issues* 7, 2004, 449–69).

19. Isabel Karpin, "Pop Justice: TV, Feminism, and the Law" in *Women, Law, and the Media*, M. Fineman and M. McCluskey, eds. (New York: Oxford University Press, 1997, 120–35).

20. Margaret Thornton, ed., *Romancing the Tomes: Popular Culture, Law and Feminism* (London: Cavendish, 2002).

21. Terry Threadgold, *Feminist Poetics: Poesis, Performing, Histories* (London: Routledge, 1997).

22. Penny Pether, "E. M. Foster's *A Passage to India*: A Passage to the Patria" in *New Macmillan Casebook on E. M. Foster*, Jeremy Tambling, ed. (New York: MacMillan & St. Martin's Press, 1995, 195–212); "Sex, Lies and Defamation: The Bush Lawter of Wessex" in *The Happy Couple: Law and Literature*, J. Neville Turner and Pamela Williams, eds. (Sydney: Federation Press, 1994, 114–36).

23. Larissa Behrendt, "The Eliza Fraser Captivity Narrative: A Tale of Frontier, Femininity, and the Legitimisation of Colonial Law" (*Saskatchewan Law Review* 63, 2000, 145–84); *Home* (Brisbane: University of Queensland Press, 2004).

24. Peter Hutchings, *The Criminal Spectre in Law, Literature, and Aesthetics: Incriminating Subjects* (London: Routledge, 2001).

25. Derek Dalton, "The Deviant Gaze: Imagining the Homosexual as Criminal Through Cinematic and Legal Discourses" in *Sexuality in the Legal Arena*, Carl Stychin and Didi Herman, eds. (London: Athlone, 2000).

26. Kirsty Duncanson, "Tracing the Law Through *The Matrix*" (*Griffith Law Review* 10:2, 2001, 160–71).

27. Merran Lawler, "There's Something Not Quite Right About Tinky-Wink: Queer Theory, the Law, and *Teletubbies*"; "Queering the *Freedom* Catalogue"; Merran Lawler, "There's Something 'Queer Eye' About *The L Word*" (manuscripts on file with author).

28. Mark Rosenthal, "The Violent Excess of the Image and the Negation of Law in *Starship Troopers*" (*Griffith Law Review* 10:2, 2001, 172–86).

29. Kieran Tranter, "Mad Max: The Car and Australian Governance" (*National Identities* 5:1, 2003, 67–81).

30. Steve Redman, *Unpopular Cultures: The Birth of Law and Popular Culture* (Manchester: Manchester University Press, 1995).

31. Steve Greenfield and Guy Osborn, *Film and the Law* (London: Cavendish, 2001).

32. Peter Goodrich, *Languages of Law: From Logics of Memory to Nomadic Masks* (London: Weidenfeld & Nicolson, 1990); *Reading the Law: A Critical Introduction to Legal Method and Techniques* (Oxford: Blackwell, 1986).

33. Costas Douzinas, *The End of Human Rights: Critical Legal Thought at the Turn of the Century* (Oxford: Hart, 2000).

34. Costas Douzinas, Ronnie Warrington, and Shaun McVeigh, *Postmodern Jurisprudence: The Law of Text in the Texts of Law* (London: Routledge, 1991).

35. Maria Aristodemou, *Law and Literature: Journeys from Her to Eternity* (New York: Oxford University Press, 2000).

36. Melanie Williams, *Empty Justice: One Hundred Years of Law, Literature, and Philosophy* (London: Cavendish, 2001).

37. Leslie J. Moran, Ian Christie, Emma Sandon, and Elena Loizidou, *Law's Moving Image* (London: Cavendish, 2004); Leslie J. Moran, *The Homosexual(ity) of Law* (New York: Routledge, 1996).

38. Costas Douzinas and Lynda Nead, eds., *Law and the Image: The Authority of Art and the Aesthetics of Law* (Chicago: University of Chicago Press, 1999).

39. Adam Gearey, *Law and Aesthetics* (Oxford: Hart, 2001).

40. Sue Chaplin, "Fictions of Femininity: Gender, Genre and the Law of Genre in Eighteenth-Century England" (*Griffith Law Review* 2:1, 2002, 34–43).

41. David Seymour, "Film and Law: In Search of a Critical Method" in *Law's Moving Image*, L. J. Moran et al., eds. (London: Cavendish, 2004, 107–20).

42. Angus McDonald, "Endless Streets, Pursued by Ghosts" in *Law's Moving Image*, L. J. Moran et. al., eds. (London: Cavendish, 2004, 121–32); "The New Beauty of a Sum of Possibilities" (*Law and Critique* 8:2, 1997, 141–59).

43. Bill Grantham, "'Get On with the Burning! Put an End to This Trial!': Representations of the Trials of Joan of Arc in the Cinema" (*Griffith Law Review* 13:2, 2004, 153–59).

44. Ari Hirvonen, ed. *Polycentricity: The Multiple Scenes of Law* (Ann Arbor: University of Michigan Press, 1998).

45. Panu Minkinnen, *Thinking Without Desire: A First Philosophy of Law* (Oxford: Hart, 1999).

46. James Boyd White, *The Legal Imagination: Studies in the Nature of Legal Thought and Expression* (Boston: Little, Brown, 1973); *Justice as Translation: An Essay in Cultural and Legal Criticism* (Chicago: University of Chicago Press, 1990).

47. Robert Ferguson, *Law and Letters in American Culture* (Cambridge, Mass.: Harvard University Press, 1984).

48. Robin West, *Narrative, Authority, and Law* (Ann Arbor: University of Michigan Press, 1993); *Caring for Justice* (New York: New York University Press, 1997).

49. Peter Brooks and Paul Gewirtz, *Law's Stories: Narrative and Rhetoric in the Law* (New Haven, Conn.: Yale University Press, 1996).

50. Wai Chee Dimock, *Residues of Justice: Literature, Law, Philosophy* (Berkeley: University of California Press, 1997); *Empire for Liberty: Melville and the Poetics of Individualism* (Princeton, N.J.: Princeton University Press, 1991).

51. Anthony Chase, *Movies on Trial: The Legal System on the Silver Screen* (New York: New Press, 2002).

52. Carol Clover, "Movie Juries" (*DePaul Law Review* 48, 1998, 389–405); "Law and the Order of Popular Culture" in *Law in the Domains of Culture*, A. Sarat and T. Kearns, eds. (Ann Arbor: University of Michigan Press, 1999, 97–119).

53. Paul Bergman, *Reel Justice: The Courtroom Goes to the Movies* (Kansas City, Mo.: McMeel & Andrews, 1996).

54. David Black, *Law in Film: Resonance and Representation* (Urbana: University of Illinois Press, 1999).

55. Richard Sherwin, *When the Law Goes Pop: The Vanishing Line Between Law and Popular Culture* (Chicago: University of Chicago Press, 2000).

56. Austin Sarat and Thomas R. Kearns, eds., *Law in the Domains of Culture* (Ann Arbor: University of Michigan Press, 2000).

57. Austin Sarat, "When Memory Speaks: Remembrance and Revenge in *Unforgiven*" (*Griffith Law Review* 10:2, 2001, 139–59).

58. Austin Sarat, "Imagining the Law of the Father: Loss, Dread, and Mourning in *The Sweet Hereafter*" (*Law and Society Review* 34:1, 2000, 3–46).

59. Susan Sage Heinzelman and Zipporah Wiseman, eds., *Representing Women: Law, Literature, and Feminism* (Durham, N.C.: Duke University Press, 1994).

60. Marianne Constable, *The Law of the Other: The Mixed Jury and Changing Conceptions of Citizenship, Law, and Knowledge* (Chicago: University of Chicago Press, 1994).

61. Hilary Schor, *Dickens and the Daughter of the House* (Cambridge: Cambridge University Press, 1999); *Scheherezade in the Marketplace: Elizabeth Gaskell and the Victorian Novel* (Oxford: Oxford University Press, 1992).

62. Austin Sarat, Lawrence Douglas, and Martha Merrill Umphrey, eds., *Law's Madness* (Ann Arbor: University of Michigan Press, 2003); *The Place of Law* (Ann Arbor: University of Michigan Press, 2003).

63. Harriet Murav, *Russia's Legal Fictions* (Ann Arbor: University of Michigan Press, 1998); *Identity Theft: The Jew in Imperial Russia and the Case of Avraam Uri Kovner* (Stanford, Calif.: Stanford University Press, 2003).

64. Nasser Hussain, *The Jurisprudence of Emergency: Colonialism and the Rule of Law* (Ann Arbor: University of Michigan Press, 2003).

65. Tom Dumm, "Toy Stories: Downsizing American Masculinity" (*Cultural Values* 1:1, 1997, 81–100).

66. Kendall Thomas, "The Eclipse of Reason: A Rhetorical Reading of Bowers v. *Hard-wick*" (*Virginia Law Review* 79, 1993, 1721–80).

67. Stephen Best, *The Fugitive's Properties: Law and the Poetics of Possession* (Chicago: University of Chicago Press, 2004).

68. Michele Goodwin, "Poetic Reflections on Law, Race and Society" (*Griffith Law Review* 10:2, 2001, 195–210).

69. Lawrence Douglas, *The Memory of Judgment: Making Law and History in the Trials of the Holocaust* (New Haven, Conn.: Yale University Press, 2001).

70. Mariana Valverde, *Law's Dream of a Common Knowledge* (Princeton, N.J.: Princeton University Press, 2003).

71. Nomi Stolzenberg, "What We Talk About When We Talk About Culture" (*American Anthropologist* 103:2, June 2001, 432–47); "Bentham's Theory of Legal Fictions—A 'Curious Double Language'" (*Cardozo Studies in Law and Literature* 11, 1999, 223–62).

72. Roger Berkowitz, "The Accusers: Law, Justice and the Image of the Prosecutors in Hollywood" (*Griffith Law Review* 13:2, 2004, 131–52).

73. Rebecca Johnson, "Leaving Normal: Constructing the Family in the Movies and in Law" in *New Perspectives on Deviance: The Construction of Deviance in Everyday Life*, Lori Beaman, ed. (Prentice-Hall, 2000, 163–79).

74. A prominent Quebec critical legal feminist currently working, with Rebecca Johnson on a discourse analysis of defenses in Canadian law.

75. Orit Kamir, *Every Breath You Take: Stalking Narratives and the Law* (Ann Arbor: University of Michigan Press, 2001).

76. Austin Sarat, ed., *Cultural Analysis, Cultural Studies, and the Law: Moving Beyond Legal Realism* (Durham, N.C.: Duke University Press, 2003).

77. And complements an e-journal such as San Francisco–based *Picturing Justice: The On-Line Journal of Law and Popular Culture* (John Denvir, ed.). Other journals in the United States carrying analyses of law and popular culture include: *Law and Literature* (Penny Pether, Peter Goodrich, and Richard Weisberg, eds.) and *Yale Journal of Law and the Humanities* (student edited).

78. Interestingly, feminist and queer theory are notable exceptions, defying the story that I am telling here of theory's "decline and fall." For they continue to flourish, in spite of theory's general withering on the vine. But this efflorescence might be the result of the feminist and queer theory's focus on *praxis* as much as their *theoria*, neither having detached the one from the other (as was often the "critical" case). These movements, therefore, constitute distinguished exceptions to my rule of legal theory's demise (exceptions that, unfortunately, may prove the rule), and I set off and exceptionalize feminist and queer theorists such as Judith Butler, Joanna Bourke, Elizabeth Grosz, Linda Hutcheon, Juliet Mitchell, and Jacqueline Rose, as well as more legally driven theorists such as Susan Bandes, Sandra Berns, Kim Crenshaw, Margaret Davies, Maria Drakopolou, Katherine Franke, Rosemary

Hunter, Aileen Moreton-Robinson, Ngaire Naffine, Jennifer Nedelsky, Helen Stacy, Sally Sheldon, and Patricia Williams. Places like Kent and Griffith, Keele and Adelaide, Buffalo and Wisconsin still remain vital centers of feminist and queer theoretical inquiry, and journals such as the *Australian Feminist Law Journal, Signs,* and *Feminist Legal Studies* are among the most interesting and lively journals on the jurisprudential and indeed theoretical scene.

79. Slavoj Žižek, *Enjoy Your Symptom!: Jacques Lacan in Hollywood and Out* (London: Routledge, 2001); *idem., The Sublime Object of Ideology* (London: Verso, 1989).

80. Mladen Dolar and Slavoj Žižek, *Opera's Second Death* (London: Routledge, 2001).

81. Alenka Zupančič, *Ethics of the Real: Kant, Lacan* (London: Verso, 2000); *idem., The Shortest Shadow: Nietzsche's Philosophy of the Two* (Cambridge, Mass.: MIT Press, 2003).

82. Renata Salecl, *(Per)versions of Love and Hate* (New York: Verso, 1998); *On Anxiety* (New York: Routledge, 2004).

83. See Slavoj Žižek, "Is There a Proper Way to Remake a Hitchcock Film?" in *Enjoy Your Symptom!* 195–212; *Pscyho,* directed by Alfred Hitchcock (USA, 1960).

84. Žižek, "Proper Way"; *Rear Window,* directed by Alfred Hitchcock (USA, 1954).

85. Žižek, "Proper Way"; *Notorious,* directed by Alfred Hitchcock (USA, 1946).

86. *Spellbound,* directed by Alfred Hitchcock (Selznick International, 1945).

87. See H.L.A. Hart, "Positivism and the Separation of Law and Morals" (*Harvard Law Review* 71, 1958, 593–629); Lon L. Fuller, "Positivism and Fidelity to Law—A Reply to Professor Hart" (*Harvard Law Review* 71, 1958, 630–72); H.L.A. Hart, *The Concept of Law* (Oxford: Oxford University Press, 1961); *The Morality of Law* (New Haven, Conn.: Yale University Press, 1964).

88. See Ronald Dworkin, "Law as Interpretation" (*Texas Law Review* 60:3, 1981–82, 527–50); Stanley Fish, "Working on the Chain Gang: Interpretation in Law and Literature" (*Texas Law Review* 60:3, 1981–82, 551–68); Ronald Dworkin, "My Reply to Stanley Fish (and Walter Benn Michaels: Please Don't Talk About Objectivity Anymore" in *The Politics of Interpretation,* W. Mitchell, ed. (Chicago: Chicago University Press, 1983, 287–313); Stanley Fish, "Wrong Again" (*Texas Law Review* 62, 1983–84, 299–316).

89. See, for example, such recent mass market publications celebrating Buffy "BS" (beyond Sunnydale) as: Diana Gallagher, *Spark and Burn* (New York: Simon Spotlight Entertainment, 2005); Nancy Holder, *Queen of the Slayers* (New York: Simon & Schuster, 2005).

90. See, for example, Žižek, *Enjoy Your Symptom!*

91. Jacques Lacan, "God and the *Jouissance* of the Woman" in *Feminine Sexuality,* ed. Juliet Mitchell and Jacqueline Rose (London: Macmillan, 1982).

92. For the use of this term, counterposed to *jouissance,* see Roland Barthes, *Plaisir du Texte* [The pleasure of the text], Richard Miller, trans.; note by Richard Howard (New York: Hill & Wang, 1975).

93. For the most sustained engagement with this term, see Slavoj Žižek, *The Indivisible Remainder* (London: Verso, 1996).

Chapter One

1. J. K. Rowling, *Harry Potter and the Philosopher's Stone* (London: Bloomsbury Publishing Plc., 1997). In the United States, the novel was distributed by Scholastic, Inc., under the rather Disneyfied title, *Harry Potter and the Sorcerer's Stone*. The American-funded and -directed film that followed the novel retained that alteration, although it resisted the temptation to further Americanize the script (aside from certain peculiarities of pronunciation). Interestingly, other anglophone countries—Australia, New Zealand, and Canada, for example—retained Rowling's original title, as well as orthography and idiom, for both novel and film.

2. HP&CS.

3. HP&PA.

4. HP&GF.

5. Anthony Holden, "Why Harry Doesn't Cast a Spell Over Me" (*Observer*, June 25, 2000).

6. Of late, however, Harry Potter and his misadventures—tortious, criminal—have attracted so much attention from academic lawyers (particularly in the United States) that one wonders if he fulfills for them the function of an "imaginary client" (like imaginary friends do for lonely children) for whom they act on fantasmatic retainer. My flippancy here, however, should not detract from the very lively and provocative debates about the various legal (sub)texts of the series: not just justice, rights, and judgment but also bureaucracy, punishment, oaths, defenses, and more. See esp. Aaron Schwabach, "Harry Potter and the Unforgivable Curses: Norm-Formation, Inconsistency, and the Rule of Law in the Wizarding World" (*Roger Williams Law Review* 11, 2005) Benjamin Barton, "Harry Potter and the Half-Crazed Bureaucracy" (*Michigan Law Review* 104, 2006). See also a special Potter-themed issue of the *Texas Wesleyan Law Review* (edited by Jeffrey E. Thomas) 12(1), 2005 and listed in the online Harry Potter Bibliography (http://www.eulenfeder.de/hpliteratur .html) as including the following legal analyses: Benjamin H. Barton, "Harry Potter and the Miserable Ministry of Magic"; Joel Fineman, "Punishment in the Harry Potter Novels"; Daniel Austin Green, "Excuse, Justification, and Authority"; Timothy S. Hall, "Magic and Contract: The Role of Intent" and "Harry Potter and Dick Whittington: Similarities and Divergences"; Andrew P. Morriss, "Making Legal Spaces for Moral Choice"; James Charles Smith, "Family Life and Moral Choices Character" and "Status, Rules and the Enslavement of the House Elves"; Aaron Schwabach, "Unforgiveable Curses and the Rule of Law"; Jeffrey E. Thomas, "Rule of Man (or Wizard) in the Harry Potter Narratives"; Danaya C. Wright, "Collapsing Liberalism's Public / Private Divide: Voldemort's War on the Family."

7. James Boyd White, *The Legal Imagination: Studies in the Nature of Legal Thought and Expression* (Boston: Little, Brown, 1973).

8. A. V. Dicey, *An Introduction to the Study of the Law of the Constitution* (London: Macmillan, 1959); *Lectures on the Relation Between Law and Public Opinion in England during the Nineteenth Century* (London: Macmillan, 1962).

9. Jacques Derrida, "Force of Law: The 'Mystical Foundation of Authority'" (*Cardozo Law Review* 11:5–6 1990, 919).

10. Stuart Hall, *Policing the Crisis: Mugging, the State and Law and Order* (London: Macmillan, 1978).

11. For examples of these frightfully "Okay, yah" preteen detectives, see Enid Blyton, *Well Done Secret Seven, Look Out Secret Seven,* and *Good Work, Secret Seven* (Leicester: Brockhampton, 1951, 1971, and 1974, respectively). And for more of Blyton's preteen twittery, this time with lashings of Turkish delight, ginger beer, and adventures, see Enid Blyton, *The Famous Five, Five Fall into Adventure,* and *Five on a Hike Together* (Geneva: Heron, 1981).

12. Eric Hobsbawn and Terence Ranger, *The Invention of Tradition* (Cambridge: University Press, 1983).

13. Sheila Rowbotham, *Woman's Consciousness, Man's World* (Harmondsworth: Penguin, 1973).

14. D. Kairys, *The Politics of the Law: A Progressive Critique* (New York: Pantheon, 1982).

15. Latin—"for a stronger reason; all the more; much more so." See Peter E. Nygh and Peter Butt, eds., *Butterworths Concise Australian Legal Dictionary* (Sydney: Butterworths, 1998, 1).

16. Cited in S. Parker and S. Bottomley, *Law in Context* (Annadale and Leichardt, Australia: Federation Press, 1994, 1997, 24).

17. Carol Gilligan, *In a Different Voice: Psychological Theory and Women's Development* (Cambridge, Mass.: Harvard University Press, 1982).

18. For an excellent overview of critical legal feminism, among other things, see Gerry Simpson and Hilary Charlesworth, "Objecting to Objectivity: The Radical Challenge to Legal Liberalism" in *Thinking About Law: Perspectives on History, Philosophy, and Sociology of Law*, Rosemary Hunter, Richard Ingleby, and Richard Johnstone, eds. (Sydney: Allen & Unwin, 1995, 86–132).

19. Kim Crenshaw, "Demarginalising the Intersection of Race and Sex: A Black Feminist Critique of Antidiscrimination Doctrine, Feminist Theory, and Antiracist Politics" (*University of Chicago Legal Forum* 1, 1989, 139).

20. For more developed versions of this argument, see William MacNeil, "Law's *Corpus Delicti*: The Fantasmatic Body of Rights Discourse" (*Law and Critique* 9:1, 1998, 37); "Taking Rights Symptomatically: *Jouissance, Coupure, Objet Petit A*" (*Griffith Law Review* 8:1, 1999, 134).

21. "Harry Potter's Chinese Adventure" (aired on "BBC News," Sept. 25, 2000), http://news.bbc.co.uk/1/hi/entertainment/941436.stm (accessed September 2006).

22. Berit Kjos, "Bewitched by Harry Potter," http://www.crossroad/to/text/articles/Harry9-99html (accessed September 2006).

23. South Carolina, most notably, but also, disturbingly, the un-Bible Beltish states of Michigan, Minnesota, and others. See Judy Blume, "Is Harry Potter Evil?" (*Censorships*

News Online 76, Winter 1999–2000), http: www.ncac.org/cen_news/cn76harrypotter.html (accessed September 2006).

24. In September 1999, Stouffer's solicitors wrote to Scholastic demanding that they cease and desist from the violation of their client's alleged copyright and trademark in the distribution of the Harry Potter books. Consequently, Scholastic immediately filed, in November 1999, for a declaratory judgment in the New York courts that they were not violating Stouffer's alleged copyright and trademark. Stouffer, in turn, proceeded to file a motion to dismiss the New York suit and to move proceedings to Pennsylvania. That motion was rejected by the New York court in August 2000. Stouffer filed her counterclaim in January 2001.

25. Which the court found was not the original title of the piece, which was "Rah and the Muggles" was added at a later date. See *Scholastic, Inc. v. Stouffer* 221 F. Supp. 2d 425 at 429 and 440 (S.D.N.Y. 2002).

26. *Scholastic v. Stouffer*, 429–31, 435–46.

27. However, Nevils in *The Legend of Rah and the Muggles* are distorted, even less humanlike forms of Muggles (*Scholastic v. Stouffer*, 432, 436); and Nimbus, in another work by Stouffer titled *Silver Linings*, is a warrior and prime minister of the cloud people of "Troposonia" (*Scholastic v. Stouffer*, 430, 436).

28. Judy Corman, a spokesperson of Scholastic, Inc., quoted in the Associated Press: "U.S. Author Sues, Claims Harry Potter Ideas Came from Her" (*South Coast Today*, March 18, 2000), http://www.onlineathens.com/stories/032000/kid_botter.html (accessed September 2006).

29. *Scholastic v. Stouffer*, 444.

30. *Ibid.*, 444–45.

31. A point also made by Nadine Epstein, "Children's Books" (*Washington Post*, Aug. 6, 2000, X10).

32. In an interview with Helena de Bertodano, Rowling said she "loved C. S. Lewis and E. Nesbit [and] the Blyton books." "Harry Potter Charms a Nation" (*Telegraph* 1156, July 25, 1998).

33. H. Carpenter, *The Inklings: C. S. Lewis, J.R.R. Tolkien, Charles Williams, and Their Friends* (London: Harper Collins, 1978).

34. See, for example, the Malory Towers series or the St. Clare's series, all published by Mammouth (London: Egmont Children's Books, 1991).

35. Revealed as such in ch. 17, "The Heir of Slytherin," in HP&CS.

36. Benedict Anderson, *Imagined Communities: Reflections on the Origin and Spread of Nationalism* (London: Verso, 1983).

37. J. K. Rowling, *Harry Potter and the Order of the Phoenix* (London: Bloomsbury Publishing, 2003).

38. J. K. Rowling, *Harry Potter and the Half-Blood Prince* (London: Bloomsbury Publishing, 2005).

Chapter Two

1. Joss Whedon, *Buffy the Vampire Slayer* (Mutant Enemy, 20th Century Fox, 1998–2003). (Hereafter cited as BtVS).

2. Constance Burge, *Charmed* (Spelling Television, WB Network, 1998–).

3. In *Charmed*, Shannon Doherty (formerly Brenda of *Beverly Hills 90210* fame), as well as Ayssa Milano and Holly Marie Combs, star as the "Charmed Ones," the Halliwell sisters Prue, Phoebe, and Piper. This sororal triumverate finds an equivalent in the admittedly nonsibling but no less enmeshed, even endogamous group in *Buffy*'s Scooby gang of Slayerettes. The original *Buffy* triad included—and still includes—Nicholas Brendan as working-class nebbish "Zeppo" Xander Harris; Alyson Hannigan as computer geek turned Wiccan gay icon Willow Rosenberg; and of course the eponymous heroine herself, SMG to her countless fans, or Sarah Michelle Gellar to the public-at-large, as everyone's favorite Vampire Slayer, Buffy Anne Summers.

4. Different regional sites are utilized, however, giving each series a somewhat altered emphasis and accent. *Charmed*'s mise-en-scène, for example, is the settled and sophisticated North, condensed in that twee-est of San Franciscan architectural clichés, the Victorian "painted lady." The effect of this *Period Living* location is to situate the series within a much older cinematic/televisual tradition—the progenitor being, of course, Hitchcock's *Vertigo*—which represents San Francisco as a genteel ghost town. *Buffy*'s backdrop is the sunny South, evoked in the very name of that "one Starbucks town," Sunnydale. Much like the Southern Californian settings of *Valley Girl*, *Legally Blonde*, and *Orange County*, Sunnydale is a distillation of the suburban provincialism of the "La-La land" fringe. In locating itself here, *Buffy* leaves *Charmed* mired in its passé rehearsal of *The Ghost and Mrs. Muir* (albeit more Mission District than Maine coastline) and propels itself into the front ranks of that most dynamic of 'nineties and 'noughties genres, the teen film.

5. *Charmed*'s title, for instance, signals its overriding concern with and focus on witchcraft, principally in the charms revealed by *The Book of Shadows* and practiced by the "Power of Three" of the Halliwells. Similarly the sobriquet "Buffy the Vampire Slayer" *seems* to say it all, providing its own unique supernatural objective, the disposition of the undead. But I emphasize "seems" because, to date, Buffy's slaying career has enjoyed a much broader ambit than this tag would indicate. She slays not only vampires (like Drusilla, Darla, Angelus, Kralik, the Master, and Vamp Willow) but also demons (consider Alcatha, Whistler, Moloch, etcetera), mummies (like Incan Princess, Ampata), even the occasional god (the gloriously named Glory) as well as *Charmed*-like witches (principally Amy Madison's mum, the developmentally arrested cheerleader from hell "Catherine the Great").

6. Nell Scovall, *Sabrina the Teen-Age Witch* (Viacom Productions, Heartbreak Films, WB Television, 1996–2003).

7. Masquerade, "All Things Philosophical on Buffy the Vampire Slayer and Angel: The Series," http://www.atpobtvs.com (accessed September 2006).

8. Joss Whedon, *Angel* (Mutant Enemy, WB Television, 1999–2004).

9. Latin—"within the power. An *intra vires* act is within the legal power or authority of a person, institution, or legislation, and therefore valid." See Nygh and Butt, *Australian Legal Dictionary*, 241.

10. Latin—"beyond the power. An *ultra vires* act is beyond the legal power or authority of a person, institution, or legislation, and therefore invalid." See Nygh and Butt, *Australian Legal Dictionary*, 438.

11. Alain Badiou, *Ethics: An Essay on the Understanding of Evil*, Peter Hallward, trans. (London: Verso, 2001, 1–3).

12. Jacques Lacan, *The Ethics of Psychoanalysis, 1959–1960*, vol. 7, *The Seminar*. Dennis Porter, trans. and notes (London: Routledge, 1992, 321).

13. L. Althusser, "Ideology and Ideological State Apparatuses" in *Lenin and Philosophy, and Other Essays*, B. Brewster, trans. (New York: Monthly Review Press, 1971, 127–88).

14. Jacques-Alain Miller, "Extimacy" in *Lacanian Theory of Discourse*, Mark Bracher et al., eds. (New York: New York University Press, 1994, 74–87).

15. Joss Whedon, "Welcome to the Hellmouth," BtVS, directed by Charles Martin, Season 1: Episode 1.

16. See, for example, Johann Wolfgang von Goethe, *Faust Parts 1 & 2: A New Version*, by Howard Brenton, from a literal translation by Christa Weisman (London: Nick Hern, 1995), Part 2, Act V, "Heaven".

17. Rob Des Hotel and Dean Batali, "The Puppet Show," BtVS, directed by Ellen Pressman, Season 1: Episode 9.

18. Whedon, "Hellmouth."

19. *Ibid.*

20. Joss Whedon, "Restless," BtVS, directed by Joss Whedon, Season 4: Episode 22.

21. Sophocles, "Antigone." In *The Three Theban Plays*, R. Fagles, trans.; Bernard Knox, intro. and notes (London: Allen Lane, 1982, 21–110).

22. Marti Noxon, "Bargaining," BtVS, directed by D. Grossman, Season 6: Episode 1.

23. Joss Whedon, "Prophecy Girl," BtVS, directed by Joss Whedon, Season 1: Episode 12.

24. Joss Whedon, "The Gift," BtVS, directed by Joss Whedon, Season 5: Episode 21.

25. Thomas Aquinas, "Selections from *Summa Theologica*" in *Lloyd's Introduction to Jurisprudence*, M.D.A. Freeman, ed. (London: Sweet & Maxwell, 1994, 134–36).

26. Aquinas, "Selections from *Summa Theologica*," 133.

27. See Anthony Giddens, *Beyond Left and Right: The Future of Radical Politics* (Cambridge: Polity Press, 1994).

28. See Badiou, *Ethics*, 85. But see esp. Alenka Zupančič, *Ethics of the Real: Kant, Lacan* (London: Verso, 2000, 90–96).

29. See Badiou, *Ethics*, 62–63; and Zupančič, *Ethics of the Real*, 87–90. For the source of this term, see Immanuel Kant, *Religion Within the Limits of Reason Alone* (New York: Macmillan, 1993, 25).

30. Sigmund Freud, *The Interpretation of Dreams*, vol. 5 in *The Complete Psychological Works of Sigmund Freud*, James Strachey, rev. and ed. (London: Institute of Psycho-Analysis and Hogarth Press, 1959, 608).

31. Ty King, "Passion," directed by M. Gershman, BtVS, Season 2: Episode 17.

32. Marti Noxon, "I Only Have Eyes for You," directed by James Whitmore, BtVS, Season 2: Episode 19.

33. Marti Noxon, "The Wish," directed by David Greenawalt, BtVS, Season 3: Episode 9.

34. Fredric Jameson, *The Political Unconscious: Narrative as a Socially Symbolic Act* (Ithaca, N.Y.: Cornell University Press, 1981).

35. Douglas Petrie, "Revelations," directed by James Contner, BtVS, Season 3: Episode 7.

36. Douglas Petrie, "Bad Girls," directed by Michael Lange, BtVS, Season 3: Episode 14.

37. David Fury, "Helpless," directed by James Cantner, BtVS, Season 3: Episode 12.

38. Marti Noxon, "Consequences," BtVS, directed by Michael Gershman, Season 3: Episode 15.

39. See esp. *Goldfinger*, directed by Guy Hamilton (Eon Productions, 1964).

40. Norman Folto and Sam Rolfe, *The Man from U.N.C.L.E.* (MGM/Arena, 1965).

41. Mel Brooks and Buck Henry, *Get Smart* (Talent Associates/Heyday, 1965–67).

42. Howard Gordon and Marti Noxon, "What's My Line? Part 1," BtVS, directed by David Soloman, Season 2: Episode 9.

43. David Greenwalt, "Faith, Hope, and Trick," BtVS, directed by James Contner, Season 3: Episode 3.

44. See Karl Llewellyn, excerpts from *My Philosophy of Law* and *The Normative, The Legal, and The Law-Jobs: The Problem of Juristic Method* in *Lloyd's Introduction to Jurisprudence*, M.D.A. Freeman, ed. (London: Sweet & Maxwell, 1994, 703–23).

45. Joss Whedon, "Graduation Day, Part 1," BtVS, directed by Joss Whedon, Season 3: Episode 21.

46. Greenwalt, "Faith, Hope, and Trick."

47. For the best introduction to and gloss on this term, see the germinal *The Politics of the Law: A Progressive Critique*, David Kairys, ed. (New York: Pantheon, 1982).

48. Noxon, "Consequences."

49. Thanks to my Griffith Law School student Jonathan Leckie for sharing his rich insights on this point.

50. John Stuart Mill, *On Liberty* (Harmondsworth: Penguin Classics, 1974, 68).

51. Immanuel Kant, *Groundwork for the Metaphysics of Morals*, Lewis M. Beck, trans. (Indianapolis: Bobbs-Merrill, 1960, 30, 421).

52. Herbert Hart, *The Concept of Law* (Oxford: Oxford University Press, 1961, 92–107, 245–46).

53. See selections from Hans Kelsen, *The Pure Theory of Law* and *General Theory of Law and State* in *Lloyd's Introduction to Jurisprudence*, M.D.A. Freeman, ed. (London: Sweet & Maxwell, 1994, 294–96, 301–4, 314–16).

54. Ronald Dworkin, *Law's Empire* (London: Fontana Press, 1986, 176–275).

55. Petre, "Bad Girls."

56. See Jeremy Bentham, selections from *An Introduction to the Principles and Morals of Legislation* in *Lloyd's Introduction to Jurisprudence*, M.D.A. Freeman, ed. (London: Sweet & Maxwell, 1994, 230).

57. Ronald Dworkin, *Taking Rights Seriously* (Cambridge, Mass.: Harvard University Press, 1977).

58. Dworkin, *Law's Empire*.

59. Piers Gray, *Marginal Men: Edward Thomas, Ivor Gurney, and J. R. Ackerley* (London: Macmillan, 1990).

60. Chris Carter, *The X Files* (Ten-Thirteen / Twentieth Century Fox, 1994).

61. Joss Whedon, "The Freshman," BtVS, directed by Joss Whedon, Season 4: Episode 1.

62. *The Parallax View*, directed by Alan Pakula (Paramount Pictures, 1974).

63. *Three Days of the Condor*, directed by Sydney Pollack (Paramount Pictures, 1975).

64. Gilles Deleuze, "What Is an Event?" in *The Fold: Leibniz and the Baroque*, Tom Conley, trans. (Minneapolis: University of Minnesota Press, 1993, 76–82); *The Logic of Sense*, Mark Lester with Charles Stivale, trans., Constance V. Boundas, ed. (New York, 1990).

65. Alain Badiou, *Ethics: An Essay on the Understanding of Evil*, Peter Hallward, trans. (London: Verso, 2001).

66. David Fury, "The I Team," BtVS, directed by James Contner, Season 4: Episode 13.

67 Marti Noxon, "Goodbye, Iowa," BtVS, directed by David Solomon, Season 4: Episode 14.

68. Joss Whedon, "Hush," BtVS, directed by Joss Whedon, Season 4: Episode 10.

69. Marti Noxon, "Living Conditions," BtVS, directed by David Grossman, Season 4: Episode 2.

70. Jane Espenson, "The Harsh Light of Day," BtVS, directed by James Contner, Season 4: Episode 3.

71. David Fury, "Primeval," BtVS, directed by James Contner, Season 4: Episode 21.

72. For the definitive study of this pairing, see Jacques Lacan, "Kant avec Sade" (*October* 51, Winter, 1989, 55–75).

73. Espenson, "The Harsh Light of Day."

74. David Petrie, "The Initiative," directed by James Contner, BtVS, Season 4: Episode 7.

75. Jane Espenson, "Pangs," directed by Michael Lange, BtVS, Season 4: Episode 8.

76. Marti Noxon, "Into the Woods," BtVS, directed by Marti Noxon, Season 5: Episode 10.

77. D. Fury, "Crush," BtVS, directed by Dan Attias, Season 5: Episode 14.

78. Whedon, "The Gift."

79. Rebecca Kirshner, "Out of My Mind," BtVS, directed by D. Grossman, Season 5: Episode 4.

80. Douglas Petrie, "Fool for Love," BtVS, directed by Nick March, Season 5: Episode 7.

81. Fury, "Crush."

82. Jane Espenson, "Interventions," BtVS, directed by Michael Gershman, Season 5: Episode 18.

83. Joss Whedon, "Buffy: The Musical" or "Once More, with Feeling," BtVS, directed by Joss Whedon, Season 6: Episode 6.

84. Drew Greenberg, "Smashed," BtVS, directed by Tari Meyer, Season 6: Episode 8.

85. Jacques Lacan, "The Mirror Stage as Formative of the Function of the I" in *Écrits: A Selection*, A. Sheridan, trans. (New York: Norton, 1977, 1–7).

86. See the U.S.-Can production, *Queer as Folk*, directed by John Greyson, et al. (Showtime, 2001–). But see also the original (and infinitely superior) UK production, *Queer as Folk*, directed by Charles MacDougall and Sarah Harding (*CITV*, 1997–99).

87. See Lacan, *The Ethics of Psychoanalysis, 1959–1960*, vol. 7 in *The Seminar of Jacques Lacan*, Jacques-Alain Miller, ed. Translated and with notes by Dennis Porter (New York: Norton, 1988, 139). See also, Jacques-Alain Miller, "Extimacy" in *Lacanian Theory of Discourse*, Mark Bracher et al., ed. (New York: New York University Press, 1994, 74–87).

88. Lacan, *Ethics of Psychoanalysis, 1959–1960*.

89. Miller, "Extimacy."

90. *Ibid.*, 85.

91. *Ibid.*

92. *Ibid.*

93. *Ibid.*

94. *Alien*, directed by Ridley Scott (20th Century Fox, 1979); *Aliens*, directed by James Cameron (20th Century Fox, 1986); *Alien3*, directed by David Fincher (20th Century Fox, 1992); *Alien Resurrection*, directed by Jean-Pierre Jeunet (20th Century Fox, 1997).

95. Literally, the "object (little) other." A term that shifts and changes in Lacan's oeuvre but remains fundamentally linked to desire, first as its object, then as its object-cause, and finally, what remains of the Real when symbolic integration has occurred. For a good overview of this concept, see the entry "*Objet Petit A*" in Dylan Evans, *An Introductory Dictionary of Lacanian Psychoanalysis* (London: Routledge, 1997, 124–26).

96. See Josh Whedon, "Angel," BtVS; or Tim Minear and Howard Gordon, "Hero," BtVS; "Angel," directed by Tucker Gates, Season 1: Episode 9.

97. Noxon, "Bargaining."

98. Jacques Lacan, "The Subversion of the Subject and the Dialectic of Desire" in *Écrits: A Selection*, A. Sheridan, trans. (New York: Norton, 1977, 314).

99. Jacques-Alain Miller, "Language: Much Ado About What?" in *Lacan and the Subject of Language*, ed. Ellie Ragland-Sullivan and Mark Bracher (London: Routledge, 1991, 30).

100. See Rob Des Hotel and Dean Batali, "Never Kill a Boy on the First Date," BtVS, directed by David Senel, Season 1: Episode 5. Of course, the other character notable for her excess of signification is none other than the "Queen of Mean" herself, the inimitable Cordelia Chase, played by Charisma Carpenter, who utters such lines as: "God, what is your

childhood trauma?" in "Welcome to the Hellmouth"; and the immortal dressing down (to Buffy in "When She Was Bad"): "Whatever's causing the Joan Collins' 'tude, deal with it, embrace the pain, spank your inner moppet, whatever.... But get over it, 'cause pretty soon you won't even have the loser friends you've got now."

101. Indeed, signification in all its infinite hermeneutical variety is positively showcased here, investing *Buffy* with the kind of pleasure that is just as much aural as the more critically touted visual kind attributed to Laura Mulvey, et al. Catchphrases (like Buffy's Seinfeld-ism in "Surprise": "Sacred duty, yada, yada, yada"), quips (for example, Spike's sneering rejoinder in "School Hard": "If every vampire who said he was at the Crucifixion was actually there, it would've been like Woodstock"), echoes (when, for instance, the Master evokes the closing of "The Untouchables" with: "Here endeth the lesson"), and allusions (in, to give one illustration, Xander's reference to *The Usual Suspects*: "Does anyone else feel we've been Keyser Soze'd?"), all resonate in each episode and reverberate throughout the series as a whole. Citations of movies (as diverse as *The Exorcist, The Sound of Music,* and *Faster, Pussycat, Kill, Kill*), comic books (with such diverse DC staples as Superman sharing space with the more rarefied Human Torch), music (The Divinyls, Michael Jackson, Cher, and others, not to mention all the countless intradiegetic performances at "The Bronze" of bands of the L.A. "indie" scene), television, of course (from *The A-Team* to *Xena,* from Snoopy to Scooby-Doo) as well as haute couture (Prada), art-house films (Bergman), and fashionable literary theory (deconstruction), all work their pun-ny way into the series' scripts.

102. See Jacques Lacan, "God and the *Jouissance* of the Woman."

103. See Slavoj Žižek, *Enjoy Your Symptom! Jacques Lacan in Hollywood and Out* (London: Routledge, 1992).

104. See Drew Goddard, "Dirty Girls," BtVS, directed by Michael Gershman, Season 7: Episode 140; Drew Z. Greenberg, "Empty Places," BtVS, directed by James A. Contner, Season 7: Episode 141; Rebecca Rand Kirshner, "Touched," BtVS, directed by David Soloman, Season 7: Episode 142; Jane Espenson and Douglas Petrie, "End of Days," BtVS, directed by Marita Grabiak, Season 7: Episode 143; and Joss Whedon, "Chosen," BtVS, directed by Joss Whedon, Season 7: Episode 144.

105. See Slavoj Žižek, "Enjoy Your Nation as Yourself" in *Tarrying with the Negative: Kant, Hegel, and the Critique of Ideology* (Durham, N.C.: Duke University Press, 1993, 206).

106. See Slavoj Žižek, "Superego by Default" in *The Metastases of Enjoyment: Six Essays on Women and Causality* (London: Verso, 1994, 54–85).

107. Defined, variously, by Lacan as that which resists symbolization, is marked by loss, and indeed, may carry with it the brute "Thing"-ness of nature—and the *jouissance* that attaches to that thing—which at once structures but disorganizes fantasy, the imaginary, and the like. See Ellie Ragland-Sullivan, "The Real" in *Feminism and Psychoanalysis,* ed. Elizabeth Wright (Oxford: Basil Blackwell, 1992, 374–77).

108. "Lack" is the constitutive principle of subjectivity in Lacanian psychoanalysis. See Jacques Lacan, "The Subversion of the Subject and the Dialectic of Desire in the Freudian Unconscious" in *Écrits: A Selection*, trans. A. Sheridan (New York: Norton, 1977, 314).

109. Nina Auerbach, *Our Vampire, Ourselves* (Chicago: University of Chicago Press, 1995).

Chapter Three

1. *Fight Club* (DVD), directed by David Fincher (Moore Park, NSW, Australia: 20th Century Fox Home Entertainment South Pacific, 1999). (Hereafter cited as FC.)

2. Chuck Palahniuk, *Fight Club* (New York: Holt, 1999).

3. *Gentleman Jim* (DVD), directed by Raoul Walsh (Warner Bros; MGM / UA Home Entertainment, 1942).

4. *Raging Bull* (DVD), directed by Martin Scorsese (Chartoff-Winkler Productions, 1980; MGM Home Entertainment).

5. Five in all (1990, 1985, 1982, 1979, 1976) with a sixth still looming (slated for 2001? then 2004? now?), but starting with the classic: *Rocky* (DVD), directed by John G. Arildsen (United Artist, 1976; MGM Home Entertainment, 2001).

6. *Million Dollar Baby* (DVD), directed by Clint Eastwood (Warner Brothers, 2004; Lakeshore Entertainment, 2005).

7. John Austin (1790–1859), British educator and legal philosopher. A former army officer who was called to the Bar in 1818. A disciple of Jeremy Bentham, Austin was the first full-time professor of English law at a British university. He was appointed Quain Professor of Jurisprudence at University College London in 1826. His lectures were published in 1832 as *The Province of Jurisprudence Determined*, and established Austin's version of Benthamic expository jurisprudence—and his "command theory of law" (law is nothing more than the command of the sovereign)—as the prevailing paradigm in English law and legal theory. He was involved in a variety of royal commissions in England and the colonies, and widely traveled on the Continent where he moved in philosophical circles that included such company as von Savigny and Niebuhr. Posthumous interest in his life and work was revived by Henry Maine, and *The Province* was reissued along with a biographical sketch by Austin's widow, Sarah (a member of a prominent family of dissenting reformers, the Taylors, that included Harriet, the wife of J. S. Mill). Austin's thought is one of the most lasting influences on analytic jurisprudence in the common law world and the Anglo-Commonwealth legal academy, for which he plays a "founding father" role. See David M. Walker, *The Oxford Companion to Law* (Oxford: Oxford University Press, 1980, 96–97).

8. Slavoj Žižek, *The Puppet and the Dwarf: The Perverse Core of Christianity* (Cambridge, Mass.: MIT Press, 2003).

9. For an excellent introduction to this fraught field, see Bruce Fink, *A Clinical Introduction to Lacanian Psychoanalysis: Theory and Technique* (Cambridge. Mass.: Harvard University Press, 1997). (Hereafter cited as CILP). See also Dylan Evans, *An Introductory Dictionary*

of Lacanian Psychoanalysis (London: Routledge, 1997); Elizabeth Wright, ed., *Feminism and Psychoanalysis* (Oxford: Basil Blackwell, 1992); J. Laplanche and J.-B. Pontalis, *The Language of Psychoanalysis*, trans. Donald Nicholson-Smith (New York: Norton, 1973). The key primary source was and remains: Jacques Lacan, *Écrits: A Selection*, ed. and trans. Bruce Fink (New York: Norton, 2002).

10. Slavoj Žižek, "The Ambiguity of the Masochist Social Link" in *Perversion and the Social Relation*, ed. Molly Ann Rothenberg, Dennis Foster, and Slavoj Žižek (Durham, N.C.: Duke University Press, 2003, 187–209).

11. H.L.A. Hart, *The Concept of Law* (Oxford: English Language Book Society / Oxford University Press, 1988). (Hereafter cited as CL.)

12. For solid overviews on the legal theory of H.L.A. Hart, see J. G. Riddall, *Jurisprudence* (London: Butterworths, 1999, 38–52); Brian Bix, *Jurisprudence: Theory and Practice* (London: Sweet & Maxwell, 2003, 33–53); Raymond Wacks, *Jurisprudence* (London: Blackstone, 1999, 58–68).

13. See entry for "Drive" in Evans, *Introductory Dictionary of Lacanian Psychoanalysis*, 46–49.

14. See Octoave Mannoni, "I Know Well, but All the Same . . . " in *Perversion and the Social Relation*, ed. Molly Anne Rothenberg, Dennis A. Foster, and Slavoj Žižek (Durham, N.C.: Duke University Press, 2003, 68–92).

15. Or "disavowal." See entry for "Disavowal (deni)" in Evans, *Introductory Dictionary of Lacanian Psychoanalysis*, 43–44.

16. Indeed, the first and foremost defect Hart identifies in primary rules is "what we may call its uncertainty" (CL, 90).

17. Alain Pottage, "The Cadastral Metaphor: Intersections of Property and Topography" in *Constituting Modernity: Private Property in the East and West*, Huri Islamoglu, ed. (London: Tauris, 2004).

18. John Austin, *The Province of Jurisprudence Determined*, ed. Wilfrid E. Rumble (Cambridge: Cambridge University Press, 1995, 194).

19. Consider the definition of law as proffered by A. Ia. Vyshinsky, principal Soviet legal theorist of the period and drafter of the Stalinist Constitution: "Law is the totality of rules of conduct which express the will of the ruling class and are laid down in a legislative manner, along with the rules and practices of communal life which are sanctioned by the power of the State. The application of these rules is backed by the coercive power of the State in order to secure, reinforce, and develop the social relationships and conditions which are agreeable to the interests of the ruling class," quoted in L. B. Curzon, *Jurisprudence* (London: Cavendish, 1995, 138). See also, on Vyshinsky and the move away from his theories in the USSR from the early to mid-1960s: W. E. Butler, *Soviet Law* (London: Butterworths, 1988, 35–36).

20. Jenifer Hart née Williams, whose particularly aristocratic form of Marxism, following in the best tradition of the Oxbridge interwar Left, is recounted in Nicloa Lacey's superb biography of Hart. See Nicola Lacey, *A Life of H.L.A. Hart: The Nightmare and the Noble Dream* (Oxford: Oxford University Press, 2004, 2–3, 67–68).

21. Lacey, *A Life of H.L.A. Hart*, 56–57.

22. Jeanne Schroeder argues with her usual persuasiveness that it is morality itself that is Hart's desire. See her brilliant article, "His Master's Voice: H.L.A. Hart and Lacanian Discourse Theory," Working Paper no. 108 (New York: Jacob Burns Institute for Advanced Legal Studies, Benjamin Cardozo School of Law, 2005).

23. For an account of this sorry episode in Hart's life, see Lacey, *A Life of H.L.A. Hart*, 338–42.

24. See Brendan Edgeworth's excellent article, contextualizing Hart in terms of welfare state laborism. Brendan Edgeworth, "H.L.A. Hart, Legal Positivism and Post-war British Labourism" (*Western Australian Law Review* 19, 1989, 275–300).

25. David Fraser, *The Man in White Is Always Right: Cricket and the Law* (Sydney: Institute of Criminology, Sydney University Law School, 1993).

26. Thomas Hughes, *Tom Brown's Schooldays* (London: Pocket Paperbacks, 1967).

27. For Hart's harrowing experience (is there any other kind?) at public school—Cheltenham College—where he was bullied as a Jew, a petit bourgeois "scholarship boy," and a poor sportsman, see Lacey, *A Life of H.L.A. Hart*, 17.

28. William Golding, *The Lord of the Flies: A Novel* (London: Faber, 1954).

29. See entry for "Mirror Stage" in Evans, *Introductory Dictionary of Lacanian Psychoanalysis*, 115–16.

30. Neil MacCormick, *H.L.A. Hart* (London: Edward Arnold, 1981, 108–9). For a clear exposition of this point, see Raymond Wacks, *Jurisprudence* (London: Blackstone Press, 1999, 64).

31. *The Valley of the Dolls* (VHS), directed by Mark Robson (20th Century Fox, 1967; Fox Video, 1997), starring Barabara Parkins, Patty Duke, and Sharon Tate.

32. "Postscript" in H.L.A. Hart, *The Concept of Law*, 2nd ed., with postscript by Penelope Bulloch and Joseph Raz (Oxford: Clarendon Press, 1994). (Hereafter cited as *PS*.)

33. A veritable pop culture cottage industry, consisting of five films of varying quality (adapted from Pierre Boulle's 1960s classic, *La Planète des Singes*), starting with the brilliant Rod Serling–scripted, Heston vehicle *Planet of the Apes*, directed by Franklin Schaeffer (1968); followed by *Beneath the Planet of the Apes*, directed by Jed Post (1970); *Escape from Planet of the Apes*, directed by Dan Taylor (1971); *Conquest of Planet of the Apes*, directed by J. Lee Thompson (1972); and finally, *Battle for Planet of the Apes*, directed by J. Lee Thompson (1973), all produced by Fox Productions. A TV series (1974) as well as a cartoon followed, until the original was "reimagined" in 2001 as *Planet of the Apes*, directed by Tim Burton (Fox, 2001).

34. Consisting of three films: *Mad Max*, directed by George Miller (Kennedy Miller Productions, 1979); *Mad Max 2: The Road Warrior*, directed by George Miller (Kennedy Miller Productions, 1981); *Mad Max 3: Beyond Thunderdome*, directed by George Miller (Kennedy Miller Productions, 1985).

35. *The Postman*, directed by Kevin Costner (Warner Bros., 1997).

36. *Waterworld*, directed by Kevin Reynolds (Universal Pictures, 1995).

37. Terry Nation, *Survivors*, (BBC 1, 1975–77).

38. Joss Whedon, *Firefly* (Mutant Enemy, Inc., 2002–3).

39. See, for example, David Bowie, "Diamond Dogs," Recording (1974, RCA).

40. Devo, *Q. Are We Not Men? A. We Are Devo!* (Warner Bros., 1978). From "Devo," meaning "devolutionary." See entry for "Artists—Biography: Devo," VH1, http://www.vh1 .com/artists/az/devo/bio.jhtml (accessed September 2006).

41. Susan Sontag, "Fascinating Fascism" in *Under the Sign of Saturn* (New York: Farrar, Stauss & Giroux, 1980, 77–105).

42. Principally, Henry Giroux. See Henry A. Giroux, "Brutalised Bodies and Emasculated Politics: *Fight Club*, Consumerism, and Masculine Violence" (*Third Text* 53, Winter 2000–2001, 31–41); "Private Satisfactions and Public Disorders: *Fight Club*, Patriarchy, and the Politics of Masculine Violence" (*JAC: A Journal of Composition Theory* 21.1, 2001, 1–31). For a more Deleuzian reading of *Fight Club*'s politics, see Bulent Diken and Carsten Begge Laustsen, "Enjoy Your Fight! *Fight Club* as a Symptom of the Network Society" (Lancaster: Department of Sociology, Lancaster University, 2001), http://www.lancs.ac.uk/fss/sociology/papers/diken-laustsen-enjoy-your-fight.pdf (accessed September 2006). See also Krister Friday, "'A Generation of Men Without History': *Fight Club*, Masculinity, and the Historical Symptom" (*Postmodern Culture* 13:3, 2002–3); A. Gronstad, "One Dimensional Men: *Fight Club* and the Poetics of the Body" (*Film Criticism* 28:1, Fall 2003, 1–23).

43. The phrase is, of course, Hart's—though initially used in connection with the work of Ronald Dworkin. See H.L.A. Hart, "American Jurisprudence Through English Eyes: The Nightmare and the Noble Dream" in *Essays in Jurisprudence and Philosophy* (Oxford: Clarendon Press, 1983, 123–44).

44. Joseph Raz, *The Authority of Law: Essays in Law and Morality* (Oxford: Clarendon Press, 1979, 37–45).

Chapter Four

1. Tolkien writes in the "Foreword to the Second Edition": "As for any inner meaning or 'message,' it has in the intention of the author none. It is neither allegorical nor topical . . . I cordially dislike allegory in all its manifestations, and always have done so since I grew old and wary enough to detect its presence," J.R.R. Tolkien, *The Lord of the Rings* (Boston: Houghton Mifflin, 1994, xvii). (Hereafter cited as LR.)

2. Thus, for example, there is Tolkien the allegorist of Catholicism, in J. Pearce, *Tolkien: Man and Myth* (London: Sage, 1998); Jungian psychology, in D. Matthews, "The Psychological Journey of Bilbo Baggins" in *A Tolkien Compass*, ed. Jared Lobdell (New York: Ballantine Books, 1975, 25–43); feminist Freudianism, in B. Partridge, "No Sex Please—We're Hobbits: The Construction of Female Sexuality in *The Lord of the Rings*" in *J.R.R. Tolkien: This Far Land*, ed. Robert Giddings (London: Vision and Barnes & Noble, 1983, 179–98); Fascism, in Robert Plank, "'The Scouring of the Shire': Tolkien's View of Fascism" in *A Tolkien*

Compass, ed. Jared Lobdell (New York: Ballantine Books, 1975, 116–25); and Faustian pacts, in R. Helms, *Myth, Magic, and Meaning in Tolkien's World* (London: Granada, 1976).

3. Though Tolkien himself would not necessarily have disapproved of these sorts of readings, his dismissal of allegory notwithstanding. He would have just relabeled them as "applicable" rather than allegorical. In support of this reading practice, Tolkien writes in the "Foreword": "I much prefer history, true or feigned, with its varied applicability to the thought and experience of readers. I think many confuse 'applicability' with 'allegory'; but the one resides in the freedom of the reader, and the other in the purposed domination of the author" (LR, xvii).

4. N. Walmsley, "Tolkien and the 60s," in Giddings, ed., *This Far Land*, 73–86. Walmsley (74) sees more than just coincidence in the publication of *The Lord of the Rings* and the first distillation of the psychotropic compound lysergic acid diethylamide (LSD), both in 1954.

5. Tolkien himself anticipates and parodies this kind of (over)reading of *War of the Ring* as an allegory of WWII when he writes in the "Foreword to the Second Edition": "The real war does not resemble the legendary war in its process or its conclusion. If it had inspired or directed the development of the legend, then certainly the Ring would have been seized and used against Sauron; he would not have been annihilated but enslaved, and Barad-dur would not have been destroyed but occupied. Saruman, failing to get possession of the Ring, would in the confusion and treacheries of the time have found in Mordor the missing links in his own researches into Ring-lore, and before long he would have made a Great Ring of his own with which to challenge the self-styled Ruler of Middle-earth. In that conflict both sides would have held hobbits in hatred and contempt: they would not long have survived even as slaves" (LR, xvii). The war "applicable" to Tolkien was, by his own acknowledgment, and as a recent study drives home, the Great War of 1914–1918 in which he served as a young officer: J. Garth, *Tolkien and the Great War: The Threshold of Middle-earth* (London: HarperCollins, 2003).

6. For Grbich's own, richly evocative term "feudalscape," see Judith Grbich, "Language as the 'Pretty Woman' of Law: Properties of Longing and Desire in Legal Interpretation and Popular Culture," in *Romancing the Tomes: Popular Culture, Law, Feminism*, ed. Margaret Thornton (London: Cavendish, 2002, 139–40).

7. In the film's prologue, Galadriel's voiceover speaks of the Ring's historical trajectory as one of "History" becoming "Legend," "Legend" becoming "Myth"; see LR-FR, disc 1, ch. 1. Jackson's script echoes Gandalf's words to Frodo in the text that with the slaying of Isildur at Gladden Fields, the Ring "passed out of knowledge and legend" (LR, 51).

8. See LR-RK, disc 2, ch. 34.

9. In the Tower of Cirith Ungol, while rescuing Frodo, Sam is described as being under the spell of the Ring he now bears: "Already the power of the Ring tempted him, gnawing at his will and reason. Wild fantasies arose in his mind; and he saw Samwise the Strong, Hero of the Age, striding with a flaming sword across the darkened land, and armies

flocking to his call as he marched to the overthrow of Barad-dur" (LR, 880–81; LR-RK disc 2, ch. 22).

10. See also, LR-FR, disc 1, ch. 1 and ch. 10.

11. Michael Hardt and Antonio Negri, *Empire* (Cambridge, Mass.: Harvard University Press, 2000).

12. H. N. Beard and D. C. Kenney and the *Harvard Lampoon* staff, *Bored of the Rings: A Parody of J.R.R. Tolkien's "The Lord of the Rings"* (Signet, 1969).

13. For the "return of the Shadow," see Galadriel's LR-FR, ch. 1. Like Sauron, write Hardt and Negri in their Preface: "Empire is materializing before our very eyes" (*Empire*, 14).

14. "The problematic of Empire," as Hardt and Negri observe in one of the most telling passages in the text, "is determined in the first place by one simple fact: that there is world order. This order is expressed as a *juridical formation*" (author's emphasis) (*Empire*, 3).

15. So Hardt and Negri state: "Empire establishes no territorial center of power and does not rely on fixed boundaries or barriers. It is a *decentered* and *deterritorializing* apparatus of rule" (*Empire*, xii).

16. "The transformation of the modern imperialist geography of the globe and the realization of the world of the market," note Hardt and Negri, "signal a passage within the capitalist mode of production . . . Capital seems to be faced with a smooth world—or really a world defined by varied and complex regimes of differentiation and reterritorialization" (*Empire*, xiii).

17. Ulrich Beck, *What Is Globalization?* trans. Patrick Camiller (Malden, Mass.: Polity Press, 2000).

18. Arjun Appadurai, *Globalization* (Durham, N.C.: Duke University Press, 2001).

19. David Held, *Democracy and the Global Order: From the Modern State to Cosmopolitan Governance* (Cambridge: Polity Press, 1995).

20. See, for example, Wayne Ellwood, *The No-Nonsense Guide to Globalization* (London: Verso, 2001); Tony Schirato and Jen Webb, *Understanding Globalization* (London: Sage, 2003); and Manfred Steger, *Globalization: A Very Short Introduction* (Oxford: Oxford University Press, 2003).

21. In all of the texts cited above, whole chapters are devoted to the globalization of the media, family, risk, economy, culture, technology, and the like. In none, however, is the law mentioned.

22. Hardt and Negri, *Empire*, 9.

23. See, for example, the otherwise excellent unpacking of the Canadian-Indonesian Bre-X mining scam and debacle by Anna Tsing, where she writes "CoWs are the magical tools of the national elite." A. Tsing, "Inside the Economy of Appearance," in Appadurai, *Globalization*, 155-189. See also, for example, W. Dierckxsens, *The Limits of Capitalism: An Approach to Globalization Without Neo-liberalism* (New York: Zed Books, 2000).

24. Ernesto Laclau and Chantal Mouffe, *Hegemony and Socialist Strategy: Towards a Radical Democratic Politics* (London: Verso, 1985).

25. Particularly when, in an interview with Slyvere Lotringer, he proclaims that, under the conditions of postmodernity, "there is no longer any law or symbolic order," rather there are only "rules." See Jean Baudrillard, *Forget Foucault* (New York: Semiotext(e) Foreign Agents Series, 1988, 75).

26. Hardt and Negri, *Empire*, 15.

27. "The Pure Theory of Law," observes Kelsen, "is a theory of positive law. It is . . . a science of law (jurisprudence) not legal politics." See Hans Kelsen, *Pure Theory of Law*, trans. Max Knight (Berkeley: University of California Press, 1967, 1).

28. Kelsen writes: "Legal sociology relates facts not valid norms as causes and affects . . . Therefore not law itself is the object of cognition for legal sociology, but certain parallel phenomenon in nature" (Kelsen, *Pure Theory of Law*, 101–2). And earlier he notes that "uncritically the science of law has been mixed with elements of psychology, sociology, ethics and political theory . . . adulterations [that obscure] the essence of the science of law." See Kelsen, *Pure Theory of Law*, 1.

29. So Kelsen argues "'pure' theory . . . because it not only describes the law and attempts to eliminate from the object of this description everything that is not strictly law: its aim is to free the science of law from alien elements. This is the methodological basis of the theory." See Kelsen, *Pure Theory of Law*, 1.

30. For extended discussions of Kelsen's hierarchy of norms, including the *grundnorm*, see Kelsen, *Pure Theory of law*, 221–76; Hans Kelsen, *General Theory of Law and State*, trans. A. Sheridan (New York: Norton, 1961, 123–61).

31. Kelsen, *General Theory of Law and State*, 116; Hans Kelsen, "Professor Stone and the Pure Theory of Law" in *Lloyd's Introduction to Jurisprudence*, ed. M.D.A. Freeman (London: Sweet & Maxwell, 2001, 289).

32. As Kelsen notes: "The presupposition of the Basic Norm does not approve any value transcending positive law" (Kelsen, *Pure Theory of Law*, 201).

33. Kelsen, *Pure Theory of Law*, 116; Kelsen, "Professor Stone," 289.

34. For the first appearance of the Queen (played by British actress Alice Krige), see *Star Trek: First Contact*, directed by Jonathan Frakes (Paramount Pictures, 1996).

35. Humphrey Carpenter, *J.R.R. Tolkien: A Biography* (London: HarperCollins, 2002); *The Inklings: C. S. Lewis, J.R.R. Tolkien, Charles Williams, and Their Friends* (London: HarperCollins, 1978).

36. J.R.R. Tolkien, *The Hobbit, or There and Back Again* (Boston: Houghton Mifflin, 1997).

37. For more details about Swampy and radical environmentalism, see the following website article: Gustavo Trompiz, "England's Eco-warriors," http://woe.edu.pl/modules.php?sid=&module=Articles&mode=show_article&art_id=200&section_id=23 (accessed September 2006).

38. Emile Durkheim, *The Division of Labor in Society?* (New York: Free Press, 1964).

39. LR-TT, disc 1, ch. 6.

40. Spoken by British actor Sir Ian McKellan as Gandalf in LR-FR, disc 1, ch. 22.

41. Max Weber, *Max Weber on Charisma and Institution Building: Selected Papers*, ed. and intro. S. N. Eisenstadt (Chicago: University of Chicago Press, 1968).

42. Anne M. Bailey and J. R. Llobera, *The Asiatic Mode of Production: Science and Politics* (London: Routledge, 1981).

43. For a further development of this thematic, see Chapter One.

44. Samuel Huntingdon, *The Clash of Civilizations and the Remaking of World Order* (New York: Simon & Schuster, 1996).

45. The expression recurs throughout the film trilogy, and its original literary source is Treebeard's poetic catalogue of Middle-earth's living creatures: "First name the four, the free peoples"—elves, dwarves, men, and ents, to which hobbits are added (LR, 413).

46. Benedict Anderson, *Imagined Communities: Reflections on the Origins and Spread of Nationalism* (London: Verso, 1983).

47. Jean François Lyotard, *The Post-modern Condition: A Report on Knowledge*, trans. Geoff Bennington and Brian Massumi (Manchester: Manchester University Press, 1984).

48. Michel Foucault, *Discipline and Punish: The Birth of the Prison*, trans. A. Sheridan (Harmondsworth: Penguin, 1979).

49. Jeremy Bentham, *Panopticon Letters*, ed. M. Bozovic (London: Verso, 1995); Foucault, *Discipline and Punish*.

50. Graham Burchell, Colin Gordon, and Peter Miller, *The Foucault Effect: Studies in Governmentality, with Two Lectures by and an Interview with Michel Foucault* (Chicago: University of Chicago Press, 1991).

51. Burchell, Gordon, and Miller, *The Foucault Effect*, 20.

52. Giorgio Agamben, *Homo Sacer: Sovereign Power and Bare Life*, trans. Daniel Heller-Roazen (Stanford, Calif.: Stanford University Press, 1998, 23–25).

53. For example, see Book Six, Chapter 5, "The Steward and the King" in *The Return of the King*, where the narrator augurs of King Elessar's reign: "In his time the City was made more fair than it had ever been, even in the days of its first glory; and it was filled with trees and with fountains, and its gates were wrought of mithril and steel, and its streets were paved with white marble; and the Folk of the Mountain laboured in it, and the Folk of the Wood rejoiced to come there; and all was healed and made good, and the houses were filled with men and women and the laughter of children, and no window was blind nor any courtyard empty; and after the ending of the Third Age of the world into the new age it preserved the memory and the glory of the years that were gone" (LR, 947).

54. His distant cousin, Diamond of Long Cleeve, of the Long Cleeve Tooks, see Appendix B (LR, 1071).

55. Lucky number thirteen, see "The Longfather-Tree of Master Samwise," Appendix C (LR, 1077).

56. Entrusted by an aged, widower Samwise, just prior to his departure for the Undying Lands, to his firstborn, Elanor (known as "the Fair"), and an heirloom of her descendants,

the Fairbairns of the Towers. See "The Longfather-Tree of Master Samwise," Appendix C (LR, 1077).

57. So Hardt and Negri write: "Empire can only be conceived as a universal republic, a network of powers and counterpowers structured in a boundless and inclusive architecture." Hardt and Negri, *Empire*, 167.

58. This conjoining of opposites is precisely the paradox that lies at the heart of *Empire*, which Hardt and Negri define as committed, conceptually, to "a perpetual and universal peace" but which is, practically, "bathed in blood" (Hardt and Negri, *Empire*, xv).

59. So much so that Hardt and Negri designate Empire as a state of "omnicrisis." They write: "we can now see that imperial sovereignty, in contrast, is organized around not one central conflict but rather through a flexible network of microconflicts. The contradictions of imperial society are elusive, proliferating, and nonlocalizable: the contradictions are everywhere. Rather than crisis, then, the concept that defines imperial sovereignty might be omni-crisis" (Hardt and Negri, *Empire*, 201).

60. Carl Schmitt, *Political Theology: Four Chapters on the Concept of Sovereignty*, trans. George Schwab (Cambridge Mass.: MIT Press, 1985, 19–20).

61. For this poetic paean to empire and God as an Englishman, see Rudyard Kipling's "Recessional":

> If drunk with sight of power, we loose
>
> Wild tongues that have not Thee in awe,
>
> Such boastings as the Gentiles use,
>
> Or lesser breeds without the Law—Lord God of Hosts, be with us yet,
>
> Lest we forget—lest we forget!

Margaret Ferguson, Mary Jo Salterv, and Jon Stallworthy, eds. *The Norton Anthology of Poetry*, 4th ed. (New York: Norton, 1996, 1078).

62. Edward Said, *Orientalism* (London: Routledge; Kegan & Paul, 1978).

63. Leopold S. Senghor, *Prose and Poetry*, sel. and trans. John Reed and Clive Wake (London: Heinemann, 1976).

64. A Maori (Indigenous New Zealander) term referring to a white or European person as opposed to a Maori. See Arthu Delbridge et al., ed. *The Macquarie Dictionary: Federation Edition* (Sydney, NSW: Macquarie University, The Macquarie Library, 2001, 1375).

65. Indeed, one could go so far as to say that *The Lord of the Rings* was a national project for Aotearoa / New Zealand. What with an estimated 1 in 60 of the population involved in its production, and a cabinet minister whose sole brief was to liaise, on behalf of the government, in the marketing of the films, *The Lord of the Rings* rivals the old Soviet bloc in its state subsidization.

66. As Hardt and Negri argue, "Empire manages hybrid identities, flexible hierarchies and plural exchanges through modulating networks of command" (Hardt and Negri, *Empire*, xii–xiii). Indeed, one might go so far as to say that Empire is the rainbow coalition of identity politics (xiii).

67. Exemplifying the way in which, as Hardt and Negri note, "imperial racist theory in itself is a theory of segregation, not a theory of hierarchy" (193).

68. In the timeline from Appendix B, 1427 marks the year in which, inter alia, King Elessar issues an edict that Men are not to enter the Shire, and he makes it a Free Land under the protection of the Northern Sceptre" (LR, 1071).

69. For the friend/enemy distinction in *Empire* see p. 13, where the enemy is at once "banalized" and "absolutized" (13). This distinction is, of course, Schmittian. See Carl Schmitt, *The Concept of the Political*, trans. and intro. George Schwabe (Chicago: University of Chicago Press, 1996).

70. Jacques Derrida, "Force of Law: 'The Mystical Foundations of Authority'" (*Cardozo Law Review* 11:5–6, 1990).

71. Slavoj Žižek, *Looking Awry: An Introduction to Jacques Lacan Through Popular Culture* (Cambridge, Mass.: MIT Press, 1991, 30).

72. Jacques Lacan, "The Mirror Stage as Formative of the Function of the I as Revealed in Psychoanalytic Experience" in *Écrits: A Selection*, trans. A. Sheridan (New York: Norton, 1977, 1–7).

73. Which, incidentally, Hardt and Negri accuse Kelsen of failing to do. That is, of explaining how legal normativity gives rise to legal sociology. They write: "Kelsen conceived the formal construction and validity of the system as independent from the material structure that organizes it, but in reality the structure must somehow exist and be organized materially. How can the system actually be constructed? That is the point at which Kelsen's thought ceases to be of any use to us: it remains merely a fantastic utopia" (*Empire*, 6). My central argument, of course, is that it is another "fantastic utopia"—The Lord of the Rings—that points the way as to how this system is constructed, deconstructed, and reconstructed.

74. For an unpacking of this concept, see Richard Dyer, *White* (London: Routledge, 1997). For an explicitly feminist and race theorist deconstruction of "whiteness," see Aileen Moreton-Robinson, *Talkin' Up to the White Woman: Indigenous Women and Feminism* (Brisbane: University of Queensland Press, 2000).

75. The term is, of course, Derridean. Jacques Derrida, "White Mythology: Metaphor in the Text of Philosophy" in *Margins of Philosophy*, trans. A. Bass (Chicago: University of Chicago Press, 1982), 207–73. For a postcolonial extension of this term, see R. Young, *White Mythologies: Writing History and the West* (London: Routledge, 1990).

76. Although the term "the multitude" is introduced right from the start of *Empire* (xv), see esp. the last chapter of the text, "The Multitude Against Empire" (393–415).

77. Hardt and Negri, *Empire*, 52–53.

78. This term references but also rebukes Homi Bhabha's tendency to sentimentalize diaspora (Hardt and Negri, *Empire*, 145), especially when one of the persistent desires diasporics have is for a *home* (Hardt and Negri, *Empire*, 155).

79. Indeed, according to Hardt and Negri, "the multitude called Empire into Being" (43).

80. So Hardt and Negri observe: "The creative forces of the multitude that sustain Empire are also capable of autonomously constructing a counter-Empire, an alternative political organization of global flows and exchanges" (xv).

81. Hardt and Negri, *Empire*, 396–407.

82. *Ibid.*, 205–18.

83. Hardt and Negri write: "we can see that the United States is privileged in a more important way by the imperial tendency of its own Constitution. The U.S. Constitution, as Jefferson said, is one of the best calibrated for extensive Empire" (182).

84. Ronald Dworkin, *Taking Rights Seriously* (Cambridge, Mass.: Harvard University Press, 1977).

85. For an explication of "negative" liberty—that is, liberty defined as negating the state's power to interfere in one's autonomic exercise of rights and freedoms, see Isaiah Berlin, "Two Concepts of Liberty" in *Four Essays on Liberty* (Oxford: Oxford University Press, 1969, 122–30).

86. Again, another term drawn from Berlin, meaning a liberty that is predicated on a set of "positive" entitlements, provided for and supplied by (usually) some form of welfare state (Berlin, "Two Concepts of Liberty," 122–30).

87. Hardt and Negri, *Empire*, 401–3.

88. *Ibid.*, 403–7.

89. Roberto M. Unger, *False Necessity: Anti-necessitarian Social Theory in the Service of Radical Democracy*, Part 1. *Politics, a Work in Constructive Social Theory* (Cambridge, UK: Cambridge University Press, 1987).

90. See esp. Part 1 of Unger's *Politics*: Roberto M. Unger, *False Necessity: Anti-necessitarian Social Theory in the Service of Radical Democracy* (Cambridge, UK: Cambridge University Press, 1987, 508–35).

91. For the introduction of this concept of "the multiple," see Alain Badiou, *Ethics: An Essay on the Understanding of Evil*, trans. Peter Hallward (London: Verso Press, 2001, 48–52).

92. For an introduction to this "sign of our times"—and its meaning of both *differing* and *deferring*, see Jacques Derrida, "*Différance*" in *Margins of Philosophy*, trans. A. Bass (Chicago: University of Chicago Press, 1982, 1–29).

Chapter Five

1. Students as eminent as, for example, Slavoj Žižek, "Gerhard Schroeder's Minority Report and Its Consequences," http://www.egs.edu/faculty/zizek/zizek-gerhard-schroeders-minority-report-and-its-consequences.html (accessed September 2006).

2. *Minority Report* (DVD), directed by Steven Spielberg (2002; 20th Century Fox Home Entertainment, 2003). (Hereafter cited as MR.)

3. See Patricia J. Williams, *The Rooster's Egg: On the Persistence of Prejudice* (Cambridge, Mass.: Harvard University Press, 1997) and Elisabeth M. Landes and Richard A. Posner,

"The Economics of the Baby Shortage" in *Economic Analysis of the Law: Selected Readings*, ed. Donald A. Wittman (Oxford: Blackwell, 2003) on the baby shortage.

4. *A.I.: Artificial Intelligence*, directed by Steven Spielberg and Stanley Kubrick (Dreamworks, 2001).

5. Of late, Phillip K. Dick has become the writer du jour in Hollywood with two more Dick-inspired films currently under way or in postproduction. *A Scanner Darkly*, directed by Richard Linklater (Warner Independent Pictures) based on a Dick novel was released in 2006; *Next*, directed by Lee Tamahori (Revolution Studies) based on a short story, "The Golden Man," is slated for 2007. With these two, which come hot on the heels of *Paycheck, Imposter*, and *Minority Report*, the total Dick filmography in English comes to eight. A French-language film, *Barjo*, directed by Jerome Boivin (France 3 Cinema, 1994), was based on Dick's *Confessions of a Crap Artist* (Vintage, 1992).

6. From his story "The Minority Report" in *The Phillip K. Dick Reader* (New York: Citadel Press, 1997, 323–54).

7. *Paycheck*, directed by John Woo (Paramount/Dreamworks, 2003).

8. Phillip K. Dick, "Paycheck" in *Dick Reader* (355–84).

9. *Imposter*, directed by Gary Fleder (Dimension Film, 2002).

10. Philip K. Dick, "Imposter" in *Selected Stories of Philip K. Dick* (Pantheon, 2002, 101–15).

11. *Screamers*, directed by Christian Duguay (Allegro Films / Fries Film Group, 1995).

12. Philip K. Dick, "Second Variety" in *Dick Reader* (385–422).

13. *Total Recall* (DVD), directed by Paul Verhoeven (Artisan Entertainment, 1990).

14. Philip K. Dick, "We Can Remember It for You Wholesale" in *Dick Reader*, 305–22.

15. For one of the best recent analyses of this film, see Peter Hutchings, "Replicating *Blade Runner*" (forthcoming, manuscript on file with author).

16. *Blade Runner*, directed by Ridley Scott (Ladd Company / Blade Runner Partnership, 1982).

17. Philip K. Dick, *Do Androids Dream of Electric Sheep?* (Garden City, N.Y.: Doubleday, 1968).

18. Patricia S. Warrick, *Mind in Motion: The Fiction of Philip K. Dick* (Carbondale and Edwardsville, Illinois: Southern Illinois University Press, 1987, 95–116); Mary Ann Doane, "Technophilia: Technology, Representation, and the Feminine," in *Liquid Metal*, ed. Sean Redmond (London: Wallflower Press, 2004, 182–90).

19. Scott Bukatman, "Prosthetic Memory: Total Recall and *Blade Runner*" in *Liquid Metal*, ed. Sean Redmond (London: Wallflower Press, 2004, 239–48); Vivian Sobchack, *Screening Space: The American Science Fiction Film* (New York: Ungar, 1987, 272–73).

20. Largely involving *explications de text* of Scott's *Blade Runner*, see Vivian Sobchack, "Cities on the Edge of Time: The Urban Science Fiction Film" in *Liquid Metal*, ed. Sean Redmond (London: Wallflower Press, 2004, 83–84); Giuliana Bruno, "Postmodernism and *Blade Runner*" in *Alien Zone*, ed. Annette Kuhn (London: Verso, 1990, 183–96).

21. Oliver Wendell Holmes, excerpts from *The Path of Law* in *The Essential Holmes: Selections from the Letters, Speeches, Judicial Opinions, and Other Writings of Oliver Wendell Holmes, Jr.*, ed. R. Posner (Chicago: University of Chicago Press, 1992, 160–62).

22. Oliver Wendell Holmes, Jr. (1841–1935), U.S. judge and jurist, b. Boston, Mass., son of physician and author Dr. Oliver Wendell Holmes, Sr. (*Autocrat at the Breakfast Table*, 1858). Studied at Harvard, graduating in Law in 1861. Fought on the Union side in the Civil War, and returned to Boston with the rank of captain. Admitted to the Massachusetts bar in 1867, and edited *American Law Review* and *Kent's Commentaries*. Taught Harvard Law School (1881), and from there elevated to the Massachusetts Supreme Court bench: Associate Justice (1882–99) and Chief Justice (1899–1902); then to Associate Justice of the U.S. Supreme Court (1902–32). Celebrated as the "Great Dissenter," a sobriquet he earned because he was so often in dissent from the conservative (indeed reactionary) majority judgments of the court in this period. His judgments were, however, profoundly influential—in the United States and abroad—and he is justly regarded as one of the great judges of the common law world, of the same stature as Sir Edward Coke; William, Lord Mansfield; and John Marshall. His most renowned work is *The Common Law*, based on his Harvard lectures. See Walker, *Oxford Companion to Law*, 577.

23. The grandson, in point of fact, of Rev. Abiel Holmes, the pastor of the 1st Congregational Church of Cambridge. See G. Edward White, *Justice Oliver Wendell Holmes: Law and the Inner Self* (Oxford: Oxford University Press, 1993, 18–19).

24. White, *Justice Oliver Wendell Holmes*, 92–94. Of late, and much more salaciously, Holmes's friendship with Henry James has come under some scrutiny in both biography and fiction. Sheldon Novick's biography of Holmes and Colm Toibin's recently published novel about James, *The Master*, suggest that the relationship was a sexual one (and James's first). See Sheldon Novick, *Honorable Justice: The Life of Oliver Wendell Holmes* (Boston: Little, Brown, 1989) and Colm Toibin, *The Master* (New York: Scribner's, 2004).

25. Catherine Drinker Bowen, *Yankee from Olympus: Justice Holmes and His Family* (Boston: Little, Brown, 1944).

26. Holmes, *The Essential Holmes*, 163.

27. Roscoe Pound, "Law in Books and Law in Action" (*American Law Review* 44:12, 1910, 12–36). The phrase is Pound's, although Langdell had written: "it was indispensable to establish at least two things; first that the law is a science; secondly, that all the available materials of that science are contained in printed books." See Christopher Columbus Langdell, *Record of the Commemoration . . . on the Two Hundred and Fiftieth Anniversary of the Founding of Harvard College* (1887) quoted in William Twining, *Karl Llewellyn and the Realist Movement* (London: Weidenfeld & Nicolson, 1973).

28. Pound, "Law in Books and Law in Action."

29. Holmes, *The Essential Holmes*, 163.

30. Karl Llewellyn, excerpts from *My Philosophy of Law* in *Lloyd's Introduction to Jurisprudence*, ed. M.D.A. Freeman (London: Sweet & Maxwell, 1994, 705).

31. For a full discussion of Llewellyn's code, see Twining, *Realist Movement*, 270–340.

32. See Jerome Frank, excerpts from *Law and the Modern Mind* in *Lloyd's Introduction to Jurisprudence*, ed. M.D.A. Freeman, 827–30 (London: Sweet & Maxwell, 2001).

33. Raymond Wacks, *Jurisprudence* (London: Blackstone Press, 1999, 135).

34. Holmes, *The Essential Holmes*, 170.

35. Brian Bix, *Jurisprudence: Theory and Context* (London: Sweet & Maxwell, 2003, 189).

36. A term of art in law referring to an assumption that something is true even though it may be untrue. Made especially in judicial reasoning to alter, sustain, or extend the operation of a legal rule. An example of a legal fiction would be the Bill of Middlesex, enabling the Court of King's Bench to take jurisdiction over a criminal matter by assuming it occurred in Middlesex, the county in which its writ ran. See Bryan Garner, ed., *Black's Law Dictionary*, 7th ed. (St Paul, Minn.: West Group, 1999, 904).

37. Hand, J. articulates this principle in *United States v. Carroll Towing Co.* (1947) F2d 169 (2d Cir). The Australian equivalent is in a judgment by J. Mason in *Wyong Shire Council v. Shirt* (1980) 146 CLR 40.

38. Two versions or variations on the definition of "efficiency" in economic transactions. A transaction is said to be Pareto optimal when two parties have bargained fully, with no loss to either, to the extent of their mutual benefit, and can go no further. A transaction is said to be Pareto superior when two parties have bargained to a point of mutual benefit beyond which, if bargaining continues, the result will be a loss, sustained by one of the parties to the benefit of the other. See Jules Coleman, "The Normative Basis of Economic Analysis" (*Stanford Law Review* 34, 1982, 1105).

39. The Kaldor-Hicks principle acknowledges that in all transactions, including the most economically "efficient" (such as wealth maximizing), there will always be someone who sustains a loss. The point is to compensate that loss through some sort of mechanism or structure (like a rule system), however notional that compensation may be. See Richard A. Posner, "Cost-Benefit Analysis: Definition, Justification, and Comment on Conference Papers" in *Cost-Benefit Analysis: Legal, Economic, and Philosophical Perspectives*, ed. Matthew Adler and Eric Posner (Chicago: University of Chicago Press, 2000, 317–42); Nicholas Mercuro and Stephen G. Medema, *Economics and the Law: From Posner to Postmodernism* (Princeton, N.J.: Princeton University Press, 1997, 130–56).

40. A wing of the Law and Economics movement associated with Profs. Ian MacNeil (Northwestern), Victor Goldberg (Columbia), et al. and arguing for a reformed rule system that will reflect the changes in the institutions that govern economic life today. So, for example, MacNeil argued for a new form of contract—in-house, standard form, and with a range of alternative dispute resolution mechanisms—amenable to and reflective of the ongoing and continuous relationships of modern business and its signal institution, the corporation, with its devices of licensing, joint ventures, and so on. See Stephen Parker and Stephen Bottomley, *Law in Context* (Annandale and Leichardt, Australia: Federation Press, 1994, 1997, 308–16).

41. A branch of Law and Economics, and most often identified with Mr. Justice Richard Posner (Chicago), and others of the Chicago School (Kronman, et al.) who sought to retain the conventional rule system of law, but resituate it on a new basis—efficiency, or Kaldor-Hicks–inspired wealth maximization. Thus contract and its rules would still obtain and regulate economic transactions—but with the difference that the old morality of bargaining—"good faith," *consensus ad idem, uberrima fides*—would be replaced by efficiency, so that, for example, efficient breaches of contract would be encouraged (rather than penalized) by the law.

42. Though Posner goes out of his way to distance and differentiate himself from utilitarianism (a case of the economist protesting too much?), see Richard A. Posner, "Utilitarianism, Economics, and Legal Theory" in *The Economic Structure of the Law: The Collected Economic Essays of Richard A. Posner*, vol. 1, ed. Francesco Parisi (Cheltenham: Edward Elgar, 2002), 140–77.

43. Jeremy Bentham, *An Introduction to the Principles and Morals of Legislation*, ed. J. H. Burns and H.L.A. Hart (London: Athlone, 1970, 11).

44. Coase never claimed, with his usual modesty and understatement, to be promulgating a scientific "theorem"; rather he attributes that coinage to his American colleague, economist George Stigler. See Parker and Bottomley, *Law in Context*, 300.

45. Ronald H. Coase, "The Problem of Social Cost," in *Law and Economics*, vol. 1, ed. Jules Coleman and Jeffrey Lange (Aldershot: Dartmouth Press, 1992, 17).

46. Elizabeth Wright, ed., *Feminism and Pscyhoanalysis: A Critical Dictionary*, advisory ed. Diane Chisholm, Juliet Flower MacCannell, and Margaret Whitford (Oxford: Blackwell, 1992, 84–88).

47. David Sugarman, "Legal Theory, the Common Law Mind, and the Making of the Textbook Tradition" in *Legal Theory and the Common Law*, ed. William Twining (Oxford: Blackwell, 1986, 26–61).

48. A. M. Polinsky, *An Introduction to Law and Economics* (Boston: Little, Brown, 1983, 11–14).

49. See, for example, Hilaire McCoubrey, Nigel D. White, *Textbook on Jurisprudence* (London: Blackstone, 1993, 243); Parker and Bottomley, *Law in Context*, 300–301; James William Harris, *Legal Philosophies* (London: Butterworths, 1997, 46–47); Wacks, *Jurisprudence*, 190.

50. Frank Easterbrook, "The Inevitability of Law and Economics" (*Legal Education Review* 1, 1989, 7).

51. Wright, *Feminism and Psychoanalysis*, 84–88.

52. *Ibid.*, 185–88.

53. *Star Trek: The Next Generation*, directed by Gene Roddenberry (Paramount, 1990–96).

54. *The Matrix* (film), directed by Andy and Larry Wachowski (Warner Brothers, 1999).

55. *Aliens*, directed by James Cameron (20th Century Fox, 1986).

56. Karl Marx, excerpts from *Capital* in *Karl Marx: Selected Writings*, ed. David McLellan (Oxford: Oxford University Press, 2000, 442–43).

57. Naomi Klein, *No Logo, No Space, No Choice, No Jobs: Taking Aim at the Brand Bullied* (London: Flamingo, 2000).

58. Louis Althusser, *Essays on Ideology* (London: Verso, 1984, 1–61).

59. Ronald H. Coase, *The Firm, the Market, and the Law* (Chicago: University of Chicago Press, 1988, 118).

60. Polinsky, *Law and Economics*, 14.

61. Milton Friedman and Rose Friedman, *Free to Choose: A Personal Statement* (New York: Harcourt Brace, 1980).

62. Berlin, *Four Essays on Liberty*, 121–31.

63. Berlin, *Four Essays on Liberty*, 131–34.

64. Cento Veljanovski, *The New Law and Economics* (Oxford: Oxford University Press, 1983, 37); Daniel Kahneman, Paul Slovic, and Amos Tversky, eds., *Judgment Under Uncertainty: Heuristics and Biases* (Cambridge, UK: Cambridge University Press, 1982).

65. Robert Cover, "Violence and the Word" (*Yale Law Journal* 95, 1986, 1601).

66. Lewis A. Kornhauser, "The New Economic Analysis of Law: Legal Rules as Incentives" in *Law and Economics*, ed. Nicholas Mercuro (Dordrecht, The Netherlands: Kluwer, 1989).

67. Stewart Macauley, "Noncontractual Relations in Business: A Preliminary Study" in *Law and Society*, ed. Roger Cotterrell (Aldershot: Dartmouth, 1994, 481–94).

68. Peter Fitzpatrick, *Dangerous Supplements: Resistance and Renewal in Jurisprudence* (London: Pluto, 1991).

69. *Brazil*, directed by Terry Gilliam (Embassy International Pictures / Universal Pictures, 1985).

70. Robert Nozick, *Anarchy, State, and Utopia* (Oxford: Blackwell, 1974, 26–27).

71. Nozick, *Anarchy, State, and Utopia*, 12–13.

72. Literally "through want of care." A decision given *per incuriam* is given "in ignorance or forgetfulness" of an earlier precedent and/or legislative provision, thereby vitiating its value as good authority. See Peter Butt and Peter Nygh, eds., *Butterworths Concise Australian Legal Dictionary* (Chatswood, Australia: Lexis Nexis Butterworths, 2004, 325).

73. Trey Parker and Matt Stone, *South Park* (Comedy Channel, 1997–).

74. Bentham, *Principles and Morals of Legislation*, 11.

75. Robert Gordon, "Critical Legal Histories" in *Critical Legal Studies*, ed. James Boyle (Aldershot: Dartmouth, 1992, 114–15).

76. Landes and Posner, "The Economics of the Baby Shortage."

77. Williams, *The Rooster's Egg*, 217–26.

78. *E.T.: The Extra-Terrestrial*, directed by Steven Spielberg (Universal, 1982).

79. Sigmund Freud, *Beyond the Pleasure Principle*, vol. 18 in *The Standard Edition of the*

Complete Psychological Works of Sigmund Freud, trans. and ed. James Strachey (London: Hogarth Press, 1966–74, 14–15).

80. Terry Eagleton, *Against the Grain: Essays, 1975–1986* (London: Verso, 1986).

81. For an objective report on this chilling phenomenon, see Clint Witchalls, "Could Reading the Thoughts of Criminals Help Free the Innocent?" (*The Guardian*, 25 March 2004).

Chapter Six

1. For the first and best fictional "hate letter" to law school (and Harvard in particular), see John Jay Osborne, Jr., *The Paper Chase* (New York: Popular Library, 1971). For a churlish (but entertaining) 1970s update, see Scott Turow, *One L: The Turbulent True Story of a First Year at Harvard Law School* (New York: Putnam, 1977). For a record-setting whinge (why not just transfer or drop out?), this time lambasting critical legal studies, see Richard D. Kahlenberg, *Broken Contract: A Memoir of Harvard Law School*, foreword by R. Coles (New York: Hill & Wang, 1992). Finally, for a refreshingly demystifying and completely hedonistic (of the gambling and crystal meth sort) tour of law school, east and west, see the recent "slacker" exposé, see Jaime Marquart and Robert Ebert Byrnes, *Brush with the Law: The True Story of Law School Today at Harvard and Stanford* (Los Angeles: Renaissance Books, 2001). Regarding "factions," see Eleanor Kerlow, *Poisoned Ivy: How Egos, Ideology, and Power Politics Almost Ruined Harvard Law School* (New York: St. Martin's, 1994). For an opposing view, this time from the professorial inside, see Derrick Bell, *Confronting Authority: Reflections of an Ardent Protester* (Boston: Beacon Hill Press, 1994). See also the now classic Patricia Williams, *The Alchemy of Race and Rights* (Cambridge, Mass.: Harvard University Press, 1991).

2. See below for *The Paper Chase* and *Legally Blonde*.

3. *The Paper Chase*, CBS, 1978; 1983–86, produced by Robert C. Thompson.

4. Halifax, Nova Scotia, Canada. Founded in 1883, Dalhousie Law School is Canada's oldest common law school and historically the curricular pioneer and model for that nation's legal education. Some notable graduates—aside from the usual suspects of prime ministers, peers, and premiers—include Mr. Justice Ronald St. John Macdonald (the first Canadian on the European Court of Human Rights), Mme. Justice Bertha Wilson (the first woman on the Canadian supreme court), and James Robinson Johnston Esq. (the first law graduate from Nova Scotia's historic black community). See John Willis, *A History of Dalhousie Law School* (Toronto: University of Toronto Press, 1979).

5. Toronto, Ontario, Canada. The alternative model in Canadian legal education was provided by Osgoode Hall Law School. While Dalhousie Law School was always a university-affiliated faculty (Dalhousie University, est. 1818) with all that implies (a tenured professoriate, full-time students, an academic study program), Osgoode Hall was run by a professional body, the Law Society of Upper Canada, and until the 1960s provided a part-time legal education somewhat akin to the English Inns of Court or the American "proprietary"

law schools. Professional training, in the form of solicitors' articles, remained paramount for entry into the "fused" Ontarian legal profession. In 1968, Osgoode Hall affiliated with York University in North Toronto, and subsequently established itself as a leading center for legal research in Canada and a rival to the Dalhousie-style, academically high-powered Faculty of Law at the University of Toronto (est. 1949 and recognized 1957). See Jerome Bickenbach and Ian Kyer, *The Fiercest Debate: Cecil A. Wright, The Benchers, and Legal Education in Ontario, 1823–1957* (Toronto: Osgoode Society, 1987).

6. Canberra, ACT, Australia. Founded in 1960 and, among the "Sandstones" (Australia's Ivy League or Oxbridge), one of the newer law schools; but one with a strong reputation and a high research profile in international and constitutional law, as befits the faculty of law of the "national" university, Australian National University.

7. Melbourne, Victoria, Australia. Founded in 1873, and long considered a leader in Australian legal education. See Alex C. Castles, *An Australian Legal History* (Sydney: Law Book Company, 1982).

8. London, England. University College London, the core constituent college of the University of London, was the first tertiary institution in the United Kingdom to teach common law continuously by establishing, in 1829, the Quain Professorship of Jurisprudence. Holders of that chair have included John Austin, Lord Lloyd of Hampstead, William Twining, and Ronald Dworkin, to name but a few. See William Twining, *Blackstone's Tower: The English Law School* (London: Sweet & Maxwell, 1994).

9. Edinburgh, Scotland. One of Britain's most eminent centers of legal education, Edinburgh University's School of Law was founded in 1707, and its graduates win the global law-and-literature gold medal, their numbers including Sir Walter Scott, Robert Louis Stevenson, and Thomas Carlyle. This literary heritage continues to the present day with a faculty that includes, as its Professor of Medico-Legal Studies, detective novelist Alexander McCall Smith. See J. W. Cairns and Hector MacQueen, "Learning and the Law: A Short History of the Edinburgh Law School" on the University of Edinburgh website, http://www.law.ed.ac .uk/Tercentenary/documents/Learningthelaw/ (accessed September 2006).

10. For an excellent history of the unique development of the American law school, see Robert B. Stevens, *Law School: Legal Education in America from 1850s to the 1980s* (Chapel Hill: University of North Carolina, 1983). For a more specialized account, see Laura Kalman, *Legal Realism at Yale, 1927–1960* (Chapel Hill, NC: University of North Carolina, 1986).

11. With NYU, the top American law schools as ranked by *U.S. News and World Report*, with Stanford, 3rd; Columbia, 4th; NYU, 5th; Chicago, 6th; Pennsylvania, 7th; and Michigan, 8th. See "America's Best Graduate Schools 2006: Top 100 Law Schools" on the USNews. com website, http://www.usnews.comsnews/edu/grad/rankings/law/brief/lawrank_brief .php (accessed September 2006).

12. See Joel Seligman, *The High Citadel: The Influence of the Harvard Law School* (Boston: Houghton-Mifflin, 1978); Richard Granfield, *Making Elite Lawyers: Visions of Law at Harvard and Beyond* (New York: Routledge, 1992).

13. As Harvard's website baldly puts it: "the world's most intellectually interesting and diverse law faculty." See The President and Fellows of Harvard College, "Harvard Law School: Faculty" on the Harvard Law School website, http://www.law.harvard.edu/faculty/ (accessed September 2006).

14. For several years now, the frontrunner in the (admittedly controversial) *U.S. News and World Report Rankings* as America's top law school.

15. William P. LaPiana, *Logic and Experience: The Origin of American Legal Education* (New York: Oxford University Press, 1994).

16. Jacques Lacan, *Le Seminaire, Livre XII. L'envers de la psychoanalyse*, ed. Jacques-Alain Miller (Paris: Editions du Seuil, 1975).

17. Lacan, *Le Seminaire*, vol. 17.

18. Leslie J. Moran, Emma Sandon, Elena Loizidou, and Ian Christie, eds. *Law's Moving Image* (London: Cavendish, 2004).

19. *The Paper Chase* (DVD), directed by James Bridges (1973; 20th Century Fox Home Entertainment, 2003). (Hereafter cited as PC.)

20. *Legally Blonde* (DVD), directed by Robert Luketic (Metro-Goldwyn-Mayer Pictures, 2001; MGM Home Entertainment, 2001). (Hereafter cited as LB.)

21. Duncan Kennedy, "Legal Education as Training for Hierarchy" in *The Politics of Law: A Progressive Critique*, ed. David Kairys (New York: Pantheon, 1982, 40–64).

22. Sigmund Freud, *The Psychopathology of Everyday Life*, trans. Alan Tyson, ed. and intro. James Strachey (New York: Norton, 1966).

23. Jacques Lacan, *Feminine Sexuality: Jacques Lacan and the école freudienne*, ed. Juliet Mitchell and Jacqueline Rose (New York: Norton, 1982).

24. Kennedy, "Legal Education as Training for Hierarchy."

25. Turow, *One L*.

26. Kahlenberg, *Broken Contract*.

27. *Gordon v. Steele* 376 F. Supp. 575 (W.D. Pa. 1974).

28. *Hawkins v. McGee* 146 A. 641 (N.H. Coos. 1929).

29. Christopher Columbus Langdell (1826–1906), American legal educator and dean, grad. Harvard Law School, 1854, and practiced law, NYC. Returned to Harvard in 1870 as Dane Professor, then Dean, teaching there for the next thirty years. Pioneered the celebrated "case method" of legal study, a mode of analysis that interrogated the particulars of a case—its facts, judgment, ratio, dissent, obiter—through a question-answer methodology sometimes known, in homage to the Platonic Dialogues, as "Socratic." Langdell's influence was enhanced by his *Cases on Contracts*, which displaced the expository textbooks of old (in which cases were merely illustrations of principles), and quickly became an American law school standard. But not all of Langdell's legacy was innovative. In fact, he represents the extension and embedding of a kind of High Formalism / Positivism in the American legal academy, wedded to the letter of the law, and hostile not only to its spirit

but also to its context—be it social, political, or economic. The Realists considered Langdell "the Enemy," and their revolution sought to overturn the, by then—the 1920s—deeply entrenched Langdellian orthodoxies in the U.S. law schools and legal consciousness. See David M. Walker *The Oxford Companion to Law* (Oxford: Oxford University Press, 1980, 714).

30. *Love Story*, directed by Arthur Hiller (Paramount, 1970).

31. Jacques Derrida, *Of Grammatology*, trans. Gayatri Chakravorty Spivak (Baltimore, Md.: Johns Hopkins University, 1976, 158).

32. Carol Gilligan, *In a Different Voice: Psychological Theory and Women's Development* (Cambridge, Mass.: Harvard University Press, 1982).

33. For the explication of this term of art, see Mari J. Matsuda, "Outsider Jurisprudence: Toward a Victim's Analysis of Racial Hate Messages" in *Group Defamation and Freedom of Speech: The Relationship Between Language and Violence*, ed. Monroe Freedman and Eric Freedman (Westport, Conn.: Greenwood, 1995, 87–123).

34. Moreton-Robinson, *Talkin' Up to the White Woman*.

35. Judith Resnik, "A Continuous Body: Ongoing Conversations About Women and Legal Education" (*Journal of Legal Education*, 53:4, Dec. 2003, 564–77, 565).

36. Deborah L. Rhode, "Midcourse Corrections: Women in Legal Education" (*Journal of Legal Education* 53:4, Dec. 2003, 475–88, 478).

37. Rhode, "Midcourse Corrections," 480.

38. Indeed, something like the much-feared "estrogen contamination" so deplored by Harvard Law School men of the 1960s and 1970s, of which Judith Richards Hope writes, quoting Patricia Schroeder, in her memoir of her life in law: *Pinstripes and Pearls* (New York: Scribner's, 2003, 14–16). Rhode, "Midcourse Corrections," 479.

39. Rhode writes in 2003: "At last count, only 23 percent of full professor[s] and 13 percent of law school deans are female, and only 4 percent of the professors and 1 percent of deans are women of color," Rhode, "Midcourse Corrections," 475.

40. Resnick, "A Continuous Body," 566. Quoting Jonathan Glazer, "Women Are Close to Being Majority of Law Students" (*New York Times*, Mar. 26, 2001, A1).

41. *Mean Girls*, directed by Mark Walters (Paramount, 2004).

42. *Heathers*, directed by Michael Lehman (New World Entertainment, 1989).

43. *Romy and Michele's High School Reunion*, directed by David Mirkin (Touchstone Pictures, 1999).

44. Kahlenberg, *Broken Contract*.

45. Turow, *One L*.

46. Jean Martin Charcot, *Clinical Lectures on Diseases of the Nervous System* (London: Routledge, 1991).

47. Sigmund Freud, *Dora: An Analysis of a Case of Hysteria*, intro. Phillip Rieff (New York: Simon & Schuster, 1997).

48. Jacques Lacan, *The Psychoses 1955–1956*, vol. 3 in *The Seminar of Jacques Lacan*, ed. Jacques-Alain Miller, trans. Russell Grigg (London: Routledge, 1981, 171); Stuart Schneiderman, *Jacques Lacan: The Death of an Intellectual* (Cambridge, Mass.: Harvard University Press, 1983, 59); Serge Leclaire, *La mort dans la vie de l'obsédé* in *La Psychanalyse 2* (1957, 129).

49. Sigmund Freud, *Psychoanalytic Notes on an Autobiographical Account of a Case of Paranoia (Dementia Paranoidia)*, vol. 12 in *The Standard Edition of the Complete Psychological Works of Sigmund Freud* (London: Hogarth Press / Institute of Psychoanalysis, 1958).

50. Joan Riviere, "Womanliness as Masquerade" in *Formations of Fantasy*, ed. Victor Burgin, James Donald, and Cora Caplan (London: Routledge, 1986, 35–44).

51. Riviere, "Womanliness as Masquerade," 35.

52. Lacan, *The Psychoses*, 179–80. See also Leclaire, *La mort dans la vie de l'obsédé*, 129.

53. Sigmund Freud, "Obsessive Action and Religious Practices," *Standard Edition*, vol. 9 (London: Hogarth Press, 1907).

54. A trust-funded twenty-something urbanite, along the lines of Paris Hilton.

55. See, for example, Slavoj Žižek, *Enjoy Your Symptom! Jacques Lacan in Hollywood and Out* (London: Routledge, 1992).

56. Jacques Lacan, "The Seminar on 'The Purloined Letter'" in *The Purloined Poe: Lacan, Derrida, and Psychoanalytic Reading*, trans. J. Mehlman; ed. J. Muller and W. Richardson (Baltimore, Md.: Johns Hopkins University Press, 1988).

57. For the concept of "hailing" or interpellation, see: Louis Althusser, "Ideology and Ideological State Apparatuses" in *Lenin and Philosophy, and Other Essays*, trans. B. Brewster (New York: Monthly Review, 1971, 127–88).

58. Althusser, "Ideology and Ideological State Apparatuses."

59. On the theme of "passionate jurisprudence," see Susan A. Bandes, *The Passions of the Law* (New York: New York University Press, 1999).

60. *Legally Blonde 2: Red, White, and Blonde* (DVD), directed by Charles Hermon-Wurfeld (MGM Home Entertainment, 2003).

61. Judith Butler, *Excitable Speech: A Politics of the Performative* (London: Routledge, 1997).

62. See esp. Renata Salecl, *The Spoils of Freedom: Psychoanalysis and Feminism After the Fall of Socialism* (London: Routledge, 1994); *Perversions of Love and Hate* (London: Verso Press, 2000).

63. Jeanne L. Schroeder, *The Vestal and the Fasces: Hegel, Lacan, Property, and the Feminine* (Berkeley: University of California Press, 1998); *The Triumph of Venus: The Erotics of the Market* (Berkeley: University of California Press, 2004).

64. Juliet Flower MacCannell, *The Regime of the Brother: After the Patriarchy* (London: Routledge, 1991).

65. Lacan, "Seminar on 'The Purloined Letter.'"

66. For the formulation of this question—the question of the Other—see Jacques

Lacan, "The Subversion of the Subject and the Dialectic of Desire" in *Écrits: A Selection*, trans. A. Sheridan (New York: Norton, 1977).

67. Slavoj Žižek, *The Sublime Object of Ideology* (London: Verso, 1989).

68. Aristotle, *Politics*, Book 3, trans. Benjamin Jowett (New York: Modern Library, 1943).

69. Panu Minkinnen, *Thinking Without Desire: A First Philosophy of Law* (Oxford: Hart, 1999).

70. See Kennedy, "Legal Education as Training for Hierarchy,", 40–64; Duncan Kennedy, "The Structure of Blackstone's Commentaries" (*Buffalo Law Review* 28, 1979, 205–382); Roberto M. Unger, *Politics, a Work in Constructive Social Theory* (Cambridge, UK: Cambridge University Press, 1987); *The Critical Legal Studies Movement* (Cambridge Mass.: Harvard University Press, 1986); Peter Cane and Mark Tushnet eds., *The Oxford Handbook of Legal Studies* (Oxford: Oxford University Press, 2003); Mark Tushnet, "Critical Legal Studies: An Introduction to its Origins and Underpinnings" (*Journal of Legal Education* 36, 1986, 505–17).

71. Lacan, "Seminar on 'The Purloined Letter.'"

72. Slavoj Žižek, *Enjoy Your Symptom!* 124–28.

73. Gilles Deleuze and Felix Guattari, *Anti-Oedipus: Capitalism and Schizophrenia*, preface by Michel Foucault (Minneapolis: University of Minnesota Press, 1983).

74. Jacques Lacan, "Kant avec Sade" (*October* 51, Winter, 1989).

75. Sigmund Freud, *Totem and Taboo: Resemblances Between the Psychic Lives of Savages and Neurotics* in *The Basic Writings of Sigmund Freud*, trans. and intro. A. A. Brill (New York: Modern Library, 1995, 775–898).

76. On another yoking of Rawls and psychoanalysis see Joan Copjec, "Sour Justice, or Liberalist Envy" in *Imagine There's No Woman: Ethics and Sublimation* (Cambridge, Mass.: MIT Press, 2002, 158–76).

77. Jacques Lacan, "God and the *Jouissance* of the Woman," 137–48.

78. Lani Guinier, Michelle Fine, and Jane Balin, *Becoming Gentlemen: Women, Law, and Institutional Change* (Boston: Beacon, 1997).

79. Deborah L. Rhode, "Missing Questions: Feminist Perspectives on Legal Education," (*Stanford Law Review* 45, July 1993, 1547–66).

80. Margaret Thornton, "F-Law Talk: Feminism in the Legal Academy" (*Australian Feminist Law Journal* 14, Mar. 2000, 116–20); "Feeling Chilly (Again) in the Legal Academy" (*Australian Feminist Law Journal* 18, June 2003, 145–51); "The Development of Feminist Jurisprudence" (*Legal Education Review* 9:2, 1998, 171–92).

81. Celia Wells, "Exceptional Women or Honorary Men? Notes from the Women Law Professors' Project" (*Current Legal Problems* 53, 2000), 181–203; "Women Law Professors—Negotiating and Transcending Gender Identities at Work" (*Feminist Legal Studies* 10, 2002, 1–38); "Ladies in Waiting: The Women Law Professors' Story" (*Sydney Law Review* 23, 2001, 167–84); "Working Out Women in Law Schools" (*Legal Studies* 21, 2001, 116–36).

82. Thornton writes as eloquently as always: "There is enormous dynamism, creativity and diversity associated with feminist legal scholarship, which moves between fringe and centre. However, I am not sure that it can still be said to be 'cutting edge' in the way that it was in the 1970s and 1980s. The move to the safety of the centre could be a dangerous sign, for the very act of attaining the object of desire may signal its disintegration. Nevertheless, despite qualified signs of acceptance, such as numerosity, I think society is far from being about to reach some ideal end state of gender justice." Thornton, "F-Law Talk," 118–19.

83. Catharine MacKinnon, "Mainstreaming Feminism in Legal Education" (*Journal of Legal Education* 53:2, June 2003, 199–212). This is not to detract from MacKinnon's very laudable efforts to construct a specifically feminist program for legal study. After all, one of the constant bleats, at least since the 1980s, of orthodox legal scholars is that critical legal studies, feminist or otherwise, lacks an agenda beyond critique: that is, they can combust (deconstruct?) but not construct. To this old saw, MacKinnon is a welcome riposte.

Chapter Seven

1. *The Castle*, directed by Rob Sitch (Village Roadshow, 1997).

2. Australian slang for truck driver. See James Lambert, ed. *Macquarie Book of Slang: Australian Slang in the Noughties* (Sydney: Macquarie University, Macquarie Library, 2000).

3. *Mabo v. The State of Queensland* (no. 2) (1992) 107 ALR 1. The case has a long and involved procedural and substantive history, the proceedings having been initiated in 1982. The original challenge concerned legislation enacted by the state of Queensland extinguishing Aboriginal land claims as contravening the Racial Discrimination Act. For a resolution of that specific issue, see *Mabo v. Queensland* (no. 1) (1988) 166 CLR 186.

4. For the standard British Commonwealth text on native title, see Kent McNeil, *Common Law Aboriginal Title* (Oxford: Oxford University Press, 1989). For a more recent comparative treatment of two major British Commonwealth jurisdictions, see Shaunnagh Dorsett, "Civilisation and Cultivation: Colonial Policy and Indigenous Peoples in Canada and Australia Post-Wik" (*Griffith Law Review* 4, 1995, 214–38).

5. Louis Althusser, "Ideology and Ideological State Apparatuses" in *Lenin and Philosophy, and Other Essays*, trans. B. Brewster (New York: Monthly Review Press, 1971, 127–88).

6. Jacques Lacan, "The Mirror Stage," 1–7.

7. At the time of this chapter's writing, the scholarly output on *Mabo* had reached a fevered pitch in Australia and around the common law world. For a selection of some of the most interesting analyses, see the special issue of *Law/Text/Culture*, titled "In the Wake of Terra Nullius" (4:1, 1998), ed. Colin Perrin. See also Elizabeth Povinelli, "The Cunning of Seduction: Real Being and Aboriginal Recognition in Settler Australia" (*Australian Feminist Law Journal* 11, Sept. 1998, 3–27); Stewart Motha, "Mabo: Encountering the Epistemic Limit

of the Recognition of 'Difference'" (*Griffith Law Review* 7:1, 1998, 79–96); Duncan Ivison, "Decolonising the Rule of Law: Mabo's Case and Post-colonial Constitutionalism" (*Oxford Journal of Legal Studies* 17, Summer 1997, 253–79); Brendan Edgeworth, "Tenure, Allodialism, and Indigenous Rights at Common Law: English, United States, and Australian Land Law Compared After *Mabo v. Queensland*" (*Anglo-American Law Review* 23, Oct./Dec. 1994, 397–433); Jeremy Webber, "The Jurisprudence of Regret: The Search for Standards of Justice in Mabo" (*Sydney Law Review* 17, March 1995, 5–28).

8. My understanding of Indigeneity, law, and culture has gained immeasurably from innumerable conversations with Christine Morris, G'Murri person, Ph.D. candidate (Griffith Law School), and friend. I want to thank her, and single out her work—on *Whalerider*, on *Thunderheart*, and on *Plains of Promise* (manuscripts on file with author)—as some of the most exciting and innovative in the cultural legal studies canon, bringing popular culture into dialogue with Indigenous jurisprudence.

9. "Ocker" in Australian slang refers to "the archetypal uncultivated Australian working man" or "a boorish, uncouth, chauvinistic Australian." The term can also refer to "an Australian male displaying qualities considered to be typically Australian" such as resourcefulness, good humor, and helpfulness. See Lambert, *Macquarie Book of Slang*, 169.

10. Northrop Frye, *The Anatomy of Criticism* (Princeton, N.J.: Princeton University Press, 1957).

11. Or "quilting point," buttoning down the dissemination of meaning. See Jacques Lacan, *The Psychoses 1955–1956*.

12. Sigmund Freud, "The Uncanny" in *Collected Papers*, vol. 4, trans. Joan Riviere (London: Hogarth, 1950, 368–407).

13. *Muriel's Wedding*, directed by P. J. Hogan (Miramax, 1994).

14. *Strictly Ballroom*, directed by Baz Luhrmann (Miramax, 1992).

15. Reg Watson, *Neighbours* (Grundy, 1985–).

16. Alan Bateman, *Home and Away* (7 Network, 1987).

17. The term is an Australian colloquialism generally used in reference to that which is distinctively Australian or specifically "the archetypal uncultivated Australian workingman." See entry for "ocker" in Bernard, J.R.L. et al., eds., *Macquarie ABC Dictionary: Australia's National Dictionary* (Sydney: Macquarie Library, 2003).

18. The extremely successful Melbourne production house behind such popular Australian television shows as "The Panel," "Frontline," "Funky Squad," and "A River Somewhere," as well as the recently released feature film, *The Dish*. See their website at http://www.workingdog.com/.

19. Australian slang for fool or idiot. See Lambert, *Macquarie Book of Slang*, 21.

20. David McLellan, ed., *Karl Marx: Selected Writings* (Oxford: Univeristy Press, 2000).

21. For details of the Australian kleptocracy, see "Alan Bond (businessman)" in Wikipedia, http://en.wikipedia.org/wiki/Alan_Bond_(businessman), and "Christopher Skase," http://en.wikipedia.org/wiki/Christopher_Skase (accessed September 2006).

22. For details of the Jabiluka protests, see "Jabiluka" in *Wikipedia*, http://en.wikipedia .org/wiki/Jabiluka (accessed September 2006). See also Takver, "Jabiluka Blockade and Protests 1998," *Radical Tradition: An Australiasian History Page*, http://www.takver.com/ history/jabiluka1998.htm (accessed September 2006).

23. For the use of this term, and an overview of the critical legal studies movement (in the United States, at least), see David Kairys, *The Politics of the Law: A Progressive Critique* (New York: Pantheon, 1982).

24. *Milirrpum v. Nabalco Pty Ltd* (1970) 17 FLR 141. See also *Coe v. Commonwealth* (1979) 24 ALR 118.

25. Australian slang for "a stupid or unfashionable male." See Lambert, *Macquarie Book of Slang*, 15.

26. Noel Pearson, "204 Years of Invisible Title," cited in Heather McRae, Garth Nettheim, Laura Beacroft, and Luke McNamara, eds., *Indigenous Legal Issues: Commentary and Materials* (Sydney: LBC Information Services, 1997, 223).

27. Determination of Moynihan J., 155–56, quoted by Toohey J. in *Mabo v. The State of Queensland* (no. 2), 107 ALR 1 in Richard Bartlett, ed., *The Mabo Decision* (Sydney: Butterworths, 1993, 149).

28. Determination of Moynihan J. quoted in Brennan J. in *Mabo* (no. 2), 9.

29. G.W.F. Hegel, *Philosophy of Right*, trans. T. M. Knox (Oxford: Clarendon, 1945).

30. Australian slang for Aboriginal. See Arthur Delbridge, ed., *The Macquarie Dictionary of Australian Colloquial Language* (Sydney: Macquarie University: Macquarie Library, 1988, 28).

31. Aileen Moreton-Robinson, *Talkin' Up to the White Woman*.

32. Though Toohey J. raises the possibility of compensation for native title land "wrongfully" extinguished by the Crown, see *Mabo* (no. 2), 169.

33. See esp. the following: *Mr. Smith Goes to Washington*, directed by Frank Capra (Columbia Pictures, 1939) and *It's a Wonderful Life*, directed by Frank Çapra (Liberty Films, 1946).

34. *Commonwealth v. Tasmania* (1983) 158 CLR 1.

35. See Ronald Dworkin, *A Matter of Principle* (Cambridge, Mass.: Harvard University Press, 1985), but also *Taking Rights Seriously* (Cambridge, Mass: Harvard University Press, 1977), and *Law's Empire* (Cambridge, Mass.: Belknap Press, 1986).

36. *Semayne's case* (1605) 5 Co Rep 91a, cited in Hilaire Bennet, *Constitutional and Administrative Law* (London: Cavendish, 1995).

37. Berlin, *Four Essays on Liberty*.

38. Berlin, *Four Essays on Liberty*.

39. *Mabo* (no. 2), 29.

40. *Mabo* (no. 2), 29.

41. *Mabo* (no. 2), 28.

42. Karl Llewellyn, *The Common Law Tradition: Deciding Appeals* (Boston: Little, Brown, 1960).

43. *Mabo* (no. 2), 29.

44. *Mabo* (no. 2), 18.

45. *Administration of Papua and New Guinea v. Daera Guba* (1973) 130 CLR at 397.

46. *Amodu Tijani v. Secretary, Southern Nigeria* 2 AC at 403–4 (1921).

47. *Calder v. Attorney-General of British Columbia* SCR at 416 (1973); 34 DLR (3d) at 218 (1973).

48. *Advisory Opinion on Western Sahara* ICJR at 39 (1975).

49. Here interpreted as a "postulate" necessary to legitimize the tenurial system, put in place in a territory recently acquired by a colonial sovereign, but not to be equated with "absolute beneficial ownership," which would extinguish all other prior—read, Indigenous—claims. See *Mabo* (no. 2), 33–34.

50. *The Case of Tanistry* (1608) Davis 28; 80 ER 516; 4th ed Dublin (1762) English translation 78, 110–11, quoted in *Mabo* (no. 2), 34, 40.

51. *Witrong and Blany* (1674) 3 Keb 401 at 402; 84 ER 789 at 789, quoted in *Mabo* (no. 2), 34, 40.

52. F. W. Maitland, *Equity, Also, the Forms of Action at Common Law: Two Courses of Lectures*, ed. W. J. Whittaker (Cambridge, UK: Cambridge University Press, 1909).

53. Noel Pearson, "From Remnant to Social Justice," cited in McRae, et al., *Indigenous Legal Issues*, 214.

54. McRae, et al., *Indigenous Legal Issues*, 219.

55. *Mabo* (no. 2), 41.

56. *Mabo* (no. 2), 55.

57. *Mabo* (no. 2), 55.

58. *Ibid.*, 35.

59. For a searching analysis of this concept, see Shaunnagh Dorsett, "'Clear and plain intention': Extinguishment of Native Title in Australia and Canada, Post-Wik" (*Griffith Law Review* 6, 1997, 96–121).

60. *Johnson v. McIntosh* (1823) 8 Wheat 543.

61. *Mabo* (no. 2), 51.

62. *Mabo* (no. 2), 51.

63. *Mabo* (no. 2), 51.

64. *Native Title Act* 1993 (Cth)

65. *Native Title Act* 1993 (Cth), s.228.

66. *Wik Peoples v. The State of Queensland* (1996) 141 CLR 129.

67. *Fejo v. Northern Territory* (1998) 156 ALR 721.

68. *Western Australia v. the Commonwealth* (1995) 183 CLR 373.

69. *Wik* has generated almost as much academic commentary in Australia as *Mabo*. For two of the best commentaries on the case, see Peter Rush, "An Altered Jurisdiction: Corporeal Traces of Law" (*Griffith Law Review* 6, 1997, 144–68); and Lee Godden, "Wik: Legal Memory and History" (*Griffith Law Review* 6, 1997, 122–43).

70. *Mabo* (no. 2), 46.

71. McRae, et al., *Indigenous Legal Issues*, 273.

72. Slavoj Žižek, *The Plague of Fantasies* (London: Verso, 1997).

73. Historically, "squatters" were those who settled on Crown land to run stock, initially without government permission, but later with a lease or license. A squatter or squattocrat is now considered one of a group of rich and influential rural land owners forming a "squattocracy." See Lambert, ed. *Macquarie Book of Slang*, 228.

74. *Wik*, 649.

75. For an interesting psychoanalytic take on Australia's race politics, and the "return of the fascist repressed" that "One Nation" promises, see Jennifer Rutherford, *The Gauche Intruder: Freud, Lacan, and the White Australian Fantasy* (Melbourne: University Press, 2000).

76. Australian slang for anything "crassly masculine." See Lambert, *Macquarie Book of Slang*, 18.

77. "Cobber" is Australian slang for mate or friend. See Lambert, *Macquarie Book of Slang*, 44.

78. Australian slang for true or genuine. See Lambert, ed. *Macquarie Book of Slang*, 81.

79. Stanley Fish, "Boutique Multiculturalism" in *The Trouble with Principle* (Cambridge, Mass.: Harvard University Press, 1999, 56–75).

80. Notably, Michael Mansell in Bain Attwood and Andrew Markus, ed. *Struggle for Aboriginal Rights* (Sydney: Allen & Unwin, 1999). See also Henry Reynolds, *Aboriginal Sovereignty: Reflections on Race, State, and Nation* (St. Leonard's, Australia: Allen & Unwin, 1996); and Scott Bennett, *White Politics and Black Australians* (St. Leonards, NSW: Allen & Unwin, 1999).

81. See, for example, Peter Read, *Belonging: Australian Place and Aboriginal Ownership* (Cambridge, UK: Cambridge University Press, 2000).

82. Leslie J. Moran, "Gothic Law" (*Griffith Law Review* 10:2, 2001, 75–100).

83. Peter Hutchings, *The Criminal Spectre in Law, Literature, and Aesthetics: Incriminating Subjects* (London: Routledge, 2001).

84. Proudhon, Pierre-Joseph, *Selected Writings of Pierre-Joseph Proudhon*, ed. Stewart Edwards; trans. Elizabeth Fraser (Garden City, N.Y.: Anchor Books, 1969).

Chapter Eight

1. Kris Berggren, "Profile Brothers Stand with Family" (*National Catholic Reporter*, April 1, 2005, 6).

2. See The Franciscan Brothers of Peace Website, http://www.brothersofpeace.org (accessed September 2006).

3. See the "Letter from Brother Paul" in which the friars volunteer their time "in the Right to Life movement (praying at abortion clinics)." Paul J. O'Donnell, "Letter from Brother Paul," Franciscan Brothers of Peace (Minneapolis), http://www.brothersofpeace .org/brpaulletter.html (accessed September 2005).

4. For a conservative theological critique of the decline of American mainline Protestantism (Episcopal, Lutheran, Presbyterian, Congregationalist, and others), see Thomas C. Reeves, *The Empty Church: Does Organized Religion Matter Anymore?* (New York: Simon & Schuster, 1996).

5. Sigmund Freud, *The Future of an Illusion*, vol. 21 in *The Complete Psychological Works of Sigmund Freud*, rev. and ed. James Strachey (London: Institute of Psycho-Analysis and Hogarth Press, 1968).

6. *Nancy B. v. Hotel Dieu de Quebec* 86 Dom LR 1992 Jan 6, 385–95.

7. *Million Dollar Baby* (DVD), directed by Clint Eastwood (Warner Brothers, 2004; Lakeshore Entertainment, 2005). (Hereafter cited as MDB.)

8. F. X. Toole, *Rope Burns: Stories from the Corner* (New York: Ecco Press and Harper Collins, 2001).

9. *The Sea Inside* (DVD), directed by Alejandro Amenábar (2004; Sogepaq and Fine Line Features, 2005). (Hereafter cited as SI.)

10. *Sister Act*, directed by Emile Ardolino (Touchstone Pictures, 1992).

11. *The Sound of Music*, directed by Robert Wise (20th Century Fox, 1965).

12. Ronald Dworkin, *Life's Dominion: An Argument About Abortion, Euthanasia, and Individual Freedom* (New York: Vintage Books, 1994). (Hereafter cited as LD.)

13. John Paul II, "Homily of Pope John Paul II at Cherry Creek State Park, Denver, Colorado, on the Feast of the Assumption, 1993" on the Augustine Club website at Columbia University, http://www.columbia.edu/cu/augustine/arch/jp2/denver17.html (accessed September 2006).

14. Paul, "Homily of Pope John Paul II," 4.

15. *Ibid.*, 3.

16. *Ibid.*, 5.

17. Ioannus Paulus PPII *Evangelium Vitae* (1995) on the Libreria Editrice Vaticana website, http://www.vatican.va/edocs/ENG0141/_INDEX.HTM (accessed September 2006).

18. Paulus, *Evangelium Vitae*, 20.

19. *Ibid.*

20. *Ibid.*

21. John Paul II, "Address of John Paul II to the Bishops of the Episcopal Conference of the United States of America (California, Nevada, and Hawaii)," October 2, 1998, on the Libreria Editrice Vaticana website, 3, http://www.vatican.va/holy_father/john_paul_ii/

speeches/1998/october/documents/hf_jp-ii_spe_19981002_ad-limina-usa_en.html   (accessed September 2006).

22. Paul, "Address of John Paul II," 6.

23. Thomas Jefferson, "1 Jan. 1802 Letter in Response to the Danbury Baptist Association" in *The Writings of Thomas Jefferson*, vol. 16, eds. Andrew A. Lipscomb, Albert E. Bagh (Washington, D.C.: Thomas Jefferson Memorial Association 1903–4, 281–82).

24. Guido Calabresi and Philip Bobbitt, *Tragic Choices* (New York: Norton, 1978).

25. Calabresi and Bobbitt, *Tragic Choices*.

26. See, for example, Emmanual Lévinas, "Ethics as First Philosophy" in *The Levinas Reader*, ed. Sean Hand (Oxford: Blackwell, 1989).

27. Costas Douzinas with Ronnie Warrington, "The Face of Justice: A Jurisprudence of Alterity" (*Social and Legal Studies*, vol. 3, 1994, 405–25); "'A Well-Founded Fear of Justice': Law and Ethics in Postmodernity," in *Legal Studies as Cultural Studies*, ed. Jerry D. Leonard, 197–229 (Albany: SUNY Press, 1995).

28. Jeffrey Minson, *Genealogies of Morals: Nietzsche, Foucault, Donzelot, and the Eccentricity of Ethics* (London: Macmillan, 1985).

29. The UK's reigning crime queen and the author of *The Mermaids Singing*, *The Wire in the Blood*, and *The Torment of Others* (HarperCollins, 1995, 1997, and 2004, respectively).

30. Thomas Harris, *Red Dragon* (New York: Dell, 1990); *The Silence of the Lambs* (New York: St Martin's Pres, 1989); *Black Sunday* (New York: Dutton, 2006).

31. Dubbed as Australia's John Grisham. See Chris Nyst, *Gettin' Square*, directed by Jonathan Teplitzky (Squared Productions, 2003); *Cop This!*, *Gone*, and *Crook as Rockwood* (Pymble, Australia: HarperCollins, 1999, 2001, and 2005, respectively). When not writing award-winning film scripts or best-selling novels, Chris Nyst is a prominent Gold Coast–based lawyer and an adjunct faculty member of the Griffith Law School, attached to its Innocence Project.

32. For more information, see "The Shipman Files" on the Cavendish Press website, http://www.cavendish-press.co.uk/shipman.htm (accessed September 2006).

33. The Associated Press and Reuters, "Australia's 'Dr. Death' linked to 87 fatalities" (MSNBC.com, May 26, 2005), http://www.msnbc.msn.com/id/7991906/ (accessed September 2006).

34. *American Psycho*, directed by Mary Harron (Universal Pictures / Edward R. Pressman Film Corporation, 2000).

35. For the key cases in this highly contested right, see: *Griswold v. Connecticut*, 381 U.S. 479 (1965); *Loving v. Virginia*, 388 U.S.1, 18 L.Ed. 2d 1010, 87 S.Ct. 1817 (1967); *Roe v. Wade*, 410 U.S. 113 (1973); *Carey v. Population Services International*, 431 U.S. 678 (1977); *Bowers v. Hardwick*, 478 U.S. 186, 92 L.Ed. 140, 106 S.Ct. 2841 (1986); *Lawrence v. Texas*, 539 U.S. (2003).

36. *Olmstead v. United States*, 277 US 438 (1928).

37. *Cruzan v. Director, Missouri Department of Health*, 497 U.S. 261 (1990).

38. *Washington v. Glucksberg*, 117 Sup Ct 2258, 138 L. Ed. 2d 772 (1997).

39. Plato, *The Republic*, trans. Desmond Lee (Middlesex: Penguin, 1987).

40. Stephen Burton, "Killing in the Name of the Other: A Lacanian Analysis of the Cinematic Serial Killer" (*Griffith Law Review* 9, 2000, 156–74).

41. For the legal history of Sampedro's case, see his sister-in-law's petition, on her dead brother-in-law's behalf, to the U.N. Human Rights Committee: *Manuela Sanlés Sanlés v. Spain*, Communication no. 1024/2001, U.N. Doc. CCPr/C/80/D/1024/2001 (2004), 2.1–2.7. See also Rod Usher, "Live and Let Die" (Time.com, Jan. 26, 1998); http://www.time.com/time/magazine/1998/int/980126/file.live_and_let_die.sh11.html and "Ramón Sampedro" on the *Wikipedia* website, http://en.wikipedia.org/wiki/Ramon_Sampedro (both accessed September 2006).

42. See *Pretty v. Director of Public Prosecutions and Secretary of State for the Home Department* [2001] UKHL 61.

43. See "Select Committee on Euthanasia," *Northern Territory Legislative Assembly*, http://www.nt.gov.au/lant/parliament/committees/rotti/parldebate.shtml (accessed September 2006) and *Wake and Gondarra v. Northern Territory and Asche* (1996) 109 NTR 1, (1996) 5 NTLR 170.

44. *Rights of the Terminally Ill Act 1995* (NT).

45. *Sanlés Sanlés v. Spain*, 2.1–2.7.

46. See Jacques Lacan, *The Ethics of Psychoanlaysis, 1959–1960*, vol. 7 in *The Seminar of Jacques Lacan*, trans. Dennis Porter, ed. Jacques-Alain Miller (New York: Norton, 1992, 270–87).

47. See Berlin, *Four Essays on Liberty*.

48. Berlin, *Four Essays on Liberty*.

49. Sigmund Freud, *Civilisation and Its Discontents*, vol. 21 in *The Complete Psychological Works of Sigmund Freud*, trans. and ed. James Strachey (London: Hogarth, 1959).

50. For a review of the provisions of the Spanish Criminal Codes, see *Sanlés Sanlés v. Spain*, 2.1.

51. *Sanlés Sanlés v. Spain*.

52. Octave Mannoni, "I Know Well But All The Same . . . " in *Perversion and the Social Relation*, ed. Molly Anne Rothenberg, Dennis A. Foster, and Slavoj Žižek (Durham, N.C.: Duke University Press, 2003, 68–92).

53. Matt Lucas and David Williams, *Little Britain* (British Broadcasting Corporation, 2003–).

54. B. B. Pande, "Right to Life or Death?: For Bharat Both Cannot Be 'Right,'" *Supreme Court Cases* 4, 1994, 19).

55. *Constitution of India*, Pt. III, Art. 21, "Protection of Life and Personal Liberty."

56. See Aldous Huxley, *Brave New World* (Penguin, 1971).

57. *Logan's Run*, directed by Michael Anderson (MGM, 1976).

58. *Soylent Green*, directed by Richard Fleisher (MGM, 1973).

59. See Slavoj Žižek, "Formal Democracy and Its Discontents" in *Looking Awry: An Introduction to Jacques Lacan Through Popular Culture* (Cambridge, Mass.: MIT Press, 1991), esp. 158–60.

60. See "Congressman Tom Delay, 22nd District of Texas" on Tom Delay's Congress website, http://tomdelay.house.gov/ (accessed September 2006).

61. Žižek, *The Plague of Fantasies*.

Conclusion

1. Diane English, *Murphy Brown* (CBS, Warner Brothers, 1988–99).

2. Russell T. Davis, *Queer as Folk* (Channel 4, 1999–); See also the American version: Ron Cowen and Daniel Lipman, *Queer as Folk USA* (Showtime, 2000–2005).

3. Darren Star, *Sex and the City* (HBO, 1998–2004).

References

Books, Articles, and Websites

Agamben, Giorgio. *Homo Sacer: Sovereign Power and Bare Life.* Translated by Daniel Heller-Roazen. Stanford, Calif.: Stanford University Press, 1998.

Althusser, Louis. "Ideology and Ideological State Apparatuses." In *Lenin and Philosophy, and Other Essays.* Translated by B. Brewster, 127–88. New York: Monthly Review Press, 1971.

———. *Essays on Ideology.* London: Verso, 1984.

Anderson, Benedict. *Imagined Communities: Reflections on the Origin and Spread of Nationalism.* London: Verso, 1983.

Apparadurai, Arjun. *Globalization.* Durham, N.C.: Duke University Press, 2001.

Aquinas, Thomas. "Selections from *Summa Theologica.*" In *Lloyd's Introduction to Jurisprudence.* Edited by M.D.A. Freeman, 134–36. London: Sweet & Maxwell, 1994.

Aristodemou, Maria. *Law and Literature: Journeys from Her to Eternity.* New York: Oxford University Press, 2000.

Aristotle. *Politics,* Book 3. Translated by Benjamin Jowett. New York: Modern Library, 1943.

Attwood, Bain, and Andrew Markus, eds. *Struggle for Aboriginal Rights.* Sydney: Allen & Unwin, 1999.

Auerbach, Nina. *Our Vampire, Ourselves.* Chicago: University of Chicago Press, 1995.

Austin, John. *The Province of Jurisprudence Determined.* Edited by Wilfrid E. Rumble. Cambridge: Cambridge University Press, 1995.

Badiou, Alain. *Ethics: An Essay on the Understanding of Evil.* Translated by Peter Hallward. London: Verso, 2001.

Bailey, Anne M., and J. R. Llobera. *The Asiatic Mode of Production: Science and Politics.* London: Routledge, 1981.

Bandes, Susan A. *The Passions of the Law.* New York: New York University Press, 1999.

Barthes, Roland. *Le Plaisir du texte* [The pleasure of the text]. Translated by Richard Miller; note by Richard Howard. New York: Hill & Wang, 1975.

Bartlett, Richard, ed. *The Mabo Decision.* Sydney: Butterworths, 1993.

Barton, Benjamin. "Harry Potter and the Half-Crazed Bureaucracy," *Michigan Law Review* 104, 2006.

Baudrillard, Jean. *Forget Foucault.* New York: Semiotext(e) Foreign Agents Series, 1988.

Beard, H. N., D. C. Kenney, and the *Harvard Lampoon* staff. *Bored of the Rings: A Parody of J.R.R. Tolkien's 'The Lord of the Rings.'* New York: Signet, New American Library, 1969.

Beck, Ulrich. *What Is Globalization?* Translated by Patrick Camiller. Malden, Mass.: Polity Press, 2000.

Behrendt, Larissa. "The Eliza Fraser Captivity Narrative: A Tale of Frontier, Femininity, and the Legitimisation of Colonial Law," *Saskatchewan Law Review* 63, 2000, 145–84.

———. *Home.* Brisbane, Australia: University of Queensland Press, 2004.

Bell, Derrick. *Confronting Authority: Reflections of an Ardent Protester.* Boston: Beacon Hill Press, 1994.

Bennet, Hilaire. *Constitutional and Administrative Law.* London: Cavendish, 1995.

Bennett, Scott. *White Politics and Black Australians.* St. Leonards, Australia: Allen & Unwin, 1999.

Bentham, Jeremy. *An Introduction to the Principles and Morals of Legislation.* Edited by J. H. Burns and H.L.A. Hart. London: Athlone, 1970.

———. Selections from *An Introduction to the Principles and Morals of Legislation.* In *Lloyd's Introduction to Jurisprudence.* Edited by M.D.A. Freeman, 229–32. London: Sweet & Maxwell, 1994.

———. *Panopticon Letters.* Edited by M. Bozovic. London: Verso, 1995.

Berggren, Kris. "Profile Brothers Stand with Family," *National Catholic Reporter*, Apr. 1, 2005, 6.

Bergman, Paul, and Michael Asimow. *Reel Justice: The Courtroom Goes to the Movies.* Kansas City, Mo.: McMeel & Andrews, 1996.

Berkowitz, Roger. "The Accusers: Law, Justice, and the Image of the Prosecutors in Hollywood," *Griffith Law Review* 13(2), 2004, 131–52.

Berlin, Sir Isaiah. *Four Essays on Liberty.* Oxford: Oxford University Press, 1969.

Bernard, J.R.L., et al., eds. *Macquarie ABC Dictionary: Australia's National Dictionary.* Sydney: Macquarie Library, 2003.

Best, Stephen. *The Fugitive's Properties: Law and the Poetics of Possession.* Chicago: University of Chicago Press, 2004.

Bickenbach, Jerome, and Ian Kyer. *The Fiercest Debate: Cecil A. Wright, The Benchers, and Legal Education in Ontario, 1823–1957.* Toronto: Osgoode Society, 1987.

Bix, Brian. *Jurisprudence: Theory and Context.* London: Sweet & Maxwell, 2003.

Black, David. *Law in Film: Resonance and Representation.* Urbana: University of Illinois Press, 1999.

Blyton, Enid. *Well Done Secret Seven*. Leicester, UK: Brockhampton, 1951.

———. *Look Out Secret Seven*. Leicester, UK: Brockhampton, 1971.

———. *Good Work, Secret Seven*. Leicester, UK: Brockhampton, 1974.

———. *The Famous Five*. Geneva: Heron, 1981.

———. *Five Fall into Adventure*. Geneva: Heron, 1981.

———. *Five on a Hike Together*. Geneva: Heron, 1981.

Bowie, David. *Diamond Dogs*. London: RCA, Olympic and Island Studios, 1974.

Brooks, Peter, and Paul Gewirtz. *Law's Stories: Narrative and Rhetoric in the Law*. New Haven, Conn.: Yale University Press, 1996.

Bruno, Giuliana. "Postmodernism and *Blade Runner*." In *Alien Zone*. Edited by Annette Kuhn, 183–96. London: Verso, 1990.

Bukatman, Scott. "Prosthetic Memory: Total Recall and *Blade Runner*." In *Liquid Metal*. Edited by Sean Redmond, 239–48. London: Wallflower Press, 2004.

Burchell, Graham, Colin Gordon, and Peter Miller. *The Foucault Effect: Studies in Governmentality*, with Two Lectures by and an Interview with Michel Foucault. Chicago: University of Chicago Press, 1991.

Burton, Stephen. "Killing in the Name of the Other: A Lacanian Analysis of the Cinematic Serial Killer," *Griffith Law Review* 9, 2000, 156–74.

Butler, Judith. *Excitable Speech: A Politics of the Performative*. London: Routledge, 1997.

Butler, William E. *Soviet Law*. London: Butterworths, 1988.

Butt, Peter, and Peter Nygh, eds. *Butterworths Concise Australian Legal Dictionary*. Chatswood, Australia: Lexis Nexis Butterworths, 2004.

Cairns, J. W., and Hector MacQueen. "Learning and the Law: A Short History of the Edinburgh Law School." University of Edinburgh website, at http://www.law.ed.ac.uk/tercentenary/documents/LearningtheLaw/ (accessed Sept. 2006).

Calabresi, Guido, and Philip Bobbitt. *Tragic Choices*. New York: Norton, 1978.

Cane, Peter, and Mark Tushnet, eds. *The Oxford Handbook of Legal Studies*. Oxford: Oxford University Press, 2003.

Carpenter, Humphrey. *The Inklings: C. S. Lewis, J.R.R. Tolkien, Charles Williams and Their Friends*. London: HarperCollins, 1978.

———. *J.R.R. Tolkien: A Biography*. London: HarperCollins, 2000.

Castles, Alex C. *An Australian Legal History*. Sydney: Law Book Company, 1982.

Chaplin, Sue. "Fictions of Femininity: Gender, Genre, and the Law of Genre in Eighteenth-Century England." *Griffith Law Review* 2(1), 2002, 34–43.

Charcot, Jean Martin. *Clinical Lectures on Diseases of the Nervous System*. London: Routledge, 1991.

Chase, Anthony. *Movies on Trial: The Legal System on the Silver Screen*. New York: New Press, 2002.

Christie, Suzanne. "Judge Judy: The Courtroom as Classroom," *Australian Feminist Law Journal* 13, Sept. 1999, 86–97.

Clover, Carol. "Movie Juries." *DePaul Law Review* 48, 1998, 389–405.

———. "Law and the Order of Popular Culture." In *Law in the Domains of Culture.* Edited by A. Sarat and T. Kearns, 97–119. Ann Arbor: University of Michigan Press, 1999.

Coase, Ronald H. *The Firm, the Market, and the Law.* Chicago: University of Chicago Press, 1988.

———. "The Problem of Social Cost." In *Law and Economics*, vol. 1. Edited by Jules Coleman and Jeffrey Lange. Aldershot, UK: Dartmouth, 1992, 17.

———. "Autobiography" at http://nobelprize.org/economics/laureates/1991/coase-autobio.html (accessed Sept. 2006).

Coleman, Jules. "The Normative Basis of Economic Analysis," *Stanford Law Review* 34, 1982, 1105.

Constable, Marianne. *The Law of the Other: The Mixed Jury and Changing Conceptions of Citizenship, Law, and Knowledge.* Chicago: University of Chicago Press, 1994.

Copjec, Joan. "Sour Justice, or Liberalist Envy." In *Imagine There's No Woman: Ethics and Sublimation*, 158–76. Cambridge, Mass.: MIT Press, 2002.

Cover, Robert. "Violence and the Word," *Yale Law Journal* 95, 1986, 1601.

Crenshaw, Kim. "Demarginalizing the Intersection of Race and Sex: A Black Feminist Critique of Antidiscrimination Doctrine, Feminist Theory, and Antiracist Politics." *University of Chicago Legal Forum* 1, 1989, 139.

Curzon, L. B. *Jurisprudence.* London: Cavendish, 1995.

Dalton, Derek. "The Deviant Gaze: Imagining the Homosexual as Criminal Through Cinematic and Legal Discourses." In *Sexuality in the Legal Arena.* Edited by Carl Stychin and Didi Herman. London: Athlone, 2000.

Delbridge, Arthur, ed. *The Macquarie Dictionary of Australian Colloquial Language.* Sydney: Macquarie University, The Macquarie Library, 1988.

———., et al., eds. *The Macquarie Dictionary: Federation Edition.* Sydney: Macquarie University, The Macquarie Library, 2001.

Deleuze, Gilles. *The Logic of Sense.* Translated by Mark Lester, with Charles Stivale. Edited by Constantin V. Boundas. New York: Columbia University Press, 1990.

———. "What Is an Event?" In *The Fold: Leibniz and the Baroque.* Translated by Tom Conley, 76–82. Minneapolis: University of Minnesota Press, 1993.

———, and Felix Guattari. *Anti-Oedipus: Capitalism, and Schizophrenia.* Preface by Michel Foucault. Minneapolis: University of Minnesota Press, 1983.

Derrida, Jacques. *Of Grammatology.* Translated by Gayatri Chakravorty Spivak. Baltimore: Johns Hopkins University, 1976.

———. "Différance." In *Margins of Philosophy.* Translated and notes by A. Bass, 1–29. Chicago: University of Chicago Press, 1982.

———. "White Mythology: Metaphor in the Text of Philosophy." In *Margins of Philosophy.* Translated by A. Bass, 207–73. Chicago: University of Chicago Press, 1982.

———. "Force of Law: The 'Mystical Foundations of Authority,'" *Cardozo Law Review* 11(5–6), 1990, 920–1045.

Devo, Q. *Are We Not Men? A. We Are Devo!*, Warner Bros., 1978. "Artists—Biography: Devo," *VH1*, Sept. 7, 2005. http://www.vh1.com/artists/az/devo/bio.jhtml.

Dicey, A. V. *An Introduction to the Study of the Law of the Constitution*. London: Macmillan, 1959.

———. *Lectures on the Relation Between Law and Public Opinion in England During the Nineteenth Century*. London: Macmillan, 1962.

Dick, Philip K. *Do Androids Dream of Electric Sheep?* Garden City, N.Y.: Doubleday, 1968.

———. *Confessions of a Crap Artist*. New York: Vintage / Random House, 1992.

———. "The Minority Report." In *The Phillip K. Dick Reader*, 323–54. New York: Citadel Press, 1997.

———. "Paycheck." In *The Phillip K. Dick Reader*, 355–84. New York: Citadel Press, 1997.

———. "Second Variety." In *The Philip K. Dick Reader*, 385–422. New York: Citadel Press, 1997.

———. "We Can Remember It for You Wholesale." In *The Philip K. Dick Reader*, 305–22. New York: Citadel Press, 1997.

———. "Imposter." In *Selected Stories of Philip K. Dick*, 101–15. New York: Pantheon / Random House, 2002.

Dierckxsens, W. *The Limits of Capitalism: An Approach to Globalization Without Neoliberalism*. New York: Zed Books, 2000.

Diken, Bulent, and Carsten Begge Laustsen. "Enjoy Your Fight! *Fight Club* as a Symptom of the Network Society." Lancaster: Department of Sociology, Lancaster University, 2001; at http://www.lancs.ac.uk/fss/sociology/papers/diken-laustsen-enjoy-your-fight.pdf (accessed Sept. 2006).

Dimock, Wai Chee. *Empire for Liberty: Melville and the Poetics of Individualism*. Princeton, N.J.: Princeton University Press, 1991.

———. *Residues of Justice: Literature, Law, Philosophy*. Berkeley: University of California Press, 1997.

Doane, Mary Ann. "Technophilia: Technology, Representation, and the Feminine." In *Liquid Metal*. Edited by Sean Redmond, 182–90. London: Wallflower Press, 2004.

Dolar, Mladen, and Slavoj Žižek. *Opera's Second Death*. London: Routledge, 2001.

Dorsett, Shaunnagh. "Civilisation and Cultivation: Colonial Policy and Indigenous Peoples in Canada and Australia Post-Wik," *Griffith Law Review* 4, 1995, 214–38.

———. "'Clear and Plain Intention': Extinguishment of Native Title in Australia and Canada, Post-Wik," *Griffith Law Review* 6, 1997: 96–121.

Douglas, Lawrence. *The Memory of Judgment: Making Law and History in the Trials of the Holocaust*. New Haven, Conn.: Yale University Press, 2001.

Douzinas, Costas. *The End of Human Rights: Critical Legal Thought at the Turn of the Century*. Oxford: Hart, 2000.

————, and Lynda Nead, eds. *Law and the Image: The Authority of Art and the Aesthetics of Law*. Chicago: University of Chicago Press, 1999.

————, with Ronnie Warrington. "The Face of Justice: A Jurisprudence of Alterity," *Social and Legal Studies* 3, 1994, 405–25.

————, with Ronnie Warrington. "'A Well-Founded Fear of Justice': Law and Ethics in Postmodernity." In *Legal Studies as Cultural Studies*. Edited by Jerry D. Leonard, 197–229. Albany: State University of New York Press, 1995.

————, Ronnie Warrington, and Shaun McVeigh. *Postmodern Jurisprudence: The Law of Text in the Texts of Law*. London: Routledge, 1991.

Drinker Bowen, Catherine. *Yankee from Olympus: Justice Holmes and His Family*. Boston: Little, Brown, 1944.

Dumm, Tom. "Toy Stories: Downsizing American Masculinity," *Cultural Values* 1(1), 1997, 81–100.

Duncanson, Kirsty. "Tracing the Law Through *The Matrix*," *Griffith Law Review* 10(2), 2001, 160–71.

Durkheim, Emile. *The Division of Labor in Society*. New York: Free Press, 1964.

Dworkin, Ronald. *Taking Rights Seriously*. Cambridge, Mass.: Harvard University Press, 1977.

————. "Law as Interpretation," *Texas Law Review* 60(3), 1981–82, 527–50.

————. "My Reply to Stanley Fish (and Walter Benn Michaels): Please Don't Talk About Objectivity Anymore." In *The Politics of Interpretation*. Edited by W. Mitchell, 287–313. Chicago: Chicago University Press, 1983.

————. *A Matter of Principle*. Cambridge, Mass.: Harvard University Press, 1985.

————. *Law's Empire*. London: Fontana, 1986.

————. *Life's Dominion: An Argument About Abortion, Euthanasia, and Individual Freedom*. New York: Vintage Books, 1994.

Dyer, Richard. *White*. London: Routledge, 1997.

Eagleton, Terry. *Against the Grain: Essays, 1975–1986*. London: Verso, 1986.

Easterbrook, Frank. "The Inevitability of Law and Economics," *Legal Education Review* 1, 1989, 7.

Edgeworth, Brendan. "H.L.A. Hart, Legal Positivism, and Post-war British Labourism," *Western Australian Law Review* 19, 1989, 275–300.

————. "Tenure, Allodialism, and Indigenous Rights at Common Law: English, United States, and Australian Land Law Compared After *Mabo v. Queensland*," *Anglo-American Law Review* 23, Oct. / Dec. 1994, 397–433.

Ellwood, Wayne. *The No-Nonsense Guide to Globalization*. London: Verso, 2001.

Evans, Dylan. *An Introductory Dictionary of Lacanian Psychoanalysis*. London: Routledge, 1997.

Farquhar, Mary, and Chris Berry. *China on Screen: Cinema and Nation*. New York: Columbia University Press, 2006.

Ferguson, Margaret, Mary Jo Salter, and Jon Stallworthy, eds. *The Norton Anthology of Poetry*, 4th ed. New York: Norton, 1996.

Ferguson, Robert. *Law and Letters in American Culture* (Cambridge, Mass.: Harvard University Press, 1984).

Fink, Bruce. *A Clinical Introduction to Lacanian Psychoanalysis: Theory and Technique.* Cambridge, Mass.: Harvard University Press, 1997.

Fish, Stanley. "Working on the Chain Gang: Interpretation in Law and Literature," *Texas Law Review* 60(3), 1981–82, 551–68.

———. "Wrong Again," *Texas Law Review* 62, 1983–84, 299–316.

———. "Boutique Multiculturalism." In *The Trouble with Principle*, 56–75. Cambridge, Mass.: Harvard University Press, 1999.

Fitzpatrick, Peter. *Dangerous Supplements: Resistance and Renewal in Jurisprudence.* London: Pluto, 1991.

Flower MacCannell, Juliet. *The Regime of the Brother: After the Patriarchy.* London: Routledge, 1991.

Foucault, Michel. *Discipline and Punish: The Birth of the Prison.* Translated by A. Sheridan. Harmondsworth, UK: Penguin, 1979.

Frank, Jerome. Excerpts from *Law and the Modern Mind.* In *Lloyd's Introduction to Jurisprudence.* Edited by M.D.A. Freeman, 827–30. London: Sweet & Maxwell, 2001.

Fraser, David. *The Man in White Is Always Right: Cricket and the Law.* Sydney: Institute of Criminology, Sydney University Law School, 1993.

Freud, Sigmund. "Obsessive Action and Religious Practices." In *The Standard Edition of the Complete Psychological Works of Sigmund Freud*, vol. 9. London: Hogarth Press, 1907.

———. *Psychoanalytic Notes on an Autobiographical Account of a Case of Paranoia (Dementia Paranoidia)*, vol. 12. *The Standard Edition of the Complete Psychological Works of Sigmund Freud.* London: Hogarth Press / Institute of Psychoanalysis, 1958.

———. *Civilisation and Its Discontents*, vol. 21. *The Standard Edition of the Complete Psychological Works of Sigmund Freud.* Translated and edited by James Strachey. London: Hogarth Press, 1959.

———. *The Psychopathology of Everyday Life.* Translated by Alan Tyso; edited and introduction by James Strachey. New York: Norton, 1966.

———. *Beyond the Pleasure Principle*, vol. 18. *The Standard Edition of the Complete Psychological Works of Sigmund Freud.* Translated and edited by James Strachey. London: Hogarth Press, 1966–74.

———. *The Future of an Illusion*, vol. 21. *The Standard Edition of the Complete Psychological Works of Sigmund Freud.* Revised and edited by James Strachey. London: Hogarth Press / Institute of Psychoanalysis, 1968.

———. *The Interpretation of Dreams*, vol. 5. *The Standard Edition of the Complete Psychological Works of Sigmund Freud.* Revised and edited by James Strachey. London: Hogarth Press / Institute of Psychoanalysis, 1968.

———. "Totem and Taboo: Resemblances Between the Psychic Lives of Savages and Neurotics," in *The Basic Writings of Sigmund Freud*. Translated and introduction by A. A. Brill. New York: Modern Library, 1995.

———. *Dora: An Analysis of a Case of Hysteria*. Introduction by Phillip Rieff. New York: Simon & Schuster, 1997.

———. "The Uncanny." In *Collected Papers*, vol. 4. Translated by Joan Riviere, 368–407. London: Hogarth Press / Institute of Psychoanalysis, 1950.

Friday, Krister. "'A Generation of Men Without History': *Fight Club*, Masculinity, and the Historical Symptom." *Postmodern Culture* 13(3), 2002–3.

Friedman, Milton, and Rose Friedman. *Free to Choose: A Personal Statement*. New York: Harcourt Brace, 1980.

Frye, Northrop. *The Anatomy of Criticism*. Princeton, N.J.: Princeton University Press, 1957.

Fuller, Lon L. "Positivism and Fidelity to Law—A Reply to Professor Hart," *Harvard Law Review* 71, 1958, 630–72.

———. *The Morality of Law*. New Haven, Conn.: Yale University Press, 1964.

Gallagher, Diana. *Spark and Burn*. New York: Simon Spotlight Entertainment, 2005.

Garner, Bryan, ed. *Black's Law Dictionary*, 7th ed. St. Paul, Minn.: West Group, 1999.

Garth, J. *Tolkien and the Great War: The Threshold of Middle-earth*. London: HarperCollins, 2003.

Gearey, Adam. *Law and Aesthetics*. Oxford: Hart, 2001.

Giddens, Anthony. *Beyond Left and Right: The Future of Radical Politics*. Cambridge: Polity Press, 1994.

Gilligan, Carol. *In a Different Voice: Psychological Theory and Women's Development*. Cambridge, Mass.: Harvard University Press, 1982.

Giroux, Henry A. "Brutalised Bodies and Emasculated Politics: *Fight Club*, Consumerism, and Masculine Violence," *Third Text* 53, Winter 2000–2001, 31–41.

———. "Private Satisfactions and Public Disorders: *Fight Club*, Patriarchy, and the Politics of Masculine Violence," *JAC: A Journal of Composition Theory* 21(1) 2001, 1–31.

Godden, Lee. "Wik: Legal Memory and History," *Griffith Law Review* 6, 1997, 122–43.

Golding, William. *The Lord of the Flies: A Novel*. London: Faber, 1954.

Goodrich, Peter. *Reading the Law: A Critical Introduction to Legal Method and Techniques*. Oxford: Blackwell, 1986.

———. *Languages of Law: From Logics of Memory to Nomadic Masks*. London: Weidenfeld & Nicolson, 1990.

Goodwin, Michele. "Poetic Reflections on Law, Race, and Society," *Griffith Law Review* 10(2), 2001, 195–210.

Gordon, Robert. "Critical Legal Histories." In *Critical Legal Studies*. Edited by James Boyle, 114–15. Aldershot, UK: Dartmouth, 1992.

Granfield, Richard. *Making Elite Lawyers: Visions of Law at Harvard and Beyond*. New York: Routledge, 1992.

Grantham, Bill. "'Get On with the Burning! Put an End to This Trial!': Representations of the Trials of Joan of Arc in the Cinema," *Griffith Law Review* 13(2), 2004, 153–59.

Gray, Piers. *Marginal Men: Edward Thomas, Ivor Gurney, and J. R. Ackerley*. London: Macmillan, 1990.

Grbich, Judith. "Language as the 'Pretty Woman' of Law: Properties of Longing and Desire in Legal Interpretation and Popular Culture." In *Romancing the Tomes: Popular Culture, Law, Feminism*. Edited by Margaret Thornton, 131–46. London: Cavendish, 2002.

Greenfield, Steve, and Guy Osborn. *Film and the Law*. London: Cavendish, 2001.

Gronstad, A. "One Dimensional Men: *Fight Club* and the Poetics of the Body," *Film Criticism* 28(1), Fall 2003, 1–23.

Guinier, Lani, Michelle Fine, and Jane Balin. *Becoming Gentlemen: Women, Law, and Institutional Change*. Boston: Beacon, 1997.

Hall, Stuart. *Policing the Crisis: Mugging, the State, and Law and Order*. London: Macmillan, 1978.

Hardt, Michael, and Antonio Negri. *Empire*. Cambridge, Mass.: Harvard University Press, 2000.

Harris, James William. *Legal Philosophies*. London: Butterworths, 1997.

Harris, Thomas. *Red Dragon*. New York: Dell, 1990.

———. *Black Sunday*. New York: Dutton, 2006.

———. *The Silence of the Lambs*. New York: St. Martin's, 1989.

Hart, H.L.A. "Positivism and the Separation of Law and Morals," *Harvard Law Review* 71, 1958, 593–629.

———. "American Jurisprudence Through English Eyes: The Nightmare and the Noble Dream." In *Essays in Jurisprudence and Philosophy*. Oxford: Clarendon Press, 1983.

———. *The Concept of Law*. Oxford: Oxford University Press, 1961.

———. *The Concept of Law*. Oxford: English Language Book Society / Oxford University Press, 1988.

———. *The Concept of Law*, 2nd ed. Edited by Penelope Bulloch and Joseph Raz. Oxford: Clarendon Press, 1994.

Hegel, G.W.F. *Philosophy of Right*. Translated by T. M. Knox. Oxford: Clarendon, 1945.

Heinzelman, Susan Sage, and Zipporah Wiseman, eds. *Representing Women: Law, Literature, and Feminism*. Durham, N.C.: Duke University Press, 1994.

Held, David. *Democracy and the Global Order: From the Modern State to Cosmopolitan Governance*. Cambridge: Polity Press, 1995.

Helms, R. *Myth, Magic, and Meaning in Tolkien's World*. London: Granada, 1976.

Hirvonen, Ari, ed. *Polycentricity: The Multiple Scenes of Law*. Ann Arbor: University of Michigan Press, 1998.

Hobsbawn, Eric, and Terence Ranger. *The Invention of Tradition*. Cambridge: Cambridge University Press, 1983.

Holden, Anthony. "Why Harry Doesn't Cast a Spell Over Me," *Observer*, June 25, 2000.

Holder, Nancy. *Queen of the Slayers*. New York: Simon & Schuster, 2005.

Holmes, Oliver Wendell. Excerpts from *The Path of Law*. In *The Essential Holmes: Selections from the Letters, Speeches, Judicial Opinions, and Other Writings of Oliver Wendell Holmes, Jr.* Edited by R. Posner, 160–62. Chicago: University of Chicago Press, 1992.

Hope, Judith Richards. *Pinstripes and Pearls*. New York: Scribner's, 2003.

Hughes, Thomas. *Tom Brown's Schooldays*. London: Pocket Paperbacks, 1967.

Huntingdon, Samuel. *The Clash of Civilizations and the Remaking of World Order*. New York: Simon & Schuster, 1996.

Hussain, Nasser. *The Jurisprudence of Emergency: Colonialism and the Rule of Law*. Ann Arbor: University of Michigan Press, 2003.

Hutchings, Peter. *The Criminal Spectre in Law, Literature, and Aesthetics: Incriminating Subjects*. London: Routledge, 2001.

———. "Replicating *Blade Runner*." Forthcoming (manuscript on file with author).

Huxley, Aldous. *Brave New World*. London: Penguin, 1971.

Ivison, Duncan. "Decolonising the Rule of Law: Mabo's Case and Post-colonial Constitutionalism," *Oxford Journal of Legal Studies* 17, Summer 1997, 253–79.

Jameson, Fredric. *The Political Unconscious: Narrative as a Socially Symbolic Act*. Ithaca, N.Y.: Cornell University Press, 1981.

Jefferson, Thomas. "1 Jan. 1802 Letter in Response to the Danbury Baptist Association." In *The Writings of Thomas Jefferson*, vol. 16. Edited by Albert Ellery Bergh. Washington, D.C.: Thomas Jefferson Memorial Association, 1903–4.

Johnson, Rebecca. "Leaving Normal: Constructing the Family in the Movies and in Law." In *New Perspectives on Deviance: The Construction of Deviance in Everyday Life*. Edited by Lori Beaman, 163–79. Upper Saddle River, N.J.: Prentice-Hall, 2000.

Kahlenberg, Richard D. *Broken Contract: A Memoir of Harvard Law School*. Foreword by R. Coles. New York: Hill & Wang, 1992.

Kahneman, Daniel, Paul Slovic, and Amos Tversky, eds. *Judgment Under Uncertainty: Heuristics and Biases*. Cambridge: Cambridge University Press, 1982.

Kairys, David, ed. *The Politics of the Law: A Progressive Critique*. New York: Pantheon, 1982.

Kalman, Laura. *Legal Realism at Yale, 1927–1960*. Chapel Hill: University of North Carolina Press, 1986.

Kamir, Orit. *Every Breath You Take: Stalking Narratives and the Law*. Ann Arbor: University of Michigan Press, 2001.

Kant, Immanuel. *Groundwork for the Metaphysics of Morals*. Translated by Lewis M. Beck. Indianapolis: Bobbs-Merrill, 1960.

———. *Religion Within the Limits of Reason Alone*. New York: Macmillan, 1993.

Karpin, Isabel. "Pop Justice: TV, Feminism, and the Law." In *Women, Law, and the Media*. Edited by M. Fineman and M. McCluskey, 120–35. New York: Oxford University Press, 1997.

Kelsen, Hans. *General Theory of Law and State*. Translated by A. Sheridan. New York: Norton, 1961.

——. *The Pure Theory of Law*. Translated by Max Knight. Berkeley: University of California Press, 1967.

——. Selections from *The Pure Theory of Law* and *General Theory of Law and State*. In *Lloyd's Introduction to Jurisprudence*. Edited by M.D.A. Freeman, 294–96, 301–4, 314–16. London: Sweet & Maxwell, 1994.

——. "Professor Stone and the Pure Theory of Law." In *Lloyd's Introduction to Jurisprudence*. Edited by M.D.A. Freeman, 289–91. London: Sweet & Maxwell, 2001.

Kennedy, Duncan. "The Structure of Blackstone's Commentaries," *Buffalo Law Review* 28, 1979, 205–382.

——. "Legal Education as Training for Hierarchy." In *The Politics of Law: A Progressive Critique*. Edited by David Kairys, 40–64. New York: Pantheon, 1982.

Kerlow, Eleanor. *Poisoned Ivy: How Egos, Ideology, and Power Politics Almost Ruined Harvard Law School*. New York: St. Martin's, 1994.

Klein, Naomi. *No Logo, No Space, No Choice, No Jobs: Taking Aim at the Brand Bullied*. London: Flamingo, 2000.

Kornhauser, Lewis A. "The New Economic Analysis of Law: Legal Rules as Incentives." In *Law and Economics*. Edited by Nicholas Mercuro. Dordrecht, The Netherlands: Kluwer, 1989.

Lacan, Jacques. *Le Seminaire*, vol. 17. *L'envers de la psychoanalyse*. Edited by Jacques-Alain Miller. Paris: Seuil, 1975.

——. "The Mirror Stage as Formative of the Function of the I as Revealed in Psychoanalytic Experience." In *Écrits: A Selection*. Translated by A. Sheridan, 1–7. New York: Norton, 1977.

——. "The Subversion of the Subject and the Dialectic of Desire in the Freudian Unconscious." In *Écrits: A Selection*. Translated by A. Sheridan, 292–325. New York: Norton, 1977.

——. *Feminine Sexuality: Jaques Lacan and the école freudienne*. Edited by Juliet Mitchell and Jacqueline Rose; translated by Jacqueline Rose. New York: Norton, 1982.

——. "God and the *Jouissance* of the Woman." In *Feminine Sexuality: Jaques Lacan and the école freudienne*. Edited by Juliet Mitchell and Jacqueline Rose; translated by Jacqueline Rose, 137–48. London: Macmillan, 1982.

——. "The Seminar on 'The Purloined Letter.'" In *The Purloined Poe: Lacan, Derrida, and Psychoanalytic Reading*. Translated by J. Mehlman; edited by J. Muller and W. Richardson. Baltimore, Md.: Johns Hopkins University Press, 1988.

——. "Kant avec Sade," *October* 51, Winter 1989, 55–75.

——. *The Ethics of Psychoanlaysis, 1959–1960*, vol. 7. *The Seminar of Jacques Lacan*. Translated by Dennis Porter, edited by Jacques-Alain Miller. New York: Norton, 1992.

———. *The Psychoses 1955–1956*, vol. 3. *The Seminar of Jacques Lacan*. Edited by Jacques-Alain Miller; translated by Russell Grigg. London: Routledge, 1993.

———. *The Four Fundamental Concepts of Psychoanalysis*, vol. 11. *The Seminar of Jacques Lacan*. Edited by Jacques-Alain Miller; translated by A. Sheridan. London: Hogarth Press, 1998.

———. *Écrits: A Selection*. Edited and translated by Bruce Fink. New York: Norton, 2002.

Lacey, Nicola. *A Life of H.L.A. Hart: The Nightmare and the Noble Dream*. Oxford: Oxford University Press, 2004.

Laclau, Ernesto, and Chantal Mouffe. *Hegemony and Socialist Strategy: Towards a Radical Democratic Politics*. London: Verso, 1985.

Lambert, James, ed. *Macquarie Book of Slang: Australian Slang in the Noughties*. Sydney: Macquarie University, Macquarie Library, 2000.

Landes, Elisabeth M., and Richard A. Posner. "The Economics of the Baby Shortage." In *Economic Analysis of the Law: Selected Readings*. Edited by Donald A. Wittman. Oxford: Blackwell, 2003.

Langdell, Christopher Columbus. *Record of the Commemoration . . . on the Two Hundred and Fiftieth Anniversary of the Founding of Harvard College* (1887). Quoted in William Twining, *Karl Llewellyn and the Realist Movement*. London: Weidenfeld & Nicolson, 1973.

LaPiana, William P. *Logic and Experience: The Origin of American Legal Education*. New York: Oxford University Press, 1994.

Laplanche, J., and J.-B. Pontalis. *The Language of Psychoanalysis*. Translated by Donald Nicholson-Smith. New York: Norton, 1973.

Lawler, Merran. "Queering the *Freedom* Catalogue." Forthcoming (manuscript on file with author).

———. "There's Something Not Quite Right About Tinky-Wink: Queer Theory, the Law, and *Teletubbies*." Forthcoming (manuscript on file with author).

———. "There's Something 'Queer Eye' About *The L Word*." Forthcoming (manuscript on file with author).

Leclaire, Serge. "La Mort dans la vie de l'obsédé," *La Psychanalyse* 2, 1957, 129.

Levinas, Emmanual. "Ethics as First Philosophy." In *The Levinas Reader*. Edited by Sean Hand. Oxford: Blackwell, 1989.

Llewellyn, Karl. *The Common Law Tradition: Deciding Appeals*. Boston: Little, Brown, 1960.

———. Excerpts from *My Philosophy of Law* and *The Normative, the Legal, and the Law-Jobs: The Problem of Juristic Method*. In *Lloyd's Introduction to Jurisprudence*. Edited by M.D.A. Freeman, 703–23. London: Sweet & Maxwell, 1994.

Lyotard, Jean François. *The Post-modern Condition: A Report on Knowledge*. Translated by Geoff Bennington and Brian Massumi. Manchester: Manchester University Press, 1984.

Macauley, Stewart. "Noncontractual Relations in Business: A Preliminary Study." In *Law and Society*. Edited by Roger Cotterrell, 481–94. Aldershot, UK: Dartmouth, 1994.

MacCormick, Neil. *H.L.A. Hart*. London: Edward Arnold, 1981.

MacKinnon, Catharine. "Mainstreaming Feminism in Legal Education," *Journal of Legal Education* 53(2), June 2003, 199–212.

MacNeil, William. "Law's *Corpus Delicti*: The Fantasmatic Body of Rights Discourse." *Law and Critique* 9(1), 1998, 37.

———. "Taking Rights Symptomatically: *Jouissance, Coupure, Objet Petit A*," *Griffith Law Review* 8(1), 1999, 134.

———. "Kidlit as Law and Literature: Harry Potter and the Scales of Justice," *Law and Literature* 14(3), 2002, 545–64.

———. "It's the Vibe! The Common Law Imaginary Down Under." In *Law's Moving Image*. Edited by Leslie J. Moran, Emma Sandon, Elena Loizidou, and Ian Christie. London: Cavendish, 2004.

———. "One *Recht* to Rule Them All! Law's Empire in the Age of *Empire*." In *The Aesthetics of Law and Culture: Texts, Images, Screens*. Edited by Peter Rush and Andrew Kenyon. Special issue of *Studies in Law, Politics and Society* 34, 2004, 279–303.

———. "You Slay Me! Buffy as Jurisprude of Desire," *Cardozo Law Review* 24(6), 2004, 2421–40.

———. "Precrime Never Pays! Law and Economics in *Minority Report*," *Continuum: A Journal of Media and Cultural Studies* 19(2), 2005, 201–20.

Maitland, F. W. *Equity, Also, the Forms of Action at Common Law: Two Courses of Lectures*. Edited by W. J. Whittaker. Cambridge: Cambridge University Press, 1909.

Manderson, Desmond. *Songs Without Music: Aesthetic Dimensions of Law and Justice*. Berkeley: University of California Press, 2000.

Mannoni, Octoave. "I Know Well, But All the Same . . . " In *Perversion and the Social Relation*. Edited by Molly Anne Rothenberg, Dennis A. Foster, and Slavoj Žižek, 68–92. Durham, N.C.: Duke University Press, 2003.

Marquart, Jaime, and Robert Ebert Byrnes. *Brush with the Law: The True Story of Law School Today at Harvard and Stanford*. Los Angeles: Renaissance Books, 2001.

Marx, Karl. Excerpts from *Capital*. In *Karl Marx: Selected Writings*. Edited by David McLellan, 452–546. Oxford: Oxford University Press, 2000.

Matsuda, Mari J. "Outsider Jurisprudence: Toward a Victim's Analysis of Racial Hate Messages." In *Group Defamation and Freedom of Speech: The Relationship Between Language and Violence*. Edited by Monroe Freedman and Eric Freedman. Westport, Conn.: Greenwood, 1995.

Matthews, D. "The Psychological Journey of Bilbo Baggins." In *A Tolkien Compass*. Edited by Jared Lobdell, 25–43. New York: Ballantine, 1975.

McCoubrey, Hilaire, and Nigel D. White. *Textbook on Jurisprudence*. London: Blackstone, 1993.

McDermid, Val. *The Mermaids Singing*. New York: HarperCollins, 1995.

———. *The Wire in the Blood*. New York: HarperCollins, 1997.

———. *The Torment of Others*. New York: HarperCollins, 2004.

McDonald, Angus. "The New Beauty of a Sum of Possibilities," *Law and Critique* 8(2), 1997, 141–59.

———. "Endless Streets, Pursued by Ghosts." In *Law's Moving Image*. Edited by Les Moran, Ian Christie, Emma Sandon, and Elena Loizidou, 121–32. London: Cavendish, 2004.

McLellan, David, ed. *Karl Marx: Selected Writings*. Oxford: Oxford Univeristy Press, 2000.

McNeil, Kent. *Common Law Aboriginal Title*. Oxford: Oxford University Press, 1989.

McRae, Heather, Garth Nettheim, Laura Beacroft, and Luke McNamara, eds. *Indigenous Legal Issues: Commentary and Materials*. Sydney: LBC Information Services, 1997.

Mercuro, Nicholas, and Stephen G. Medema. *Economics and the Law: From Posner to Postmodernism*. Princeton, N.J.: Princeton University Press, 1997.

Milbank, Jenni. "It's About *This*: Lesbians, Prison, Desire," *Current Legal Issues* 7, 2004: 449–69.

Mill, John Stuart. *On Liberty*. Harmondsworth, UK: Penguin Classics, 1974.

Miller, Jacques-Alain. "Language: Much Ado About What?" In *Lacan and the Subject of Language*. Edited by Ellie Ragland-Sullivan and Mark Bracher, 21–35. London: Routledge, 1991.

———. "Extimacy." In *Lacanian Theory of Discourse*. Edited by Mark Bracher et al., 74–87. New York: New York University Press, 1994.

Minkinnen, Panu. *Thinking Without Desire: A First Philosophy of Law*. Oxford: Hart, 1999.

Minson, Jeffrey. *Genealogies of Morals: Nietzsche, Foucault, Donzelot, and the Eccentricity of Ethics*. London: Macmillan, 1985.

Moran, Leslie J. *The Homosexual(ity) of Law*. New York: Routledge, 1996.

———. "Gothic Law," *Griffith Law Review* 10(2), 2001, 75–100.

———, Ian Christie, Emma Sandon, and Elena Loizidou, eds. *Law's Moving Image*. London: Cavendish, 2004.

Moreton-Robinson, Aileen. *Talkin' Up to the White Woman: Indigenous Women and Feminism*. Brisbane, Australia: University of Queensland Press, 2000.

Motha, Stewart. "Mabo: Encountering the Epistemic Limit of the Recognition of 'Difference,'" *Griffith Law Review* 7(1), 1998, 79–96.

Murav, Harriet. *Russia's Legal Fictions: Law, Meaning, and Violence*. Ann Arbor: University of Michigan Press, 1998.

———. *Identity Theft: The Jew in Imperial Russia and the Case of Avraam Uri Kovner*. Stanford, Calif.: Stanford University Press, 2003.

Novick, Sheldon. *Honorable Justice: The Life of Oliver Wendell Holmes*. Boston: Little, Brown, 1989.

Nozick, Robert. *Anarchy, State, and Utopia*. Oxford: Blackwell, 1974.

Nygh, Peter E., and Peter Butt, eds. *Butterworths Concise Australian Legal Dictionary*. Sydney: Butterworths, 1998.

Nyst, Chris. *Cop This!* Pymble, Australia: HarperCollins, 1999.

———. *Gone*. Pymble, Australia: HarperCollins, 2001.

———. *Crook as Rockwood*. Pymble, Australia: HarperCollins, 2005.

Osborne, John Jay, Jr. *The Paper Chase*. New York: Popular Library, 1971.

Palahniuk, Chuck. *Fight Club*. New York: Holt, 1999.

Pande, B. B. "Right to Life or Death? For Bharat Both Cannot Be 'Right,'" *Supreme Court Cases* 4, 1994, 19.

Parker, Stephen, and Stephen Bottomley. *Law in Context*. Annadale and Leichardt, Australia: Federation Press, 1994, 1997.

Partridge, B. "No Sex Please—We're Hobbits: The Construction of Female Sexuality in *The Lord of the Rings*." In *J.R.R. Tolkien: This Far Land*. Edited by Robert Giddings, 179–98. London: Vision and Barnes & Noble, 1983.

Pearce, J. *Tolkien: Man and Myth*. London: Sage, 1998.

Perrin, Colin. "Special Issue: In the Wake of Terra Nullius," *Law / Tex / Culture* 4(1), 1998.

Pether, Penny. "Sex, Lies and Defamation: The Bush Lawyer of Wessex." In *The Happy Couple: Law and Literature*. Edited by J. Neville Turner and Pamela Williams, 114–36. Sydney: Federation Press, 1994.

———. "E. M. Foster's *A Passage to India*: A Passage to the Patria." In *New Macmillan Casebook on E. M. Foster*. Edited by Jeremy Tambling, 195–212. New York: Macmillan & St. Martin's, 1995.

Plank, Robert. "'The Scouring of the Shire': Tolkien's View of Fascism." In *A Tolkien Compass*. Edited by Jared Lobdell, 116–25. New York: Ballantine Books, 1975.

Plato. *The Republic*. Translated by Desmond Lee. Middlesex: Penguin, 1987.

Polinsky, A. M. *An Introduction to Law and Economics*. Boston: Little, Brown, 1983.

Posner, Richard A. "Cost-Benefit Analysis: Definition, Justification, and Comment on Conference Papers." In *Cost-Benefit Analysis: Legal, Economic, and Philosophical Perspectives*. Edited by Matthew Adler and Eric Posner, 317–42. Chicago: University of Chicago Press, 2000.

———. "Utilitarianism, Economics, and Legal Theory." In *The Economic Structure of the Law: The Collected Economic Essays of Richard A. Posner*, vol. 1. Edited by Francesco Parisi, 140–77. Cheltenham: Edward Elgar, 2002.

Pottage, Alain. "The Cadastral Metaphor: Intersections of Property and Topography." In *Constituting Modernity: Private Property in the East and West*. Edited by Huri Islamoglu. London: Tauris, 2004.

Pound, Roscoe. "Law in Books and Law in Action," *American Law Review* 44(12), 1910, 12–36.

Povinelli, Elizabeth. "The Cunning of Seduction: Real Being and Aboriginal Recognition in Settler Australia," *Australian Feminist Law Journal* 11, Sept. 1998, 3–27.

Proudhon, Pierre-Joseph. *Selected Writings of Pierre-Joseph Proudhon*. Edited by Stewart Edwards; translated by Elizabeth Fraser. Garden City, N.Y.: Anchor, 1969.

Ragland-Sullivan, Ellie. "The Real." In *Feminism and Psychoanalysis*. Edited by Elizabeth Wright, 374–77. Oxford: Basil Blackwell, 1992.

Raz, Joseph. *The Authority of Law: Essays in Law and Morality*. Oxford: Clarendon, 1979.

Read, Peter. *Belonging: Australian Place and Aboriginal Ownership*. Cambridge: Cambridge University Press, 2000.

Redman, Steve. *Unpopular Cultures: The Birth of Law and Popular Culture*. Manchester: Manchester University Press, 1995.

Reeves, Thomas C. *The Empty Church: Does Organized Religion Matter Anymore?* New York: Simon & Schuster, 1998.

Resnik, Judith. "A Continuous Body: Ongoing Conversations About Women and Legal Education," *Journal of Legal Education* 53(4), Dec. 2003, 564–77, 565.

Reynolds, Henry. *Aboriginal Sovereignty: Reflections on Race, State, and Nation*. St. Leonard's, Australia: Allen & Unwin, 1996.

Rhode, Deborah L. "Missing Questions: Feminist Perspectives on Legal Education," *Stanford Law Review* 45, July 1993, 1547–66.

———. "Midcourse Corrections: Women in Legal Education," *Journal of Legal Education* 53(4), Dec. 2003, 475–88, 478.

Riddall, J. G. *Jurisprudence*. London: Butterworths, 1999.

Riviere, Joan. "Womanliness as Masquerade." In *Formations of Fantasy*. Edited by Victor Burgin, James Donald, and Cora Caplan. London: Routledge, 1986.

Rosenthal, Mark. "The Violent Excess of the Image and the Negation of Law in *Starship Troopers*," *Griffith Law Review* 10(2), 2001, 172–86.

Rowbotham, Sheila. *Woman's Consciousness, Man's World*. Harmondsworth, UK: Penguin, 1973.

Rowling, J. K. *Harry Potter and the Philosopher's Stone*. London: Bloomsbury, 1997.

———. *Harry Potter and the Chamber of Secrets*. London: Bloomsbury, 1998.

———. *Harry Potter and the Prisoner of Azkaban*. London: Bloomsbury, 1999.

———. *Harry Potter and the Goblet of Fire*. London: Bloomsbury, 2000.

———. *Harry Potter and the Order of the Phoenix*. London: Bloomsbury, 2003.

———. *Harry Potter and the Half-Blood Prince*. London: Bloomsbury, 2005.

Rush, Peter. "An Altered Jurisdiction: Corporeal Traces of Law," *Griffith Law Review* 6, 1997, 144–68.

Rutherford, Jennifer. *The Gauche Intruder: Freud, Lacan, and the White Australian Fantasy*. Melbourne: University Press, 2000.

Said, Edward. *Orientalism*. London: Routledge; Kegan & Paul, 1978.

Salecl, Renata. *The Spoils of Freedom: Psychoanalysis and Feminism After the Fall of Socialism*. London: Routledge, 1994.

————. *(Per)versions of Love and Hate*. London: Verso Press, 2000.

————. *On Anxiety*. New York: Routledge, 2004.

Sarat, Austin. "Imaging the Law of the Father: Loss, Dread, and Mourning in *The Sweet Hereafter*," *Law and Society Review* 34(1), 2000, 3–46.

————. "When Memory Speaks: Remembrance and Revenge in *Unforgiven*," *Griffith Law Review* 10(2), 2001, 139–59.

————, ed. *Cultural Analysis, Cultural Studies, and the Law: Moving Beyond Legal Realism*. Durham, N.C.: Duke University Press, 2003.

————, Lawrence Douglas, and Martha Merrill Umphrey, eds. *Law's Madness*. Ann Arbor: University of Michigan Press, 2003.

————, Lawrence Douglas, and Martha Merrill Umphrey, eds. *The Place of Law*. Ann Arbor: University of Michigan Press, 2003.

————, and Thomas R. Kearns, eds. *Law in the Domains of Culture*. Ann Arbor: University of Michigan Press, 2000.

Schirato, Tony, and Jen Webb. *Understanding Globalization*. London: Sage, 2003.

Schmitt, Carl. *Political Theology: Four Chapters on the Concept of Sovereignty*. Translated by George Schwab. Cambridge, Mass.: MIT Press, 1985.

————. *The Concept of the Political*. Translated and with introduction by George Schwabe. Chicago: University of Chicago Press, 1996.

Schneiderman, Stuart. *Jacques Lacan: The Death of an Intellectual*. Cambridge, Mass.: Harvard University Press, 1983.

Schor, Hilary. *Scheherezade in the Marketplace: Elizabeth Gaskell & the Victorian Novel*. Oxford: Oxford University Press, 1992.

————. *Dickens and the Daughter of the House*. Cambridge: Cambridge University Press, 1999.

Schroeder, Jeanne L. *The Vestal and the Fasces: Hegel, Lacan, Property, and the Feminine*. Berkeley: University of California Press, 1998.

————. *The Triumph of Venus: The Erotics of the Market*. Berkeley: University of California Press, 2004.

————. "His Master's Voice: H.L.A. Hart and Lacanian Discourse Theory," Working Paper no. 108. New York: Jacob Burns Institute for Advanced Legal Studies, Benjamin Cardozo School of Law, 2005.

Schwabach, Aaron. "Harry Potter and the Unforgiveable Curses: Norm-Formation, Inconsistency, and the Rule of Law in the Wizarding World." TJSL Legal Studies Research Paper No. 05-13 *Roger Williams University Law Review*, 2005.

Seligman, Joel. *The High Citadel: The Influence of the Harvard Law School*. Boston: Houghton-Mifflin, 1978.

Senghor, Leopold S. *Prose and Poetry*. Selected and translated by John Reed and Clive Wake. London: Heinemann, 1976.

Seymour, David. "Film and Law: In Search of a Critical Method." In *Law's Moving Image*. Edited by Les Moran, Ian Christie, Emma Sandon, and Elena Loizidou, 107–20. London: Cavendish, 2004.

Sherwin, Richard. *When the Law Goes Pop: The Vanishing Line Between Law and Popular Culture*. Chicago: University of Chicago Press, 2000.

Simpson, Gerry, and Hilary Charlesworth. "Objecting to Objectivity: The Radical Challenge to Legal Liberalism." In *Thinking About Law: Perspectives on History, Philosophy, and Sociology of Law*. Edited by Rosemary Hunter, Richard Ingleby, and Richard Johnstone, 86–132. Sydney: Allen & Unwin, 1995.

Sobchack, Vivian. *Screening Space: The American Science Fiction Film*. New York: Ungar, 1987.

———. "Cities on the Edge of Time: The Urban Science Fiction Film." In *Liquid Metal*. Edited by Sean Redmond. London: Wallflower Press, 2004.

Sontag, Susan. "Fascinating Fascism." In *Under the Sign of Saturn*, 77–105. New York: Farrar, Stauss & Giroux, 1980.

Sophocles. "Antigone." In *The Three Theban Plays*. Translated by R. Fagles; introduction and notes by Bernard Knox, 21–110. London: Allen Lane, 1982.

Steger, Manfred. *Globalization: A Very Short Introduction*. Oxford: Oxford University Press, 2003.

Stevens, Robert B. *Law School: Legal Education in America from 1850s to the 1980s*. Chapel Hill: University of North Carolina, 1983.

Stolzenberg, Nomi. "Bentham's Theory of Legal Fictions—A 'Curious Double Language,'" *Cardozo Studies in Law and Literature* 11, 1999, 223–62.

———. "What We Talk About When We Talk About Culture," *American Anthropologist* 103(2), June 2001, 432–47.

Sugarman, David. "Legal Theory, the Common Law Mind, and the Making of the Textbook Tradition." In *Legal Theory and the Common Law*. Edited by William Twining, 26–61. Oxford: Blackwell, 1986.

Thomas, Jeffrey E., ed. "Harry Potter and the Law." 12 *Texas Wesleyan Law Review*, 427 (2005).

———. "The Eclipse of Reason: A Rhetorical Reading of *Bowers v. Hardwick*," *Virginia Law Review* 79, 1993, 1721–80.

Thornton, Margaret. "The Development of Feminist Jurisprudence," *Legal Education Review* 9(2), 1998, 171–92.

———. "F-Law Talk: Feminism in the Legal Academy." *Australian Feminist Law Journal* 14, March 2000, 116–20.

———. "Feeling Chilly (Again) in the Legal Academy." *Australian Feminist Law Journal* 18, June 2003, 145–51.

———, ed. *Romancing the Tomes: Popular Culture, Law, Feminism*. London: Cavendish, 2004.

Threadgold, Terry. *Feminist Poetics: Poesis, Performing, Histories*. London: Routledge, 1997.

Toibin, Colm. *The Master*. New York: Scribner's, 2004.

Tolkien, J.R.R. *The Lord of the Rings*. Boston: Houghton Mifflin, 1994.

———. *The Hobbit, or There and Back Again*. Boston: Houghton Mifflin, 1997.

Toole, F. X. *Rope Burns: Stories from the Corner*. New York: Ecco Press and Harper Collins, 2001.

Tranter, Kieran. "Mad Max: The Car and Australian Governance," *National Identities* 5(1), 2003, 67–81.

Tsing, A. "Inside the Economy of Appearance." In *Globalization*. Edited by Arjun Apparadurai. Durham, N.C.: Duke University Press, 2001.

Turow, Scott. *One L: The Turbulent True Story of a First Year at Harvard Law School*. New York: Putnam, 1977.

Tushnet, Mark. "Critical Legal Studies: An Introduction to Its Origins and Underpinnings." *Journal of Legal Education* 36, 1986, 505–17.

Twining, William. *Karl Llewellyn and the Realist Movement*. London: Weidenfeld & Nicolson, 1973.

———. *Blackstone's Tower: The English Law School*. London: Sweet & Maxwell, 1994.

Unger, Roberto M. *The Critical Legal Studies Movement*. Cambridge, Mass.: Harvard University Press, 1986.

———. *Politics, a Work in Constructive Social Theory*. Cambridge: Cambridge University Press, 1987.

———. *False Necessity: Anti-necessitarian Social Theory in the Service of Radical Democracy*, Part 1. *Politics, a Work in Constructive Social Theory*. Cambridge: Cambridge University Press, 1987.

Valverde, Mariana. *Law's Dream of a Common Knowledge*. Princeton, N.J.: Princeton University Press, 2003.

Veljanovski, Cento. *The New Law and Economics*. Oxford: Oxford University Press, 1983.

Wacks, Raymond. *Jurisprudence*. London: Blackstone Press, 1999.

Walker, David M. *The Oxford Companion to Law*. Oxford: Oxford University Press, 1980.

Walmsley, N. "Tolkien and the 60s." In *J.R.R. Tolkien: This Far Land*. Edited by Robert Giddings, 73–86. London: Vision and Barnes & Nobles, 1983.

Warrick, Patricia S. *Mind in Motion: The Fiction of Philip K. Dick*. Carbondale and Edwardsville: Southern Illinois University Press, 1987.

Webber, Jeremy. "The Jurisprudence of Regret: The Search for Standards of Justice in Mabo," *Sydney Law Review* 17, March 1995, 5–28.

Weber, Max. *Max Weber on Charisma and Institution Building: Selected Papers*. Edited and introduction by S. N. Eisenstadt. Chicago: University of Chicago Press, 1968.

Wells, Celia. "Exceptional Women or Honorary Men? Notes from the Women Law Professors' Project," *Current Legal Problems* 53, 2000, 181–203.

———. "Ladies in Waiting: The Women Law Professors' Story," *Sydney Law Review* 23, 2001, 167–36.

———. "Working Out Women in Law Schools," *Legal Studies* 21, 2001, 116–36.

———. "Women Law Professors—Negotiating and Transcending Gender Identities at Work," *Feminist Legal Studies* 10, 2002, 1–38.

West, Robin. *Narrative, Authority, and Law*. Ann Arbor: University of Michigan Press, 1993.

———. *Caring for Justice*. New York: New York University Press, 1997.

White, G. Edward, *Justice Oliver Wendell Holmes: Law and the Inner Self*. Oxford: Oxford University Press, 1993. 18–19.

White, Hilaire McCoubrey Nigel D. *Textbook on Jurisprudence*. London: Blackstone, 1993.

White, James Boyd. *The Legal Imagination*. Boston: Little, Brown, 1973.

———. *Justice as Translation: An Essay in Cultural and Legal Criticism*. Chicago: University of Chicago Press, 1990.

Williams, Melanie. *Empty Justice: One Hundred Years of Law, Literature, and Philosophy*. London: Cavendish, 2001.

Williams, Patricia. *The Alchemy of Race and Rights*. Cambridge, Mass.: Harvard University Press, 1991.

———. *The Rooster's Egg: On the Persistence of Prejudice*. Cambridge, Mass.: Harvard University Press, 1997.

Willis, John. *A History of Dalhousie Law School*. Toronto: University of Toronto Press, 1979.

Witchalls, Clint. "Could Reading the Thoughts of Criminals Help Free the Innocent?" *The Guardian*, March 25, 2004.

Wolfgang von Goethe, Johann *Faust Parts 1 & 2: A New Version*, by Howard Brenton, from a literal translation by Christa Weisman, London: Nick Hern, 1995.

Wright, Elizabeth, ed. *Feminism and Psychoanalysis: A Critical Dictionary*. Advisory editors Diane Chisholm, Juliet Flower MacCannell, and Margaret Whitford. Oxford: Basil Blackwell, 1992.

Young, Alison. *Judging the Image: Art, Value, Law*. London: Routledge, 2005.

Young, Robert. *White Mythologies: Writing History and the West*. London: Routledge, 1990.

Žižek, Slavoj. *The Sublime Object of Ideology*. London: Verso, 1989.

———. "Formal Democracy and Its Discontents." In *Looking Awry: An Introduction to Jacques Lacan Through Popular Culture*. Cambridge, Mass.: MIT Press, 1991.

———. *Looking Awry: An Introduction to Jacques Lacan Through Popular Culture*. Cambridge, Mass.: MIT Press, 1991.

———. "Enjoy Your Nation as Yourself." In *Tarrying with the Negative: Kant, Hegel, and the Critique of Ideology*. Durham, N.C.: Duke University Press, 1993.

———. "Superego by Default." In *The Metastases of Enjoyment: Six Essays on Woman and Causality*, 54–85. London: Verso, 1994.

———. *The Indivisible Remainder*. London: Verso, 1996.

———. *The Plague of Fantasies*. London: Verso, 1997.

———. *Enjoy Your Symptom! Jacques Lacan in Hollywood and Out*. London: Routledge, 1992, 2001.

———. "Is There a Proper Way to Remake a Hitchcock Film?" In *Enjoy Your Symptom! Jacques Lacan in Hollywood and Out*, 195–212. New York: Routledge, 1992, 2001.

———. "The Ambiguity of the Masochist Social Link." In *Perversion and the Social Relation*. Edited by Molly Ann Rothenberg, Dennis Foster, and Slavoj Žižek, 187–209. Durham, N.C.: Duke University Press, 2003.

———. *The Puppet and the Dwarf: The Perverse Core of Christianity*. Cambridge, Mass.: MIT Press, 2003.

———. "Gerhard Schroeder's Minority Report and Its Consequences" at http://www.egs .edu/faculty/zizek/zizek-gerhard-schroeders-minority-report-and-its-consequences .html (accessed Sept. 2006).

Zupančič, Alenka. *Ethics of the Real: Kant, Lacan*. London: Verso, 2000.

———. *The Shortest Shadow: Nietzsche's Philosophy of the Two*. Cambridge, Mass.: MIT Press, 2003.

Primary Legal Sources

Cases

Administration of Papua and New Guinea v. Daera Guba, 130 CLR (1973).

Advisory Opinion on Western Sahara, ICJR at 39 (1975).

Amodu Tijani v. Secretary, Southern Nigeria, 2 AC (1921).

Bowers v. Hardwick, 478 U.S. 186, 92 L.Ed. 140, 106 S.Ct. 2841 (1986).

Calder v. Attorney-General of British Columbia, SCR (1973).

Carey v. Population Services International, 431 U.S. 678 (1977).

The Case of Tanistry, 80 ER 516 (1608).

Coe v. Commonwealth, 24 ALR 118 (1979).

Commonwealth v. Tasmania, 158 CLR 1 (1983).

Cruzan v. Director, Missouri Department of Health, 497 U.S. 261 (1990).

Fejo v. Northern Territory, 156 ALR 721 (1998).

Gordon v. Steele, 376 F. Supp. 575 (W.D. Pa. 1974).

Griswold v. Connecticut, 381 U.S. 479 (1965).

Hawkins v. McGee, 146 A. 641 (N.H. Coos. 1929).

Johnson v. McIntosh, 8 Wheat 543 (1823).

Lawrence v. Texas, 539 U.S. (2003).

Loving v. Virginia, 388 U.S. 1, 18 L.Ed. 2d 1010, 87 S.Ct. 1817 (1967).

Mabo v. The State of Queensland (no. 1), 166 CLR 186 (1988).

Mabo v. The State of Queensland (no. 2), 107 ALR 1; 175 CLR 1 (1992).

Milirrpum v. Nabalco Pty Ltd., 17 FLR 141 (1970).

Nancy B. v. Hotel Dieu de Quebec, 86 Dom LR, 385–95 (Jan. 6, 1992).

Olmstead v. United States, 277 U.S. 438 (1928).

Pretty v. Director of Public Prosecutions and Secretary of State for the Home Department, UKHL 61 (2001).

Roe v. Wade, 410 U.S. 113 (1973).

Sanlés Sanlés v. Spain, Communication no. 1024 / 2001, U.N. Doc. CCPr/C/80/D/1024/2001 (2004), 2.1.

Scholastic, Inc. v. Stouffer, 221 F.Supp. 2d 425 (SDNY 2002).

Semayne's Case, 5 Co Rep 91a (1605).

United States v. Carroll Towing Co., F.2d 169 (2d Cir. 1947).

Wake and Gondarra v. Northern Territory and Asche, 109 NTR 1; 5 NTLR 170 (1996).

Washington v. Glucksberg, 117 Sup. Ct. 2258, 138 L.Ed. 2d 772 (1997).

Western Australia v. the Commonwealth, 183 CLR 373 (1995).

Wik Peoples v. The State of Queensland, 141 CLR 129 (1996).

Witrong and Blany, 84 ER 789 (1674).

Wyong Shire Council v. Shirt, 146 CLR 40 (1980).

Legislation

Constitution of India.

Native Title Act 1993 (Cth).

Rights of the Terminally Ill Act 1995 (NT).

Filmography

A.I.: Artificial Intelligence. Directed by Steven Spielberg and Stanley Kubrick. Dreamworks, 2001.

Aliens. Directed by James Cameron. 20th Century Fox, 1986.

American Psycho. Directed by Mary Harron. Universal Pictures / Edward R. Pressman Film Corporation, 2000.

Barjo. Directed by Jerome Boivin. France 3 Cinema, 1994.

Battle for Planet of the Apes. Directed by J. Lee Thompson. Fox, 1973.

Beneath the Planet of the Apes. Directed by Jed Post. Fox, 1970.

Blade Runner. Directed by Ridley Scott. The Ladd Company, 1982.

Brazil. Directed by Terry Gilliam. Universal Pictures, 1985.

The Castle. Directed by Rob Sitch. Village Roadshow, 1997.

Conquest of Planet of the Apes. Directed by J. Lee Thompson. Fox, 1972.

Escape from Planet of the Apes. Directed by Dan Taylor. Fox, 1971.

E.T.: The Extra-Terrestrial. Directed by Steven Spielberg. Universal, 1982.

Fight Club. DVD. Directed by David Fincher. 20th Century Fox Home Entertainment South Pacific Pty. Ltd., [1999] 2000.

Gentleman Jim (VHS). Directed by Raoul Walsh. MGM / UA Home Entertainment Inc., [1942] 2001.

Gettin' Square. Directed by Jonathan Teplitzky; written by Chris Nyst. Squared Productions, 2003.

Goldfinger. Directed by Guy Hamilton. Eon Productions, 1964.

Heathers. Directed by Michael Lehman. New World Entertainment, 1989.

Imposter. Directed by Gary Fleder. Dimension Films, 2002.

It's a Wonderful Life. Directed by Frank Capra. Liberty Films, 1946.

Legally Blonde (DVD). Directed by Robert Luketic. Metro-Goldwyn-Mayer Pictures, 2001; MGM Home Entertainment, 2001.

Legally Blonde 2: Red, White and Blonde (DVD). Directed by Charles Hermon-Wurfeld. MGM Home Entertainment, 2003.

Logan's Run. Directed by Michael Anderson. MGM, 1976.

The Lord of the Rings: The Fellowship of the Ring (special extended edition DVD). Directed by Peter Jackson. New Line Home Entertainment, [2001] 2002.

The Lord of the Rings: The Return of the King (special extended edition DVD). Directed by Peter Jackson. New Line Home Entertainment, [2003] 2004.

The Lord of the Rings: The Two Towers (special extended edition DVD). Directed by Peter Jackson. New Line Home Entertainment, [2002] 2003.

Love Story. Directed by Arthur Hiller. Paramount, 1970.

Mad Max. Directed by George Miller. Kennedy Miller Productions, 1979.

Mad Max 2: The Road Warrior. Directed by George Miller. Kennedy Miller Productions, 1981.

Mad Max 3: Beyond Thunderdome. Directed by George Miller. Kennedy Miller Productions, 1985.

The Man from U.N.C.L.E. Directed by Norman Folto and Sam Rolfe. MGM / Arena, 1965.

The Matrix. Directed by Andy and Larry Wachowski. Warner Brothers, 1999.

Mean Girls. Directed by Mark Walters. Paramount, 2004.

Million Dollar Baby (DVD). Directed by Clint Eastwood. Warner Brothers, 2004; Lakeshore Entertainment, 2005.

Minority Report (DVD). Directed by Steven Spielberg. 20th Century Fox Home Entertainment, [2002] 2003.

Mr. Smith Goes to Washington. Directed by Frank Capra. Columbia Pictures, 1939.

Muriel's Wedding. Directed by P. J. Hogan. Miramax, 1994.

Notorious. Directed by Alfred Hitchcock. USA, 1946.

The Paper Chase (DVD). Directed by James Bridges. 20th Century Fox Home Entertainment, [1973] 2003.

The Parallax View. Directed by Alan Pakula. Paramount Pictures, 1974.

Paycheck. Directed by John Woo. Paramount Pictures, 2003.

Planet of the Apes. Directed by Franklin Schaeffer. Fox, 1968.

Planet of the Apes. Directed by Tim Burton. Fox, 2001.

The Postman. Directed by Kevin Costner. Warner Bros., 1997.

Psycho. Directed by Alfred Hitchcock. Shamley Productions, 1960.

Raging Bull (DVD). Directed by Martin Scorsese. MGM Home Entertainment, [1980] 2000.

Rear Window. Directed by Alfred Hitchcock. Paramount Pictures, 1954.

Rocky (DVD). Directed by John G. Arildsen. MGM Home Entertainment, [1976] 2001.

Romy and Michele's High School Reunion. Directed by David Mirkin. Touchstone Pictures, 1999.

Screamers. Directed by Christian Duguay. Allegro Films, 1995.

The Sea Inside (DVD). Directed by Alejandro Amenábar. Sogepaq and Fine Line Features, [2004] 2005.

Sister Act. Directed by Emile Ardolino. Touchstone Pictures, 1992.

The Sound of Music. Directed by Robert Wise. 20th Century Fox, 1965.

Soylent Green. Directed by Richard Fleisher. MGM, 1973.

Spellbound. Directed by Alfred Hitchcock. Selznick International, 1945.

Star Trek: First Contact. Directed by Jonathan Frakes. Paramount Pictures, 1996.

Strictly Ballroom. Directed by Baz Luhrmann. Miramax, 1992.

Three Days of the Condor. Directed by Sydney Pollack. Paramount Pictures, 1975.

Total Recall. Directed by Paul Verhoeven. Artisan Entertainment, 1990.

The Valley of the Dolls (VHS). Directed by Mark Robson. 20th Century Fox; Fox Video, 1967.

Waterworld. Directed by Kevin Reynolds. Universal Pictures, 1995.

Television Series

Angel. Joss Whedon. Mutant Enemy, WB Television, 1999.

Buffy the Vampire Slayer. Joss Whedon. Mutant Enemy, 20th Century Fox, 1998–.

Charmed. Constance Burge. Spelling Television, WB Network, 1998–.

Firefly. Joss Whedon. Mutant Enemy, 20th Century Fox Television, 2002–3.

Get Smart. Directed by Mel Brooks and Buck Henry. Talent Associates / Heyday, 1965–67.

Home and Away. Alan Bateman. 7 Network, 1987.

Little Britain. Matt Lucas and David Williams. British Broadcasting Corporation, 2003–.

Neighbours. Reg Watson. Grundy, 1985–.

The Paper Chase. Directed by James Bridges, Written by James Bridges and Jon J. Osborne Jr. CBS, 1978; 1983–86.

Queer as Folk. Directed by Charles MacDougall and Sarah Harding. CITV, 1997–99.

Queer as Folk. Directed by John Greyson. Showtime, 2001–.

Sabrina the Teen-Age Witch. Nell Scovall. Viacom Productions, Heartbreak Films, WB Television, 1996–.

South Park. Trey Parker and Matt Stone. Comedy Channel, 1998–.

Star Trek: The Next Generation. Directed by Gene Roddenberry. Paramount, 1990–96.

Survivors. Terry Nation. BBC 1, 1975–77.

The X Files. Chris Carter. Ten-Thirteen / 20th Century Fox, 1994.

Buffy the Vampire Slayer Episodes

"Bad Girls," by Douglas Petrie; directed by Michael Lange. Season 3: Episode 14.

"Bargaining," by Marti Noxon; directed by D. Grossman. Season 6: Episode 1.

"Buffy: The Musical" or "Once More, With Feeling," written and directed by Joss Whedon. Season 6: Episode 6.

"Chosen," written and directed by Joss Whedon. Season 7: Episode 144.

"Consequences," by Marti Noxon; directed by Michael Gershman. Season 3: Episode 15.

"Crush," by David Fury; directed by Dan Attias. Season 5: Episode 14.

"Dirty Girls," by Drew Goddard; directed by Michael Gershman. Season 7: Episode 18.

"Empty Places," by Drew Z. Greenberg; directed by James A. Contner. Season 7: Episode 19.

"End of Days," by Jane Espenson and Douglas Petrie; directed by Marita Grabiak. Season 7: Episode 143.

"Faith, Hope and Trick," by David Greenwalt; directed by James Contner. Season 3: Episode 3.

"Fool For Love," by Douglas Petrie; directed by Nick March. Season 5: Episode 7.

"The Freshman," written and directed by Joss Whedon. Season 4: Episode 1.

"The Gift," written and directed by Joss Whedon. Season 5: Episode 21.

"Goodbye, Iowa," by Marti Noxon; directed by David Solomon. Season 4: Episode 14.

"Graduation Day, Part 1," written and directed by Joss Whedon. Season 3: Episode 21.

"The Harsh Light of Day," by Jane Espenson; directed by James Contner. Season 4: Episode 3.

"Helpless," by David Fury; directed by James Cantner. Season 3: Episode 12.

"Hush," written and directed by Joss Whedon. Season 4: Episode 10.

"I Only Have Eyes for You," by Marti Noxon; directed by James Whitmore. Season 2: Episode 19.

"The I Team," by David Fury; directed by James Contner. Season 4: Episode 13.

"The Initiative," by Douglas Petrie; directed by James Contner. Season 4: Episode 3.

"Interventions," by Jane Espenson; directed by Michael Gershman. Season 5: Episode 18.

"Living Conditions," by Marti Noxon; directed by David Grossman. Season 4: Episode 2.

"Out of My Mind," by Rebecca Rand Kirshner; directed by David Grossman. Season 5: Episode 4.

"Passion," by Ty King; directed by M. Gershman. Season 2: Episode 17.

"Primeval," by David Fury; directed by James Contner. Season 4: Episode 21.

"Prophecy Girl," written and directed by Joss Whedon. Season 1: Episode 12.

"The Puppet Show," by Rob Des Hotel and Dean Batali. Directed by Ellen Pressman. Season 1: Episode 9.

"Restless," written and directed by Joss Whedon, Season 4: Episode 22.

"Revelations," by Douglas Petrie; directed by James Contner. Season 3: Episode 7.

"Smashed," by Drew Greenberg; directed by Tari Meyer. Season 6: Episode 8.

"Touched," by Rebecca Rand Kirshner; directed by David Soloman. Season 7: Episode 142.

"Welcome to the Hellmouth," by Joss Whedon; directed by Charles Martin, Season 1: Episode 1.

"The Wish," by Marti Noxon; directed by David Greenawalt. Season 3: Episode 9.

"What's My Line? Part 1," by Howard Gordon and Marti Noxon; directed by David Soloman. Season 2: Episode 9.

Index